GENGHIS KHAN
AND THE MONGOL
WAR MACHINE

GENGHIS KHAN AND THE MONGOL WAR MACHINE

Chris Peers

Pen & Sword
MILITARY

First published in Great Britain in 2015 by
PEN AND SWORD MILITARY
an imprint of
Pen and Sword Books Ltd
47 Church Street
Barnsley
South Yorkshire S70 2AS

ISBN 978 1 78340 056 0

A CIP record for this book is available from the British Library

Printed and bound in England
by CPI Group (UK) Ltd, Croydon, CR0 4YY

Typeset in Times by CHIC GRAPHICS

Pen & Sword Books Ltd incorporates the imprints of Pen & Sword
Archaeology, Atlas, Aviation, Battleground, Discovery, Family
History, History, Maritime, Military, Naval, Politics, Railways,
Select, Social History, Transport, True Crime, Claymore Press,
Frontline Books, Leo Cooper, Praetorian Press, Remember When,
Seaforth Publishing and Wharncliffe.

For a complete list of Pen and Sword titles please contact
Pen and Sword Books Limited
47 Church Street, Barnsley, South Yorkshire, S70 2AS, England
E-mail: enquiries@pen-and-sword.co.uk
Website: www.pen-and-sword.co.uk

Contents

List of Plates

1. The open grassland, or steppe, of central Mongolia. (Fotolia)
2. The barren wastes of the Gobi Desert. (Fotolia.)
3. Typical Mongol ponies. (Fotolia)
4. Modern statues of Mongol warriors, outside the Genghis Khan Museum in Ulaanbaatar. (Fotolia)
5. The Battle of Huan-erh-tsui in 1211, as depicted in the *Jami al-tawarikh* of Rashid ud-Din.
6. Mongol cavalry pursuing a routed enemy, from Rashid ud-Din.
7. Lance-armed Egyptian Mamluks pursue Mongol mounted archers. From the fourteenth-century *History of the Tartars* by the Armenian historian Hayton of Coricos.
8. The only near-contemporary portrait of Genghis Khan.
9. Stages in the construction of a modern replica of a Mongolian composite bow (photos courtesy of Green Man Longbows). This photograph shows the wooden core of the bow, with separate plates of horn ready to be attached.
10. Preparing the core for the attachment of the 'siha'.
11. The core of the bow with the siha and central hand grip glued in place.
12. The horn is strapped tightly in place while the glue dries.
13. Bundles of shredded sinew, which will be soaked in glue and applied to the wooden core.
14. The finished weapon.
15. Drawing a composite bow.
16. Another view of the draw.
17. A variety of siege techniques is illustrated in this picture of the siege of Baghdad, taken from Rashid ud-Din's history.
18. Mongol tent, on a huge wagon, from Colonel Yule's edition of Marco Polo's *Travels*, 1876.

Timeline: The Mongol Conquests and the Career of Genghis Khan

c. 800 AD	Emergence of Mongol tribes.
907	Foundation of Khitan Liao dynasty.
960	Foundation of Sung dynasty in China.
1138	Foundation of Tangut Hsi Hsia dynasty.
1125	Liao overthrown by Jurchens. Qara-Khitai state established.
c. 1150	Kabul Khan forms first Mongol confederation.
1161	Kabul Khan defeated by Jurchens.
c. 1162	Birth of Temujin.
c. 1170	Death of Temujin's father, Yesugei.
1177	Temujin escapes from Tayichi'ut captivity.
1178	Temujin marries Borte and swears allegiance to Toghril.
1179	Abduction of Borte and war with the Merkits.
c. 1180–1210	Drought in Mongolia.
1186	Khwarizmian Empire founded.
c. 1189	Temujin becomes Khan, takes title of Genghis.
c. 1190	Genghis defeated by Jamuqa at Dalan-baljut.
1195	Genghis joins Jurchens in war against Tatars.
1201	Battle of Koyiten. Jamuqa defeated and Tayichi'uts destroyed.
1202	Genghis defeats Tatars at Dalan-nemurges.
1203	First campaign against Naimans. Split with Toghril. Genghis defeated at Qalaqaljit Sands. 'Baljuna Covenant'. Keraits defeated at Jer-qabchiqay Pass.
1204	Second war with Naimans. Genghis victorious at Mount Naqu-kun. Merkits defeated at Black Steppe.

1205	Capture of Jamuqa. First Mongol raids against Hsi Hsia.
1206	Genghis proclaimed ruler of Mongolia.
1209	Uighurs submit to Genghis.
1209–1210	First war with Hsi Hsia.
1211	Invasion of Chin Empire. Genghis victorious at Battle of Huan-erh-tsui.
1215	Capture of Chung-tu.
1215–1216	Samukha's raid into China.
1216	Wars against Tumads and Merkits. Kirghiz revolt suppressed. First clash with Khwarizmians. Victory over Chin at Shen-shui.
1217	Mukhali appointed viceroy in China.
1218	First invasion of Korea. Jebei conquers Qara-Khitai. Mukhali defeats Chin at Battle of Lang-ya Ling.
1219	Genghis invades Khwarizmian Empire.
1220	Capture of Bokhara and Samarkand. Mukhali defeats Chin at Huang-ling-kang.
1221	Battles of Parvan and the Indus River. Defeat of Jalal ud-Din. Invasion of India.
1221–1223	Jebei and Subotei's Black Sea campaign.
1222–1227	War with Sung Chinese.
1223	Russians defeated at Battle of Kalka River. Mongols repulsed by Bulgars. Death of Mukhali. Mongols defeat Sung at Battle of Wu-ma Hills.
1224	Second invasion of Hsi Hsia. Tanguts again submit.
1225	Tanguts form alliance with Chin. Third Mongol invasion of Hsi Hsia.
1227	Death of Genghis. Final defeat of Hsi Hsia. Succession of Ogodei Khan.
1228	Jalal ud-Din defeated at Battle of Isfahan.
1231	Death of Jalal ud-Din.
1234	Capture of K'aifeng. End of the Chin dynasty.
1237–1241	Mongol invasion of Europe.
1241	Death of Ogodei.

1256	Mongol invasion of Middle East.
1260	Accession of Kubilai as Great Khan. Mongols defeated by Egyptians at Ain Jalut.
1268	Civil war between Kubilai and Kaidu. Fragmentation of Mongol Empire.
1271	Kubilai proclaims Yuan dynasty in China.
1279	Final defeat of Sung.
1368	Fall of Yuan dynasty.

The Family Tree of Genghis Khan ('Great Khans' and the period of their reigns in capitals)

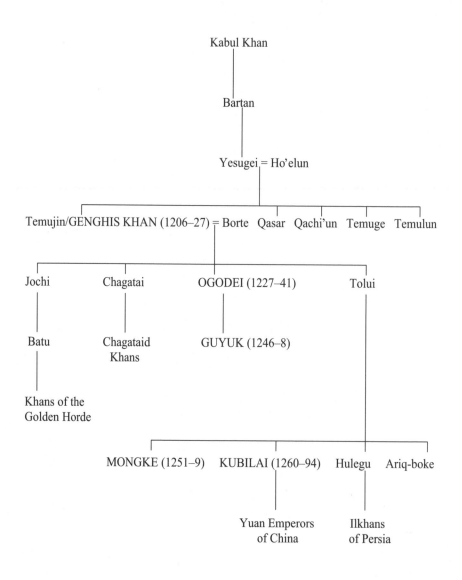

Kabul Khan

Bartan

Yesugei = Ho'elun

Temujin/GENGHIS KHAN (1206–27) = Borte Qasar Qachi'un Temuge Temulun

Jochi Chagatai OGODEI (1227–41) Tolui

Batu Chagataid Khans GUYUK (1246–8)

Khans of the Golden Horde

MONGKE (1251–9) KUBILAI (1260–94) Hulegu Ariq-boke

Yuan Emperors of China Ilkhans of Persia

Who's Who in Thirteenth-Century Mongolia

Ala-qush-digit-quri: Chief of the Ongguts and commander of the Onggut contingent in the Mongol army in 1206.

Ala-qush Tagin: Chief of the Ongguts, successor to Ala-qush-digit-quri and ally of Genghis in the wars in China.

Ambakai: Nephew of Kabul Khan, executed by the Jurchens in 1161.

Bekter: Half-brother of Temujin, killed by the latter in a childhood quarrel.

Belgutei: Half-brother of Temujin.

Bo'orchu: One of Genghis' 'four war-horses'.

Boroqul: One of Genghis' 'four war-horses', killed by the Tumads in 1216.

Borte: Genghis' senior wife.

Buyiruq Khan: Naiman chief defeated by Genghis in 1202.

Chagatai: Second son of Genghis and founder of the 'Chagatai Horde'.

Chaghan: Officer of Tangut origin, commander of Genghis' guard in 1206.

Chila'un-ba'atur: One of Genghis' 'four war-horses'.

Dorbei Doqshin: Mongol officer. Victor in the Tumad War of 1216, sent to invade India in 1221.

Gemyabek: Mongol officer, killed by the Russians in 1223.

Ho'elun: Wife of Yesugei and mother of Temujin.

Inancha-bilge Khan: Naiman chief, father of Tayang Khan.

Ja'afar: Muslim merchant and spy in Genghis' employ.

Jamuqa: Chief of the Jajirat Mongols, childhood friend and later rival of Genghis. Executed in 1205.

Jarchi'udai: Chief of the Uru'ut Mongols and father of Jelme.

Jebei: Former Tayichi'ut prisoner of war, one of Genghis' 'four hounds'. Conqueror of Qara-Khitai and commander of Russian expedition, died c. 1223.

Jelme: Son of Jarchi'udai and one of Genghis' 'four hounds'.

Jirqo'adai – see Jebei.

Jochi: Eldest son of Genghis, died 1227.

Kabul Khan: Great-grandfather of Genghis and founder of first Mongol confederation. Defeated by Chin in 1161.

Kokse'u-sabraq: Naiman general.

Kubilai Khan: Grandson of Genghis and founder of the Yuan dynasty in China.

Kuchluq: Naiman prince, son of Tayang Khan. Took over Qara-Khitai, and was defeated and killed by Jebei in 1218.

Megujin-se'ultu: Tatar Khan, defeated by Genghis in 1195.

Metiken: Grandson of Genghis, killed at Bamiyan in 1221.

Monglik: Friend of Genghis' father Yesugei and father of Teb Tengri.

Mukhali: One of Genghis' 'four war-horses', and his viceroy in China. Died in 1223.

Ogodei: Genghis' third son and successor.

Ong Khan – see Toghril.

Qachi'un: Brother of Temujin.

Qadaqan: Grandson of Genghis.

Qasar: Brother of Temujin, renowned for his strength and skill as an archer.

Qorchi: Mongol officer, originally a defector from Jamuqa, whose imprisonment was the cause of the Tumad War of 1216.

Qubilai: One of Genghis' 'four hounds'. His name is spelt thus in this narrative to distinguish him from Kubilai, Genghis' grandson.

Qultuqan Mergen: Merkit prince, son of Toqto'a, defeated by Jochi in 1216.

Quyildar: Mongol officer, commander of the Mangquts at the Battle of Qalaqaljit Sands.

Samukha: Mongol officer, served in China 1214 to 1216.

Senggum: Kerait prince, son of Toghril, defeated by Genghis in 1203.

Shigi-qutuqu: Adopted Tatar orphan, rose to high office under Genghis. Commander at the Battle of Parvan in 1221.

Sorqan-shira: Tayichi'ut Mongol, early supporter of Genghis.

Subotei: Mongol officer of Uriangqat origin, joint commander with Jebei on Russian expedition. Also served in China and continued his career under Genghis' successor Ogodei. Often regarded as the greatest of the Mongol commanders.

Taichar: Brother of Jamuqa, killed c. 1182.

Tarqutai: Tayichi'ut chief and rival of Genghis, defeated in 1201.

Tayang Khan: Naiman chief, defeated by Genghis at Mount Naqu-kun in 1205.

Teb Tengri: Mongol shaman, originally a supporter of Genghis, later turned against him and was killed by Temuge in 1206.

Tekechuk: Mongol officer, defeated at Valiyan in 1221.

Temuge: Brother of Temujin.

Temujin: Son of Yesugei, known from c. 1195 as Genghis Khan.

Temulun: Sister of Temujin.

Toghril: Chief of the Keraits, ally and later rival of Genghis, defeated in 1203.

Tolui: Son of Genghis.

Toqto'a: Chief of the Merkits, defeated and killed at the Erdish River in 1205.

Toquchar: Mongol officer, killed at Nishapur in 1220.

Yesugei: Chief of the Borjigin Mongols. Father of Temujin, the future Genghis Khan. Murdered by Tatars c.1170.

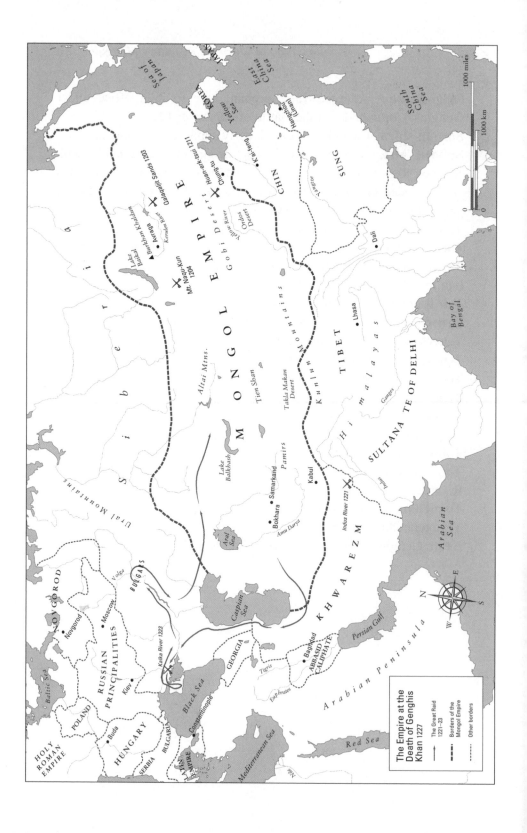

The Empire at the
Death of Genghis
Khan 1227

The Great Raid
1221–23

Borders of the
Mongol Empire

Other borders

MONGOL EMPIRE

Siberia

Ural Mountains

Altai Mtns.

Lake Baikal

Burkhan Khaldun
Avraga
Qalaqaljit Sands 1203
Kerulen River
Mt. Naqu-Kun 1204
Huan-erk-tsui 1211
Chung-tu

Gobi Desert

Ordos Desert

Yellow River

CHIN

Yellow Sea

KOREA

Kai-feng

JAPAN

Sea of Japan

East China Sea

Seoul

South China Sea

SUNG

Hangzhou (Linan)

Yangtze

Dali

Tien Shan

Takla Makan Desert

Kunlun Mountains

TIBET

Lhasa

Himalayas

Ganges

Bay of Bengal

SULTANATE OF DELHI

Lake Balkhash

Pamirs

Samarkand

Bokhara

Amu Darya

Aral Sea

Kabul

Indus River 1221

Indus

KHWAREZM

Arabian Sea

Caspian Sea

Volga

BULGARS

NOVGOROD

Novgorod

Moscow

RUSSIAN PRINCIPALITIES

Kiev

Kalka River 1223

POLAND

HOLY ROMAN EMPIRE

HUNGARY

Buda

SERBIA

BULGARIA

Constantinople

LATIN EMPIRE

Black Sea

GEORGIA

Tigris

Euphrates

Baghdad

ABBASID CALIPHATE

Persian Gulf

Arabian Peninsula

Red Sea

Nile

Mediterranean Sea

Baltic Sea

N E S W

1000 miles

1000 km

Introduction

In many respects Genghis Khan needs no introduction. Eight hundred years after he launched his career of conquest he remains one of the best-known figures in history, not only in his home country of Mongolia but across the globe. 'The East', says Urgunge Onon in the introduction to his translation of the *Secret History*, 'has known only three great men.' These, in his view, were the Buddha, Confucius and Genghis Khan. At first sight this verdict is startling; two famous men of peace sitting side by side with the most successful conqueror in history. But among present-day Mongolians Genghis enjoys a status not far short of divinity, while the neighbouring People's Republic of China lays claim to him with almost equal enthusiasm. He has become a sort of global brand, with his image appearing on products from beer bottles to postcards as far west as Turkey. In 1995 the *Washington Post* voted him 'the most important man of the last thousand years'. It is well known that he founded the biggest land-based empire the world has ever seen, stretching from the Black Sea in the west to Korea in the east, uniting peoples who until then knew nothing of each other's existence. And yet it is surprising how little we really know about him – or rather how far the popular perception differs from what we do know.

My aim in this book is to try to explain how Genghis achieved what he did, and to try to answer some of the questions that are still being debated today. Was he a true empire-builder, or just the world's most successful bandit? Was he a genius who single-handedly altered the course of world history, or did he ride to success on the back of forces stronger than any human will? How did the Mongols conquer most of the known world? We can talk about motivation, courage, discipline and even military technology, but how exactly did these translate into success on the battlefield? Much of Genghis' story is not for the squeamish. Behind such abstract words as 'conquest' and 'empire' lies the grisly reality that these were obtained by killing other people, or at least by terrifying them into submission. Did Genghis and his followers really kill the millions and produce the wastelands that they are reputed to have done?

The Sources
I have tried – as far as is possible when relying on translated works – to answer these questions by going back to the original sources. Very few of these, in fact, are 'original sources' in the sense that a modern historian would use the term; they are not, for example, contemporary eyewitness reports or administrative documents preserved in state archives. Instead they are mostly chronicles written within a few years or decades of the events they describe, but nevertheless subject to selectivity and bias. They are, however, essential if Genghis' story is to be understood at all. For all practical purposes the only source for his early life – and the only Mongolian source for his career of conquest – is the book generally known as the *Secret History of the Mongols*. This work was probably written originally in Mongolian, using the script which Genghis adopted from the Turkish-speaking Uighurs, and at some point had come to be regarded as taboo to non-Mongols, hence the term 'Secret'. However it has survived to the present day only in the form of a fourteenth-century Chinese transcription, under the title *Yuan Ch'ao Pi Shih*. We do not know the name of the author or precisely when it was written; the epilogue states that it was finished 'in the Year of the Rat and the Month of the Roebuck', but in the Mongol chronology a Rat Year recurred every twelve years, and there is still debate about which cycle is meant. Urgunge Onon, whose English translation is referred to in this book, argues persuasively for the year 1228, though some material must have been added later. This is only a year after the death of Genghis Khan, so the *Secret History* can be regarded as a near-contemporary source for the events it describes. This does not of course mean that it is necessarily

accurate. Much of the material dealing with Genghis' ancestors is clearly mythical, and some historians – notably Arthur Waley, who published one of the first English translations – have regarded the whole work as fiction. Most scholars do not accept this argument, however, and Morgan has pointed out that the *Secret History* can to some extent be validated by comparison with a now lost work, the *Altan Debter* or *Golden Book*, which was used as a source by the Persian writer Rashid ud-Din. This is fortunate, because without the *Secret History* it is hard to see how any convincing account of Genghis and his era could be written. Nevertheless, from a Western viewpoint it is a particularly frustrating document, because it virtually ignores what we tend to see as the most significant aspect of Genghis' career – the extension of his conquests after the unification of Mongolia itself. In fact it is not really what the modern reader would regard as a 'history' at all. Its focus is mainly genealogical, recording events because of the light which they shed on the relationships between members of the Khan's family, and the privileges of various eminent Mongols which they legitimised, rather than because of their wider significance. For this reason the *Secret History* concentrates mainly on Genghis' ancestry, his early years and the wars which gave him control of Mongolia, culminating in the great assembly or 'quriltai' in 1206, at which he was proclaimed supreme ruler. The *History* is by no means a eulogy, and includes several episodes which do not seem intended to enhance its subject's reputation, but a recurring theme is the double-dealing of his various rivals and allies, who one by one attempted to stab him in the back and therefore had to be eliminated in self-defence. This process is assisted by the different flaws of character which make all these individuals unfit to rule, at least in comparison with Genghis. The result of this bias is that a narrative based on the *Secret History* – as the following account of his rise to power necessarily is – has a feeling of inevitability which could not have been apparent at the time. Mongolia, before Genghis unified it, had been fought over for several decades by a collection of warlords, all happy to eliminate their opponents by poisoning, assassination by hired thugs and other gangster methods. The reader should bear in mind that all we have today is an account written by the henchmen of the most successful gangster. The events which followed Genghis' takeover in Mongolia are covered in much less detail, even those involving the conquest of China which absorbed the bulk of Mongol energies for seven decades, and the campaigns in the west are mentioned almost as an afterthought. It is as though there was no need to explain to the Mongols how or why their ancestors managed to conquer most of the known world; once they had been unified and provided with effective leadership, the rest was inevitable. If this reflects a genuine contemporary Mongol perspective, though, it is one which does in fact explain a lot. The veterans of several decades of warfare against the most formidable of enemies – their fellow steppe dwellers – may well have found the campaigns against more 'civilised' victims easy going by comparison.

The accounts of the 'civilised' victims themselves are naturally less sympathetic to the Mongols, which is why two of the Persian sources are especially valuable, because they were written by men who had attained high office in the service of later Mongol khans. Ata Malik Juvaini was Governor of Baghdad under Genghis' grandson Hulegu, and his *History of the World Conqueror* covers not only the life of Genghis but the reigns of his successors up to about 1260. Next to the *Secret History* this has been the most valuable source for the early Mongols, although it is not always easy to read; the narrative is not consistently presented in chronological order, so that Juvaini sometimes deals with the same events under different headings, and it is interrupted by countless digressions and quotations from earlier Islamic literature. The other important Persian chronicler is Rashid ud-Din, who was chief minister of Ghazan Khan, ruler of the Ilkhanid Mongol state which Hulegu's family established in the Middle East. Rashid wrote around the end of the thirteenth century and naturally had to rely on earlier sources – including Juvaini – for the events of Genghis' reign, but he nevertheless records a large amount of useful information which would otherwise have been lost. Unfortunately only part of his modestly-titled *Jami al-tawarikh* or *Collection of Histories* is available in translation. Also valuable is the *Tabaqat-i Nasiri* of

Juzjani, who had actually served in the Khwarizmian army at the time of the Mongol invasion of 1219, and wrote his book about 1260 while in exile in Delhi. Not surprisingly he is fiercely anti-Mongol, but much of what he says is corroborated by Juvaini's contemporary account.

To Genghis and his followers China was by far the most important region outside Mongolia, and the bulk of their resources were devoted to conquering it. Therefore Chinese sources are invaluable for understanding the Mongol conquests, but unfortunately few of them are available in English. I have relied heavily on H. Desmond Martin's work for the campaigns in China, and for the useful information on the Mongol army recorded by Meng Hung. The latter was a thirteenth-century general who wrote a perceptive report for the Sung Emperor on the invaders and the prospects for defeating them. Chinese official records tend to be short on military detail, but Hsiao has translated some relevant sections of the Official History of the Yuan dynasty which was established by another grandson of Genghis, Kubilai. Also useful is Waley's translation of the account by Li Chih-ch'ang of the visit of the Taoist sage Ch'ang Ch'un to Genghis in 1222.

When the expanding Mongol empire began to threaten Europe from the 1240s onwards several missions were sent east on behalf of the Papacy, ostensibly as ambassadors to the Great Khans, but in reality principally as spies, with instructions to report on the Mongols' military abilities and other matters of practical concern. John de Plano Carpini and William of Rubruck have left especially valuable records, which are covered by De Rachewiltz in his *Papal Envoys to the Great Khans*. Dating from half a century later, but still valuable for our purpose, is the better-known account of Marco Polo, who served at the court of Kubilai Khan in China.

Needless to say I am indebted to numerous more recent scholars whose works are listed in the Bibliography. Any reader wanting a more in-depth or wide-ranging study of Mongol history that is attempted here are recommended to consult these, in particular the books by De Hartog, Morgan and Rachtnevsky. There are many different ways of rendering Mongol, Chinese and Persian names into

English, and the inconsistencies between various authorities can be confusing. In most cases I have tried to minimise the confusion for the reader by using the form of a particular name from the source in which it is most likely to be encountered – thus Mongol names tend to be taken from Onon's translation of the *Secret History*, and Chinese ones from H. D. Martin. The latter therefore appear in the old Wade-Giles transliteration, which remains the most accessible system for English speakers. The choice between Genghis, Chinggis, Chinggiz and the numerous other ways in which the Khan's title has been written is based purely on its familiarity to the general reader.

Chapter 1

Genghis' World

The Country and the People

Mongolia consists mainly of a high plateau at the eastern end of the belt of open grassland, or steppe, which stretches across most of Asia between the latitudes of forty and fifty degrees north. Further north lies the Siberian forest, and to the south, where not bounded by mountain ranges, the steppe merges imperceptibly into scrub and stony desert. The whole region is very distant from the sea, and so is subject to seasonal extremes of climate which, together with shortage of rainfall, make it generally unsuitable for agriculture. Therefore in pre-modern times its principal inhabitants were nomadic herdsmen who lived off their herds of sheep, cattle, camels and horses. Both the land and the people have traditionally been seen as remote and backward, but this stereotype is misleading. For one thing, through the southern part of the steppe zone ran the greatest east-west trade route of the ancient and medieval worlds, known from its most prestigious commodity as the Silk Road, which connected China, via a series of local middlemen, with the Mediterranean. The route not only allowed ideas and inventions to flow between the steppe and the agricultural civilisations to the south, but supported a string of wealthy cities along its course, from Hami on the borders of China west to Bokhara on the Oxus River, and beyond to Baghdad. The steppe itself had also been the source of world-changing technological developments, many of them based around the most characteristic of its wild fauna, the horse. Horses had probably first been ridden near the southern end of the Ural Mountains around 4000 BC, and 2,000 years later, in the same region, they were being yoked to the earliest war chariots. The spread of this military technology has been linked to the dispersal of Indo-European languages across an area from Europe to India, suggesting that the steppe warriors had dominated their sedentary cousins from a very early date. By historical times the theme of nomadic horsemen descending from the high grasslands to pillage and conquer had become a familiar one, from the Skythians who wrecked the Assyrian capital at Nineveh in 612 BC to the Huns of Attila, who in the fifth century AD nearly did the same to Constantinople. Most important of all were the Turks, who during the six centuries after AD 600 moved south and west in a series of waves, eventually coming to dominate most of the Middle East, while at the same time their relatives did the same in northern China.

But although Mongolia had been the original homeland of many of the Turkish tribes, it remained something of a backwater. Here the steppe zone reached its greatest altitude above sea level, and its greatest distance from the sea. Thus the country was dry, cold and bleak even by Central Asian standards, and migration within the steppe zone had always tended to be from the east towards the milder and wetter west. By the twelfth century AD the people still living on the high plateau were incredibly hardy, but also relatively poor. They were divided among several tribal confederations, of which the Mongols themselves were among the least important. In the west, in the foothills of the Altai Mountains, lived the Naimans, who are generally regarded as of Turkish origin, although the distinction between Turk and Mongol was mainly linguistic rather than cultural, and is not always detectable in our sources. The Naimans were mostly Buddhists or Nestorian Christians, having been converted by the Uighurs, sedentary Turks whose territory in the Tarim Basin of what is now the Chinese province of Xinjiang bordered theirs to the south. Possibly it was distant rumours of Christians in this remote region that had given rise to the European legend of Prester John, a mythical Christian potentate who at various times during the twelfth and thirteenth centuries was supposed to be heading west to help his coreligionists in their wars with the Muslims.

The Naimans were former allies of another Turkish people, the Kirghiz, who had briefly dominated the whole of Mongolia in the ninth century, but had since been driven by their numerous enemies into the forests along the River Yenisei further north. East of the Naimans were another powerful group, the Keraits, also mainly Nestorian, who occupied the central Mongolian steppe between the Orkhon and Onon rivers. The northern neighbours of the Keraits were the Merkits, who lived on the lower Selengge River south of Lake Baikal. The Merkit country was mostly forested and the people were as much hunters as stock breeders, although the distinction between the two groups was very fluid. In daily life the Merkits rode reindeer rather than horses, but it is obvious from the sources that they maintained significant cavalry armies, which suggests that their economy must somehow have supported large numbers of livestock as well as people. The Oirats living further north and west, east of the upper Yenisei valley, had a similar lifestyle but were fewer in numbers.

In eastern Mongolia, between the Kerulen River and the Khingan Mountains which marked the border with Manchuria, the dominant people were the Tatars. They are characterised in the *Secret History* as the deadly enemies of the Mongols, but in fact it seems that the two clans later known as 'Mongqol' or Mongol – the Borjigin and the Tayichi'ut – had originally been branches of the Tatar people. The Tayichi'ut inhabited the edge of the forest zone in the north of the Tatar territory and had a reputation as great hunters, while the Borjigin further south were classic stockbreeding nomads. Other tribes in the region included the Jalair, said to have originated as a band of Turkish refugees, who lived between the Merkits and the Keraits; the Onggirats in the far southeast; and the Ongguts, who at some unknown date had migrated south of the Gobi Desert as far as the borders of China, but still maintained contacts with their relatives further north. Despite their apparent isolation, however, most of these tribes had been involved to some degree in the power politics of East Asia, and by the thirteenth century the road south to China was already a well-trodden one.

The Road to Empire
One of the most dramatic features of the millennium or so after AD

300 was the long series of incursions by armies from Central Asia into the settled empires on the coastal fringes of the continent. According to the traditional view, the Huns, Magyars, Turks and Mongols were all part of the same process, the driving force behind which was the imbalance in wealth between the prosperous civilisations of the littoral zones of Asia and Europe and the barren steppes of the interior. The pastoral economies of the grasslands were rich in livestock and certain natural resources, but were not self-sufficient in grain and other agricultural produce, in textiles, or in goods which required specialist craftsmen to produce. The theory is that the nomads needed to acquire these from their settled neighbours, either by trade, or by war and the imposition of tribute. Thus the Mongol conquests have sometimes been seen as the culmination of 'a primitive attempt to abolish inequality: as the most stupendous and continuous programme of forced aid ever carried out'. But recent research has modified this view in several important respects. Firstly, archaeological work in previously neglected regions of Central Asia has established that steppe societies were far more self-sufficient than had been appreciated. Metalworking was widespread, exploiting extensive local reserves of iron and copper; crops could be grown in irrigated areas and along rivers fed by meltwater from the mountains; and even where most of his food came from animals, the average nomad was better nourished than his contemporaries in farming countries. Equally important was the role of long-distance trade. This not only supported the city states of the Silk Road which connected China and the Mediterranean, but diffused precious metals and other goods among the nomads, as tolls or tribute, or by stimulating demand for horses, hides and other local products. The tribute exacted from China by nomad invaders often included items like silk and gold, but these were easily-transported prestige goods which may have been more of symbolic value to the victors than essential to their societies. It has been noted that the loot which they took by force was more often people and livestock, which represented moveable wealth in their economy, than the grain which they were supposed to need for survival. One analysis has gone so far as to turn the whole argument on its head, maintaining

that the Central Asians were more often than not the victims of aggression by the surrounding empires – especially China – and that our idea of the former as 'barbarians' stems solely from an uncritical reliance on biased Chinese records.

So we need not suppose that the Mongols were driven to expand outwards by vague world-historical forces, nor that poverty and envy of their settled neighbours were inevitable results of their lifestyle. It may nevertheless be true that a particular trigger for their conquests was a period of drought which is known to have affected the eastern steppes during the late twelfth century. However, the most recent tree ring data from Mongolia provides a more detailed and more complex picture. The growth rings on trees vary in thickness from one year to another, being wider in seasons with plenty of rain, so if samples can be found going back far enough they can give an indication of the weather conditions in a specific year. It appears that a period of drought did begin in the 1180s, and continued until 1211, which was an exceptionally wet year. The following two years were again dry, but then for twelve years from 1214 there was a succession of heavy rains. This is significant because the increased rainfall would have improved growing conditions not only for the trees, but for the grass on which the Mongols relied to feed their herds. In fact productivity might have increased by a factor of four or five, enabling much larger numbers of horses, cattle and sheep to be maintained. It would also of course be easier to move large armies across the steppe if more forage was available for the horses. The era of drought might be tied in with the period of violence on the steppe as the tribes fought over scarce grazing grounds, culminating in their enforced unification after 1206. The increased rainfall came too late to account for Genghis' rise to power, but it could have greatly improved both the economy and the logistic flexibility of his new empire from 1211 onwards. It is also possible that it encouraged more widespread acceptance of his regime, in accordance with the Chinese tradition that associated good weather with Heaven's endorsement of a monarch's right to rule.

The apparently barren steppe was also rich in other ways. The

Mongols' use of regular autumn hunts as training for war is well known, but the grassland fauna is less often appreciated as a logistic factor in their campaigns. Modern ecologists recognise what they call a 'shifting baseline syndrome' – a reference to the fact that our expectations are now so diminished that we find it impossible to appreciate how much more productive most natural environments were before the era of mass overexploitation. But there is reason to believe that the wild game of the Central Asian steppe was once as abundant as the buffalo herds of the North American plains in the nineteenth century, and far more diverse. According to the *Secret History*, when Genghis despatched his general Subotei in pursuit of the sons of Toqto'a in 1216, his main concern was that the men might be distracted by the abundance of wild animals they would encounter, and tempted into exhausting their horses by chasing them. And Juvaini tells how, when Genghis summoned his son Jochi to join him after the capture of Samarkand, the latter arrived from the steppes to the north driving herds of wild asses in front of him 'like sheep'. On this occasion the animals were not eaten, but captured when exhausted, branded and presumably drafted as baggage animals. At the same time Chagatai and Ogodei went hunting swans at Qara Kol, the 'Black Lake' in Uzbekistan, and sent fifty camel-loads of the birds every week to their father 'as a sample'. With such abundance of food available, there can have been little difficulty in supplying the Mongol warriors or their families in their own environment. And as hunters, the Mongols would also have been skilled at making use of wild animal products such as bone, hides and glue to repair their armour and other equipment. The main constraint on the mobility of the nomads and their armies was undoubtedly the availability of grass and water for the horses, an issue to which we will return in Chapter 3.

If their nomadic lifestyle did not automatically make the Central Asian tribes more aggressive, or force them to attack their neighbours out of sheer desperation, it certainly contributed to their effectiveness if they did decide to go to war. Hunting encouraged familiarity with weapons – bows and arrows in particular. Herdsmen often worked without supervision and needed to be self-reliant, but at the same time to be able to cooperate with their neighbours in occasional large-scale migrations. Most nomads did not wander across the steppe at will, but followed regular traditional routes between summer and winter pastures, so that twice a year the whole community would move together with their tents, wagons and other possessions. Such a migration could involve transporting several thousand people over a distance of hundreds of miles, while at the same time ensuring their security against predators, both human and animal. This was excellent training for the logistical side of warfare, and at the same time it instilled in the people a respect for the virtues of discipline and loyalty. An army of stockbreeders was also highly mobile, because of its easy access to large numbers of horses, and could take its food supply and even its families with it on campaign with a minimum of disruption to the economy. This is why, despite the disparity in numbers between the sparsely-populated steppe and the surrounding agricultural civilisations, the people of the former managed not only to retain their independence over thousands of years, but on occasion to impose their authority on the farmers.

The Nomads and China
Of all the settled lands around the edges of the steppe the one closest to Mongolia, and most intimately involved with events there, was China. Along the northern frontier of China a series of nomad invaders from the north managed to establish themselves at various times in the settled zone, only to be gradually absorbed into the larger native population. Then the Chinese would resume the initiative and push their garrisons and agricultural colonies out into the steppes, until they eventually overreached themselves and the whole cycle began again. Under the T'ang dynasty of the seventh to ninth centuries AD Chinese power had extended far into Central Asia, but in 907 the T'ang empire collapsed and China was divided among numerous mutually hostile warlords in an era known as the 'Five Dynasties and Ten Kingdoms'. At that time several tribes from the north had taken advantage of the confusion to migrate into north China. Among these were the Sha-t'o Turks, who had been brought in by the T'ang as mercenaries, the Tanguts from the Tibetan

borderlands who were recognised by the T'ang as subordinate 'kings' in the Ordos steppe of the upper Yellow River in return for similar services, and the Khitans from what is now Manchuria, newly united under their own self-styled 'emperor' of the Liao dynasty. In 960 a Chinese officer named Chao K'uang-yin managed to bring most of the country under his control and established a new native dynasty, the Sung, but the Khitans retained control of sixteen districts in the northeast. They also pushed their frontier west into what was later to become known as Mongolia, holding a line of garrisons along the Orkhon River and imposing a temporary peace in that turbulent region. The Sung were also forced to recognise the Tangut state of Hsi Hsia in the northwest as an independent, if nominally subordinate, kingdom. The Sung made a lasting peace with the Khitans in 1004, but in 982 they launched the first in a long series of unsuccessful campaigns against Hsi Hsia. One reason for their hostility was that the Tanguts controlled not only the best horse-rearing lands in the empire, but also the economically valuable trading cities along the Silk Road. Another was that the interlopers refused to acknowledge the Sung emperors as their overlords as they had with the T'ang; in 1040 their ruler Chao Yuan-hao even proclaimed himself emperor, thus putting himself on an equal footing with the Sung emperor as the head of a fully independent state.

The Chinese campaigns against Hsi Hsia continued until 1119, but succeeded only in weakening the Sung state. Although greatly outnumbered, the Tanguts had superior cavalry and were usually fighting on the defensive, so they were almost invariably victorious. But by this time an even greater threat had emerged at the other end of the Sung's northern frontier. One of the Khitan's Manchurian subject peoples, the Jurchens, had rebelled against their overlords, and in 1115 had set up their own Chinese-style dynasty, the Chin or 'Golden' under Wan-yen Akuta. The Sung Emperor Hui-tsung, instead of supporting the Liao as a friendly buffer state, stabbed them in the back in the hope of regaining the lost sixteen districts, but succeeded only in distracting the Khitans long enough to enable the Jurchens to overrun the entire northeastern frontier. Many of the

Khitan ruling classes fled westwards into Central Asia, where they established the state of Qara-Khitai west of the Altai Mountains, while others became reluctant subjects of the Jurchens. In 1127 the Chin armies captured the Sung capital at K'aifeng and took possession of the whole of the northern half of the empire, forcing the Sung to retreat to a new capital at Hangchow in the south, now known as 'Lin-an' or 'Temporary Peace'. Over the next half-century both the Chin and the Sung tried repeatedly to overthrow the other and reunite the empire, but the result was only to weaken both.

What was more, the Jurchen regime had already established itself as the natural enemy of whoever controlled Mongolia. In many ways the Chin had become a typical Chinese dynasty, but it had never turned its back on the steppes as most other successful invaders tended to do. Neither, however, did it try to maintain a direct military presence as the Khitans had done. Instead it abandoned the Orkhon garrisons and pursued a 'forward policy' in Mongolia, by supporting its own protégés among the contending nomad chiefs who moved into the vacuum left behind. However, the way in which this policy had been executed was remarkably inept. According to the Sung general Meng Hung, the Jurchen rulers had reversed a longstanding Chinese embargo on supplying iron to the steppe tribes, and in fact had made the situation worse by refusing to accept the old Sung iron currency as legal tender. The people had therefore sold their useless coins as scrap to merchants who had transported them to Mongolia, where they were forged into weapons and armour. This may have been a factor in the increased availability of metal in the Mongol armies, but it is unlikely to have been as significant as Meng Hung suggests. The Turks and other steppe peoples had in fact been famous as iron workers since at least the fifth century AD, and most of their supplies of metal undoubtedly came from within Central Asia itself.

More serious for the Chin was that their meddling in steppe politics had made them some formidable enemies. In the mid-twelfth century they had supported the Tatars, which made them natural opponents of the Borjigin Mongols, who had made a successful bid for independence under Kabul Khan, the great-grandfather of the future Genghis Khan. Kabul seems to have been on the way to establishing some sort of central control over all the various Mongolian tribes, but Jurchen plotting sabotaged the attempt. The Chin emperor first invited Kabul to a conference in his capital at Chung-tu (modern Beijing), then connived at a botched attempt to assassinate him on his way home. Finally, in 1161, the Chin sent troops to support a Tatar army which smashed the Borjigin confederation. Ambakai, Kabul's nephew, was handed over to the Jurchens by the Tatars and humiliatingly put to death by being impaled on a wooden donkey with knives set into its back. But the Tatars were unable to consolidate their victory, and as soon as the Jurchen troops were withdrawn Mongolia collapsed into anarchy. The Chin emperors nevertheless continued to consider themselves the overlords of the Mongol chiefs, awarding them empty titles and demanding tribute in return.

One Borjigin who managed to maintain a small following in these turbulent times was Kabul's grandson Yesugei. He supported a Kerait neighbour, Toghril, in his bid to become chief of that tribe, and was rewarded with the status of 'anda', or blood brother. But he also earned the renewed hatred of the Tatars, and one day about the year 1170, after visiting a Tatar camp, he fell ill and died. His family always believed, as the *Secret History* alleges, that he had been poisoned. Yesugei left behind a widow, Ho'elun, and five young children, of whom the eldest was eight-year-old Temujin. Temujin also had two half-brothers by a junior wife of Yesugei. The boy had been named after a Tatar captive taken at the time of his birth, a traditional way of celebrating a victory over the old enemy. The name is derived from the Turkish and Mongolian word for iron, implying a worker in that metal, and so is a near equivalent of the English Smith. But Temujin was to become far better known by the title he took for himself in later life – Genghis Khan. The outline of his early career given in the *Secret History* contains a number of mythological elements – such as the clot of blood which he was supposedly clutching in his hand when he was born – but also vividly depicts the anarchy of the times and the precariousness of life for a boy without powerful protectors. Ho'elun fell out with two noblewomen of the Tayichi'ut clan, who persuaded Yesugei's people to desert her and follow one of their leading men, Tarqutai, leaving the widow and her seven children and stepchildren to fend for themselves. They survived by fishing, hunting and gathering wild plants, but life was difficult and the boys often quarrelled over the meagre spoils. It was at this time that Temujin killed his first victim – his half-brother Bekter, shot with an arrow in retaliation for stealing a small fish that he and his brother Qasar had caught. Their mother was furious with her sons for fighting with their own kinsfolk at a time when, as the *Secret History* puts it, 'apart from our shadows we have no friends, apart from our tails we have no fat'. (The latter is an allusion to the fat-tailed sheep, which in times of scarcity lives on its reserves like a camel on its hump.) Her lecture on the need for the family to stick together, quoted at length by the same source, seems to have had a major influence on Temujin, who throughout his life insisted on the value of family solidarity and mutual loyalty.

Chapter 2

War on the Steppes

By 1177 Temujin was approaching manhood, and the Tayichi'ut chief Tarqutai seems to have realised that he could one day become a threat. Ho'elun's family must have got wind of a plot to abduct the boy, because the *Secret History* describes them building a barricade of logs in the forest from behind which they could defend themselves. When the Tayichi'uts came and demanded that they hand over Temujin, he escaped on horseback while his siblings fought a delaying action. Qasar, who was already known as a powerful archer, shot arrows from the shelter of the barricade, while his brothers Qachi'un and Temuge, and their younger sister Temulun, prepared to fight from the cover of a narrow gorge. But the enemy ignored them and rode after their older brother, whom they eventually captured after cornering him in a thicket. It is not clear what Tarqutai intended to do with his prisoner, but he first ordered him to be fastened into a 'cangue' – a wooden plank with holes through which the head and hands were secured – and displayed in each of his people's camps in turn, perhaps to convince those who were inclined to sympathise with Yesugei's son that his was now a lost cause. But in the tent of one man, Sorqan-shira, Temujin did meet with sympathy, and his host's sons loosened the ropes that fastened the cangue to make him more comfortable. The following evening the prisoner was taken to eat by an inexperienced young man who was holding one end of the rope attached to the cangue. Seeing his opportunity Temujin jerked the rope, pulling the youth towards him, knocked him down with the edge of the board, and ran for the nearby Onon River, where he submerged himself until only his head was visible. The guard gave the alarm and the Tayichi'uts started after him. It was now dark, but the moon was full, and Temujin would certainly have been recaptured but for the appearance of Sorqan-shira, who not only decided not to give him away, but distracted the pursuers by suggesting other places they should search. He later gave the fugitive temporary shelter in his camp and provided him with a horse. Eventually Temujin returned to his mother.

Though still poor, and forced to subsist on marmots and field mice, the family was beginning to assemble a small herd of horses. The *Secret History* tells how one day rustlers swept down and drove off eight of them, leaving only a chestnut on which one of the brothers, Belgutei, had been out hunting marmots. Temujin took this horse and tracked the thieves for three days, until he met a youth named Bo'orchu tending his father's herd. Bo'orchu not only showed Temujin the direction the thieves had taken, but immediately offered to accompany him. This was another example of Temujin's extraordinary ability to win friends, though it is likely that Bo'orchu was simply bored with his task and eager for any adventure. Together they located the rustlers' camp and drove off the stolen horses, while Temujin shot arrows at a lone pursuer until he gave up the chase in the gathering dusk. The two became firm friends, and Bo'orchu later came to join Temujin's small band. Another reinforcement arrived at about the same time. While Yesugei was still alive he had betrothed Temujin to Borte, the daughter of Dei-sechen, a chief of the Onggirats, and the boy now brought her home as his bride. With her came a dowry, a valuable black sable jacket, which her husband realised could be turned into the political support he so badly needed. So he went in search of his father's old friend, Toghril of the Keraits, and presented him with the jacket as a token of allegiance. Toghril was sufficiently impressed to promise Temujin that he would provide troops to reunite the scattered Borjigins and restore him to his rightful place as their chief. On the way back home the boy received another valuable addition to his group in the person of Jelme, son of Jarchi'udai of the Uru'ut clan, whose father had apparently dedicated him to Temujin's service when the latter was born, in the days when Yesugei was powerful enough to be a patron worth cultivating. But it says much for either Jarchi'udai's faith or Temujin's growing charisma that the old man still thought it was worthwhile keeping to the bargain. Jelme eventually rose to become one of Genghis' four leading generals.

In the following year, while the family was camped near the source of the Kerulen River, they were surprised at dawn by another raiding party. An old servant woman gave the alarm, and supposing that the attackers were Tayichi'uts come to kill him, Temujin mounted a horse and escaped, followed by his mother, brothers and sister. The *Secret History* describes how Ho'elun took her daughter Temulun on the front of her saddle while leading another horse. But the result was that there was no mount left for Borte, who was forced to hide under a load of wool in a cart driven by the old servant. They were quickly overtaken and captured by the enemy, who in fact turned out to be Merkits pursuing a very old feud – for Ho'elun was herself a Merkit, who had been abducted by Yesugei in similar circumstances many years before. Three of the Merkits went after the fleeing men, who presumably did not stop to find out how few they were, but kept riding until they reached the forests on the slopes of Mount Burkhan Khaldun. Temujin stayed in hiding for three days until his companions rode out and assured him that the enemy had gone. The *Secret History* tells how he expressed his gratitude to the servant who had raised the alarm, and to Burkhan Khaldun, which was henceforth regarded by the Mongols as a sacred mountain: 'I was greatly afraid. Every morning I shall sacrifice to Burkhan Khaldun, and every day I will pray to it. The seed of my seed shall know this.' The whole affair seems rather discreditable to the future Khan and to his mother, who surely could have allowed Borte to ride the spare horse. One even wonders whether Ho'elun was an accessory to her fellow Merkits' plan. However, the real motive behind the tale is not entirely clear. To suppose that the *Secret History* relates any incident for no other reason than that it happened, in the style of a modern historical work, would be to misunderstand its purpose. One objective seems to have been to establish the credentials of Burkhan Khaldun as a holy place;

another was perhaps to set the scene for forthcoming events. This is not the first instance of this source telling a story that one might have thought Genghis would rather have suppressed. When Yesugei first took his young son to meet Borte, he left him in her father's camp with instructions to look out for him because he was frightened of dogs. This is sometimes taken as an example of the *Secret History*'s admirable honesty in giving a 'warts and all' portrait of its hero, but it is nevertheless an unusual detail to encounter in such a source. Onon suspects that it may be a coded reference to a threat from human enemies, which subsequent events had clearly shown to be well founded.

Temujin's First Campaigns

Temujin's next move was to go to visit Toghril and call in the favour he was owed. The Kerait leader not only agreed to field an army to attack the Merkits, but suggested to Temujin that he should also seek help from another family friend, Jamuqa, with whom he had been close as a boy. At this point the true value of the connections that Temujin and his father had maintained with the various tribal aristocracies became apparent, because Jamuqa was by now chief of the Jajirat clan, and the *Secret History* in different passages describes his following as totalling either 10,000 or 20,000 men. With Toghril providing a similar number, the youth who only a short time before had been a poverty-stricken fugitive suddenly found himself at the head of a formidable army. The actual numbers are probably greatly exaggerated, but the reversal of fortune must have been real enough. Furthermore, Jamuqa had some useful intelligence about the Merkit commanders and their dispositions. Their 'beki' or prince, Toqto'a, he said, was camped between the Orkhon and Selengge Rivers. He was a nervous character, who 'takes the flapping of the saddle cloth for the beating of drums', while his two subordinates were cowardly and treacherous. Jamuqa's information proved to be accurate. He joined up with Toghril, and the combined force crossed the Kilko River on rafts made of logs tied together with sedges. Then they advanced up the Selengge towards Toqto'a's camp, which was apparently defended by only 300 men. On learning of the enemy's approach the Merkits fled, and the Keraits and Mongols galloped through the camp, looting and cutting down any fugitives they could overtake. Temujin rode ahead calling out for Borte, and the couple were reunited in the midst of the slaughter.

After their victory Temujin and Jamuqa exchanged gifts and renewed the oath of brotherhood that they had first made as children. They travelled together for a year and a half, but eventually Jamuqa suggested that they should separate. The *Secret History* implies that his idea may have been simply to make the best use of the available grazing, but Borte persuaded Temujin that his friend was planning some kind of treachery. This was about 1182, and the future Genghis Khan was around twenty years old. By this time he was already the leader of a substantial following, and it is likely that Jamuqa saw his friend's growing popularity as a threat to his own position. If so he was right to do so, because after the split many of Jamuqa's men left him to follow Temujin. According to the *Secret History* one of these, Qorchi, related to his new master a dream which foretold that he would one day become 'master of the nation'. Temujin's reply suggests that the idea was not altogether new to him: 'If what you say is true . . .' he told Qorchi, 'I will make you the commander of ten thousand households.' Over the next few years more and more of the Mongol bands rallied to Temujin's cause, and in about 1189, with the approval of his old protector Toghril, he was formally proclaimed Khan of the Mongols, with authority over thirteen camps. At this point the *Secret History* starts to refer to him not as Temujin but as Genghis Khan, though it is not clear exactly when he adopted this title. 'Khan' was a title already in widespread use to denote the ruler of a tribe or nation. The precise meaning of Genghis, or 'Chinggis' as it is often written, has always been controversial, but the consensus still seems to be in favour of a derivation from 'tengiz', or 'oceanic', which in the Turkish and Mongol languages has the additional sense of 'universal'. An alternative theory associates it with the word 'ching'; 'firm' or 'strong'. Ratchnevsky suggests that the former was the original meaning, but that the Mongols themselves eventually forgot it, leading to confusion with the idea of strength or ferocity. According to Juvaini the title was coined by a Mongol shaman, Teb Tengri, who was instrumental in promoting the cause of the new khan, but later fell out with him and was murdered by his brother, Temuge.

Jamuqa, however, had no intention of accepting his rival's claims, and soon found an opportunity to declare war. His younger brother Taichar had stolen some horses from one of Genghis' allies, a man named Jochi-darmala, who pursued Taichar and shot him dead. On the pretext of avenging his brother, Jamuqa raised an army said to be 30,000 strong and met Genghis in battle at Dalan-baljut. We have no details of the encounter, except that Genghis was beaten and forced to go into hiding in the woods along the Onon River, while Jamuqa committed some inexplicable atrocities against his prisoners, boiling many of them alive in cauldrons. This sounds a rather unlikely charge, but if Jamuqa had begun to act in a brutal and arbitrary fashion after his victory it could explain why the flow of deserters to Temujin, instead of lessening, actually gathered pace. Among the clan chiefs who now brought their warriors to him were Jelme's father Jarchi'udai, Quyildar of the Mangquts, and Yesugei's old friend 'Father' Monglik with his seven sons. Soon Genghis was able to rally his people, despite an unfortunate incident when fighting broke out between the Jurkin and the other clans over precedence at a feast. The *Secret History* then continues with the news that war had broken out between the Tatars and the Chin emperor, but it seems that this may conceal an obscure passage in Genghis' career. Chinese sources date this event to 1195, six years later, and Ratchnevsky quotes one of them, Chao Hung, as saying that the Khan once spent ten years as a slave of the Chin. It is conceivable that this episode occurred in the aftermath of the defeat by Jamuqa, but perhaps more likely that the allegation was concocted later by Chinese propagandists. It is certainly hard to see how Genghis could ever have recovered his position in Mongolia after such a long absence, given the number of potential rivals for the title of khan.

The war of 1195 occurred when the Tatar Khan Megujin-se'ultu refused to pay the tribute due to the Chin, and a Jurchen army advanced north into the steppes, driving the rebels before it. Genghis immediately saw this as an opportunity to destroy the hated Tatars, and sent a message to Toghril proposing a joint campaign. Once again Toghril was eager to help, and within three days he had assembled an army. Megujin-se'ultu had built a stockaded camp on the Ulja River and was preparing to make a stand against the Chin, but when Genghis and Toghril descended on him from the opposite direction he was taken by surprise. The Tatar chief was killed in the ensuing fight, while many of those working on the defences were taken prisoner. The victors then went to meet the Chin commander, who rewarded them with Chinese titles. Toghril became a 'Wang', or king, and was known subsequently by the Mongolian version of the title, 'Ong Khan'. Genghis, who was obviously still regarded as the junior partner in the alliance, was given the rank of 'Ja'ut-quri', or commander of a frontier district. The men of the Jurkin clan had failed to join the campaign, and on his return to his camp Genghis found that they had caused more trouble, killing ten men and stealing a quantity of clothing before taking to flight. He therefore led the army out again and found the Jurkin on an island in the Kerulen River. He defeated them, executed their chiefs, and 'reorganised' the people, distributing them among the other clans. This was perhaps the first instance of a method which he was later to use much more widely to prevent the establishment of rival power-bases by tribal chieftains. However, in this case it failed, as Jurkin warriors are later recorded as part of a coalition fighting against him.

The Tayichi'uts and the Tatars
In 1201, clearly fearful of the combined power of Toghril and Genghis, the Tayichi'uts, Merkits, Naimans and various smaller tribes formed a confederacy under the leadership of Jamuqa. In the following year the opposing armies met in battle at a place called Koyiten. After an indecisive struggle up and down the slopes of a mountain, during which Genghis had his horse shot under him, a great storm broke and forced both sides to abandon the battle. Jamuqa's coalition, probably never very well organised, disintegrated as the different contingents each headed for their home territories. (The *Secret History* ascribes this disaster to two shamans

in Jamuqa's army, who bungled an attempt to employ magic rain stones against their enemies.) Toghril and Genghis rode in pursuit, the latter following a band of Tayichi'uts under A'uchu-ba'atur, while the Ong Khan went after Jamuqa himself. Eventually Genghis caught up with the Tayichi'uts, and another protracted struggle took place. The two armies fought until nightfall, then camped on the battlefield, still in close proximity. Genghis had again been in the thick of the fighting, and was wounded in the neck by an arrow: the *Secret History* tells the famous story of how Jelme saved his life by sucking the clotted blood from the wound, then sneaked into the enemy camp to steal a bowl of curds for him to drink. But in the morning it became apparent that the enemy had scattered, and by then Genghis had recovered sufficiently to lead a fresh pursuit. Among the fugitives the victors overtook a woman who addressed the Khan by name, and turned out to be the daughter of Sorqan-shira, the man who had rescued him from the Tayichi'ut camp many years before. She brought in her father and the rest of his family, who claimed that they had only been waiting for the right moment to defect; among them was a young man called Jirqo'adai, who confessed to having shot Genghis' horse at the Battle of Koyiten. Impressed by both his honesty and his marksmanship, the Khan took him into his service, bestowing on him the name of Jebei, 'the Arrow'.

In the aftermath of the victory the Tayichi'ut aristocracy were eliminated, says the *Secret History*, 'so that they blew in the wind like ash'. This was not a general massacre, however, for the same source then describes how most of the people were incorporated into Genghis' growing empire. His old enemy Tarqutai was captured by three of his own followers, who put him in a cart and started for Genghis' camp with the idea of handing him over. On the way, however, they repented of their treachery and let him go. They were later brought before Genghis, who explained that he would spare them, but that if they had gone through with their plan to betray their rightful lord he would have had them executed. Thus he publicly reinforced the message that what he valued in men above all else was loyalty. So far, in fact, Genghis' success seems to have been based mainly on his ability to inspire the devotion of a diverse collection of followers, and to organise them into a coherent force. He had not distinguished himself by any outstanding personal feats of arms, nor had he particularly shone as a battlefield tactician. He had up to this point enjoyed no easy victories, except when he possessed overwhelming numbers, as in the rescue of Borte from the Merkits, or the advantage of surprise, as against the Tatars on the Ulja River. He and his army were undergoing a tough apprenticeship, having to rely on luck and determination to survive in conflicts with foes as formidable as they were themselves. But at last this hard training was bearing fruit.

Jamuqa's alliance never reassembled, and Genghis' rivals became increasingly isolated from each other. In 1202 he marched against the Tatars, bringing them to battle at Dalan-nemurges. His orders issued before the clash, reported by the *Secret History*, suggest a new emphasis on discipline. No one, he said, was to stop to loot until the enemy was completely routed, and if they were forced to retire temporarily his troops were to rally at the place where they began the attack, rather than dispersing to their homes as was the usual practice. The result was a decisive victory, with the Tatar camp and most of their people falling into the hands of the Mongols. Three of Genghis' officers who had stopped to round up horses and goods from the enemy camp were punished by having all their plunder confiscated, and subsequently deserted to the Keraits. The Tatars were the first of the major tribes to be completely at Genghis' mercy, and as hereditary enemies and the murderers of his father, they suffered a particularly harsh fate. All the males who were taller than the linchpin of a wagon were killed, while the women and small children were distributed among the victors as slaves. A few men, however, were warned by Genghis' half-brother Belgutei and managed to escape. Genghis himself took two Tatar sisters as wives, despite the fact that one of them was already married to a Tatar fugitive who was still at large. One day, says the *Secret History*, Genghis heard the woman sigh deeply, and realising that she must have recognised someone from her past life, he immediately ordered all the men in the camp to parade in their units.

One man was left standing alone, and confessed that he was the missing husband, who had hoped to remain undetected in the crowd. Genghis' reaction reveals not just his ruthlessness, but also his continuing insecurity. 'What has he come looking for?' he asked. 'We measured those like him against a linchpin. What do you expect?' So this man was also killed.

The Split with the Keraits
In the same year Toghril's Keraits fought a successful campaign against the Merkits, and then he and Genghis joined forces to attack Buyiruq Khan, one of the leaders of the Naimans. Whether there was any underlying motive for this war, or whether their policy was now to suppress all political rivals in Mongolia, is not clear. Buyiruq refused battle and tried to escape west across the Altai Mountains, but was caught at Lake Kishil-bashi and his forces scattered. But on their way home the two allies found their way blocked by another Naiman army under Kokse'u-sabraq. They were unable to join battle at once as dusk was falling, so they camped for the night and prepared to attack on the following day. However, during the hours of darkness Toghril decamped and moved off up the Qara Se'ul River, leaving his camp fires burning, so that it was not until dawn that Genghis realised that he had been abandoned. He at once gave orders to avoid pursuit by the stronger Naiman forces by crossing the mountains that bordered the river valley, and his army emerged unscathed onto the Sa'ari Steppe. The *Secret History* adds that from then on he no longer regarded the Naimans as worth fighting. He had perhaps been influenced by their failure to attack him when he was vulnerable, but in fact Kokse'u-sabraq had instead marched in pursuit of the Keraits. He overtook Toghril and defeated him, capturing his wife and his son Senggum as well as the bulk of his herds. The *Secret History* attributes Toghril's desertion of Genghis to Jamuqa's intrigues, but whatever the reason for his actions Toghril seems to have no hesitation in appealing to Genghis once again. The latter agreed to help, and sent his four best generals, the 'war-horses' Mukhali, Boroqul, Bo'orchu and Chila'un-ba'atur, who liberated the captives and returned them to their people. A grateful Toghril, now

apparently conscious of his declining health and aware of Senggum's lack of leadership qualities, now declared Genghis to be his 'son' and successor as khan of the Keraits.

This was an obvious slight to Senggum, who responded by entering into negotiations with Jamuqa and trying to turn his father against Genghis. The *Secret History* depicts Toghril as an increasingly feeble and rather pathetic character, who tried to keep the peace between his 'sons', but eventually agreed to let Senggum have his way. The latter's plan was to pretend to agree to a marriage between his sister and Genghis' eldest son Jochi, then to capture the Khan and his entourage at the betrothal feast. Genghis set out for the feast with only ten men, but the Keraits had been discussing the plot too freely in their camp, and two sympathisers arrived to warn him in time to make his escape. He shook off pursuit by fleeing through the Great Khingan Mountains on the borders of Manchuria, and rejoined his army in time to prepare it for the inevitable clash. At the Qalaqaljit Sands he was engaged by a Kerait force which was under the nominal command of Toghril, but in fact it had been drawn up for battle by the old enemy Jamuqa. Both armies seem to have been deployed in depth. The *Secret History* gives a comprehensive list of the tribal contingents on both sides. Jamuqa placed the Jirkins in the vanguard, followed in succession by the Tumen-Tubegens, the Olon-dongqayits, the Torqods and the Kerait main body, each placed to guard the rear of the units in front. On Genghis' side the Uru'uts and Mangquts volunteered to lead the attack and drove off the Jirkins, only to be attacked by the Tumen-Tubegens, who wounded and unhorsed Quyildar, the commander of the Mangquts. While the latter rallied around their fallen chief, the Uru'uts under Jarchi'udai made a heroic stand, defeating the next three waves of the enemy in turn. Senggum then advanced with the bulk of the Keraits – without orders we are told – but the attack faltered when he was hit in the cheek by an arrow. But despite the heroics described by the *Secret History* it is evident that Genghis was in fact defeated, because he is then described as breaking off the engagement and halting briefly to collect stragglers, among whom was his son Ogodei, who had been badly wounded in the neck and was brought in by Boroqul. Rashid ud-Din adds that it was only the wounding of Senggum that had prevented the Keraits from totally routing the Mongols. In the *Secret History*'s version the Khan kept repeating, 'If the enemy come, we will fight', but when the dust of the advancing Keraits was seen they continued to retreat, eventually arriving at Dalan-nemurges, the scene of the victory over the Tatars. If the *Secret History*'s figures are even approximately correct the defeat must have been serious, because when he finally reassembled his army Genghis had only 2,600 men still under his command. He divided them into two equal columns which moved down opposite banks of the Qalqa River towards the country of the Onggirats, where he hoped to find reinforcements.

Meanwhile Toghril had been persuaded that Genghis had lost too many men in battle or to desertion to be able to recover his strength, and had abandoned the pursuit to look after his wounded son. So the Khan was able to negotiate unmolested with the Onggirats, collect further stragglers – who eventually included his brother Qasar – and gradually rebuild his strength in the forests around Lake Baljuna in the far southeast of Mongolia. Some recruits arrived from further afield, including two Khitan princes, Ila Ahai and Tuka, who hoped for support against the Jurchens. Some Muslim traders, including a certain Ja'afar, who later performed useful service in China, may also have made contact with Genghis at this time. Juvaini and the Chinese sources all refer to what became known as the 'Baljuna Covenant', by which Genghis declared a special bond with nineteen loyal followers who had remained with him throughout this darkest hour, and 'drunk the muddy water' of the lake with him. According to Juvaini the names of all those who accompanied Genghis at Baljuna were recorded, down to the slaves and grooms, who rather surprisingly included 'Turks, Tajiks and Indians'. The *Secret History*, however, does not mention this episode, possibly because some of the men involved later fell from favour. It does, however, quote from a series of messages which Genghis sent from his hideout in an attempt to provoke dissension among his enemies. Qasar, who had left his family in the Kerait camp, also used his situation to open negotiations with Toghril.

The messengers returned to report that the old man had split with Jamuqa, and that he and Senggum were camped at the Jer-qabchiqay Pass, feasting and apparently unprepared for war. Genghis responded without hesitation. Toghril had also despatched a messenger – or spy – Iturgen, who as he approached Genghis' camp saw the Mongol army advancing in battle array, in an attempt to take the Keraits by surprise. Iturgen turned and galloped back to warn his master, but a Mongol named Chaqurqan brought down his horse with an arrow shot at extreme range, and the scout was captured and executed by Qasar. Consequently the Keraits were completely unprepared when Genghis surrounded and besieged their camp. They nevertheless resisted for three days, but eventually Toghril and his son broke out and escaped, and the survivors surrendered. In contrast to the Tatars, the Keraits were treated relatively leniently. The people were mainly distributed among the Mongol commanders to form part of their retinues. Badai and Kishiliq, the two men who had first warned the Khan of Senggum's treachery, were rewarded with the golden tent and other personal possessions that had belonged to Toghril. The Ong Khan himself fled to the Naimans, where he was killed by a sentry who failed to recognise him. Senggum was abandoned in the Chol Desert by his groom, who went to report to Genghis what he had done and was executed for his pains. However, his former master survived and fled as far west as Kashgar, in the country of the Uighurs, before he too met his death.

The Naiman War

Now all of Genghis' Mongolian rivals had been vanquished apart from the Naimans and Jamuqa, who had now gone to join them. The ruler of the Naimans, Inancha-bilge Khan, was old, and his heir was a stupid and irresponsible young man known as Tayang Khan (another empty Chinese title, meaning in this case 'Great King'). According to the *Secret History* he and his mother mocked Genghis and his followers as uncouth barbarians, boasting that they would round them up as slaves, and joking that they might allow the Mongol women to milk the Naiman cattle as long as they washed their hands first. Their general Kokse'u-sabraq, who had already encountered the Mongols at first hand, advised caution, but in 1204 Tayang sent a messenger to the Ongguts, asking them to join him in a war against Genghis. The Onggut chief Ala-qush-digit-quri refused, and instead warned Genghis of the impending attack. When the news arrived the Khan established a camp at Keltegei Cliffs on the River Qalqa. The account in the *Secret History* of the preparations which took place there is the first detailed discussion of the organisation of the Mongol army, and it seems that many of its best-known features were introduced at this time. The soldiers were organised into units of ten, a hundred and a thousand, under officers appointed personally by the Khan. One thousand picked 'heroes' formed an elite guard unit under Arqai-qasar. There was also a smaller bodyguard for Genghis himself, consisting of seventy day guards and eighty night guards.

Then when his preparations were complete, in the early summer of 1204, Genghis rode out to meet the Naimans. On top of Mount Qangqarqan, overlooking the Sa'arl Steppe, they encountered a screen of enemy scouts, and in the ensuing skirmish a Mongol horse was captured and taken back to Tayang Khan. Genghis was aware that his mounts were still lean after the winter, and the march had tired them, so he accepted advice to camp on the steppe and rest. Because Tayang was known to lack determination, the Mongols were ordered to light extra camp fires, five per man, to give the enemy the impression of overwhelming numbers. The *Secret History* tells how scouts returned to the Naiman camp with the discouraging news that 'there are more fires than stars'. Tayang was so worried that he proposed to retreat and try to lure the Mongols into an ambush, but his son Kuchluq regarded this as cowardice, pointing out that Genghis could not have that many men since so many of the Mongols were on their side, with Jamuqa. What was more the captured horse showed how out of condition Genghis' mounts must be. Kuchluq went on to lament the fact that Kokse'u-sabraq was getting too old to take the field, and suggested that his grandmother should be sent for, as she would do a better job of commanding the army than Tayang. The Naiman Khan, insulted, agreed to fight. He crossed the Orkhon River and marched towards Genghis' position, but then seems to have lost his nerve again, because as the Mongols deployed for battle the Naimans fell back and took up a defensive position on the slopes of Mount Naqu-kun.

According to the *Secret History*, Genghis personally took charge of the vanguard, with his brother Qasar commanding the main body. He issued his orders according to what must by now have been a standard tactical doctrine, with the troops marching in 'bush clump' formation, deploying in 'lake array', and charging with a 'chisel attack' (see pages 70–1 for a discussion of what these terms may have meant). Certainly the order of the Mongol army as it advanced must have been impressive, because the same source goes on to describe how Tayang Khan's morale collapsed even before a blow had been struck. In a well-known but rather puzzling passage, it relates how Tayang asked Jamuqa, who was standing by his side, who the enemy were and what they were doing. Jamuqa replied with a series of tall tales about the prowess of Genghis' men, which frightened his ally into retreating further and further towards the top of the mountain. He then sent a message to his rival Genghis, assuring him that he had neutralised the Naiman threat, and that he had himself deserted them. Eventually the Naimans were forced to camp for the night on the summit, where Genghis surrounded them. During the night they tried to break out, but many were killed by falling from the rocks, and in the morning the Mongols mopped up the survivors with ease. The Naimans were crushed beyond recovery, though Kuchluq managed to escape to the west. The Mongols who had followed Jamuqa also went over to Genghis, but their former leader was nowhere to be found.

The whole story is rather difficult to believe, as no motive is given for Jamuqa's betrayal of the Naimans, and it is in any case implausible that Tayang should have been so demoralised that he allowed his army to be destroyed without a fight. We might also expect, if Jamuqa had decided to help Genghis, that he would have joined him after the battle, whereas he is next heard of as a refugee in the mountains, hunting wild sheep with a handful of companions. Rashid ud-Din says that in fact he did unintentionally demoralise the Naimans, but only because he panicked himself. The passage in the

Secret History is surely an excuse to reproduce a number of verses which were current, extolling the valour and ferocity of the Mongol leaders. Jebei, Jelme, Qubilai and Subotei are described as four hounds fed on human flesh, who chase the enemy as wolves do sheep. The Uru'uts and Mangquts go into battle rejoicing and riding in circles, like foals kicking their legs in excitement as they are released in the morning. Qasar is a giant who can swallow a man whole, while Genghis himself has the look of a starved falcon eager for flesh. It must have made stirring reading for a Mongol audience, but for us it is unfortunate that the real events of the most decisive battle in Genghis' early career have been obscured in this fashion.

After his victory at the Battle of Mount Naqu-kun, however it was achieved, Genghis turned his attention to the Merkits. In the autumn he met Toqto'a in battle on the Black Steppe and defeated him. The Merkit leaders escaped, but many of their people were captured. They were treated leniently, but subsequently rose in rebellion twice, obliging Genghis to disperse the survivors among the rest of his followers. Toqto'a joined up with Kuchluq the Naiman and fought another battle with Genghis at the Erdish River, where Toqto'a was killed and many of his men drowned in the river as they fled. Finally, in 1205, Jamuqa was brought in by his remaining followers. Predictably Genghis executed the men who had betrayed their master, and then, according to the *Secret History*, forgave Jamuqa and urged him to join the Mongols. Jamuqa, however, replied that the two men could never trust each other again, and was put to death at his own request. Whether this is true, or whether this source is merely trying to avoid accusing Genghis of murdering his childhood companion, we do not know. Understandably, Morgan suggests that in relating this version of events the author of the *History* was displaying a rather cynical sense of humour. But the result was that Genghis now had undisputed control over the whole of Mongolia. After he had 'unified the people of the felt-walled tents', says the *Secret History*, 'they assembled at the source of the Onon River in the Year of the Tiger'. This was 1206, and the event was one of the most significant in world history – the great assembly, or 'quriltai', at which the united Mongol nation formally came into being.

Mopping up in Central Asia

The 'quriltai' of 1206 may have marked an important stage in Genghis' rise to power, but the expansion of his empire was by no means at an end. In 1207 he sent his son Jochi to establish Mongol authority over the Oirats and Kirghiz who occupied the forests west of Lake Baikal. According to the *Secret History* they all submitted voluntarily, and Jochi added 20,000 warriors to the Mongol strength without losing a man or a horse, to his father's great satisfaction. Unrest continued sporadically for several years, however. In 1216 the Tumads, another people living in the same region who had previously sent tribute to Genghis, imprisoned Qorchi, the Mongol officer whom Genghis had appointed to govern them. (The *Secret History* dates these events to a decade earlier, but most scholars follow Rashid ud-Din, who places the suppression of the Tumad revolt in 1217.) The Khan had given Qorchi permission to take thirty Tumad girls as his wives, but the insensitive way in which he had done this had upset the tribesmen. When the news reached Genghis he sent another official, Quduqa, to secure Qorchi's release. That the Khan resorted to diplomacy rather than immediately sending a military expedition suggests that he knew that Qorchi had provoked the trouble, but on his arrival Quduqa was also held prisoner. This time a war party was despatched under the leadership of Boroqul, one of the four 'war-horses' and an adopted son of Genghis of whom, according to Rashid ud-Din, he was particularly fond. Boroqul set out along the narrow trails through the forest, but one evening he marched into an ambush and was killed. According to the *Secret History* he was scouting ahead of the army at the time with only three companions. This disaster so angered Genghis that he prepared to ride out himself to avenge Boroqul. The Khan was dissuaded by Bo'orchu and Mukhali, and eventually the task was delegated to Dorbei Doqshin, who according to the *Secret History* planned his campaign meticulously. Strict discipline was imposed on the troops, who were ordered to travel not by the man-made routes which were being watched by the Tumad sentries, but by wild animal trails, cutting down trees and clearing the undergrowth if necessary. The *Secret History* implies that the Mongol troops were nervous in the vast Siberian forests, as would be natural for those brought up on the open steppe, because they were given staffs with which they were to beat anyone ahead of them who refused to advance. Meanwhile patrols acting as decoys moved along the normal trails to deceive the enemy into thinking that the army was following Boroqul's route. In this way Dorbei Doqshin climbed over a supposedly impassable mountain, and descended on the enemy camp as though 'through the top of the Tumad people's smoke holes' as they were feasting. The prisoners were released, and the Tumads were divided in the usual way among the followings of Genghis' leading nobles. One hundred of them were allocated in perpetuity as servants to Boroqul's descendants.

Simultaneously with Dorbei Doqshin's expedition, Jochi and a promising officer named Subotei were sent with 20,000 men to eliminate the last of the Merkits, who under Toqto'a's son Qultuqan Mergen ('the archer') had established themselves west of the Altai Mountains and begun launching raids into Mongolia. The Merkits fled west before this overwhelming force, but were eventually overtaken and destroyed. Juvaini says that this encounter took place between the Rivers Qaili and Qaimich, which Martin places north of the Irghiz River on what is now the Kazakhstan steppe. Qultuqan was captured and Jochi wanted to spare him because of his legendary skill as an archer, but his father would not allow it and the last Merkit prince was executed, along with the rest of his family.

The Kirghiz further north also revolted around this time. Rashid ud-Din says that they had already rebelled before Boroqul's death, but Martin, following the *Meng-wu-erh Shih*, argues that it was that disaster that had persuaded them that the time was right to challenge the Mongols. Genghis had asked the Kirghiz to send troops to help against the Tumads, but they had refused, so late in 1216 Jochi was sent to deal with them. His march took him across the Tannu Ula Mountains which separate northwestern Mongolia from Siberia, and into the valley of the upper Yenisei River. The Kirghiz gave battle on the far side of the mountains but were defeated, and Jochi rode north down the Yenisei, travelling on the frozen river, according to the *Meng-wu-erh Shih*, in preference to the forests on either bank. Near present-day Abakan, west of the Sayan Mountains, the Mongols found an extensive area of open grassland and fields of grain, surrounded by the forest, which was the main centre of Kirghiz power. There the rebels surrendered and agreed to provide hostages, and Jochi returned victorious to Mongolia. This was the furthest that Genghis' armies ever penetrated into the northern forests. But by this time greater events were unfolding far to the south.

Chapter 3

The Khan's Armies

The Organisation of the Mongol Army
We have seen how Genghis, like many of his leading followers, started his career without the benefit of a traditional tribal power-base. In his case this handicap resulted from the death of his father and the defections which followed, but for others it was inevitable, thanks to their relatively humble origins. Paradoxically, however, this was one of the reasons for Genghis' success: with no traditional political structure to worry about, he could start from scratch and organise his diverse forces in a new way. The solution he adopted was to group them not by their tribal origin but into units of standard sizes, commanded by men whom he promoted on the basis of merit and not birth. This system was even able to incorporate other, non-Mongol steppe nomads with a minimum of trouble, enabling ever bigger forces to be raised as the conquests gathered pace. It seems from Genghis' pronouncements in the *Secret History* and elsewhere that he was old-fashioned enough to regard his empire ultimately as the private possession of his own family and the closely-related Mongol aristocracy, but he was always willing to employ – and richly reward – capable individuals from outside that restricted circle. He also had the undoubted gift of inspiring loyalty. As explained in Chapter 2, one of his 'four war-horses', Bo'orchu, had met Genghis as a result of a chance encounter when the latter was pursuing some stolen horses. Bo'orchu had risked the wrath of his father by abandoning his own herds to help his new friend, and was later to become one of the Khan's most trusted advisors. The man who was to become the best known of all the Mongol generals,

Subotei, was the son of a blacksmith of the Uriangqat, a reindeer-herding tribe of the northern forests, while Chaghan, the commander of the Guard, was a Tangut who had been adopted as a child. Others were former enemies, or even prisoners of war. Jebei 'the Arrow', who has been described as 'probably the greatest cavalry general in the history of the world', was fighting with the Tayichi'uts when he was captured after the Battle of Koyiten. And the three leading civil administrators of the empire, Shigi-qutuqu, Ta-ta T'ong-a and Yeh-lu Chu-tsai, were respectively of Tatar, Uighur and Khitan origin. Shigi-qutuqu had been found as a young boy in an abandoned Tatar camp and adopted into Genghis' family, where his organisational skills soon became apparent. The result of this pragmatic policy was that Genghis was exceptionally well served by his subordinates, and unlike most of his opponents he seems never to have been forced to adapt his strategy to take into account the potential disloyalty of his officers or men.

Describing Genghis' reorganisation of the Mongol peoples at the 'quriltai' of 1206, the *Secret History* names eighty-five 'commanders of thousands', plus three chiefs who led larger tribal contingents not yet incorporated into the new system – Alchi guregen with 3,000 Onggirats, Butu guregen with 2,000 Ikires, and Ala-qush-digit-quri guregen at the head of 5,000 Ongguts. The 'thousands', or 'minghans', were civil as well as military units, being based on communities of a thousand households, each of which was responsible for supplying a fighting man. They were further organised into higher-level formations of 10,000, known as 'toumans', and subdivided into 'hundreds' and 'tens', each under their own commanders. These were of course 'paper' strengths which may not always have been achieved in reality: we know from the Official History of the Yuan dynasty that later in the century 'toumans' were often no more than 3,000 strong. The commanders of each 'ten thousand' were appointed from among those who had been the Khan's most loyal companions during his rise to power; among them were Bo'orchu and Mukhali, who was honoured partly for his own contribution and partly for the sake of his father, who had been killed two years earlier after he gave his own horse to Genghis during a skirmish with the Naimans. These two men were also placed in overall charge of the units responsible for the western and eastern flanks of the army respectively (the 'Right Wing' and 'Left Wing' in Mongol terminology, according to which – as in ancient Chinese tradition – the army was always envisaged as facing south). The nominal strength of the army was 95,000 men, 'excluding the people of the forest', who presumably served in their traditional tribal units like the contingents mentioned above. Writing towards the end of the thirteenth century, Marco Polo also mentions a unit of 100,000 men, known as a 'tuk', but it is unlikely that in Genghis' day any field army was so large as to require such a subdivision.

Genghis subsequently ordered his bodyguard to be enlarged from the original seventy day guards and eighty night guards to the strength of a full 'touman' of 10,000. This was done by transferring the best men, especially the sons of officers, from the 'line' units. The expanded guard, like many of the other institutions of Mongol government, was probably inspired by Khitan practice, because the Liao emperors had had similar bodyguards of 10,000 or 20,000 men. The Kerait khans may also have copied the idea for their 1,000-strong 'day guard', and it has been suggested that it was via the Keraits that the idea was transmitted to the Mongols. The *Secret History* provides a detailed account of the commanders appointed to the various 'thousands' of Genghis' guard, and of the regulations governing their duties and the punishments for evading them. Security was so tight around the Khan's tent at night that a person could be arrested for entering the area patrolled by the night guards, or even for asking how many guards were on duty. The same source also records Genghis' decree that each individual guardsman was considered to be senior in rank to a commander of a thousand in the rest of the army. The guards now became the regular core of the army: 'In times of peace, let them stand guard. But on days of battle, let them stand to the fore as warriors.' The night guards, who now numbered a full thousand, also seem to have had certain judicial duties, performed under the supervision of Shigi-qutuqu. Nevertheless, Genghis emphasised that their primary function was to protect his person, so they were not to fight in battle unless he was present, and any officer trying to order them to do so was to be punished.

Rashid ud-Din gives an order of battle from the time of Genghis' death in 1227 which suggests that, although the strength of the army had increased since 1206, it was still relatively small in comparison with those of its enemies. It now comprised 62,000 men in the Army of the Left Wing; 38,000 in the Army of the Right Wing; 1,000 men of the Khan's guard in the centre; 4,000 each for his sons Jochi, Chagatai and Ogodei; and 16,000 commanded by the other members of the Khan's family. The total strength according to this list was 129,000, although this did not include the numerous non-Mongol units. Of course this was the total of the armed force available for the whole empire, and it was never all concentrated in any one place. Campaigns were undertaken by task forces built around the units belonging to their generals, who were usually commanders of toumans. Sometimes this gives us a fairly accurate guide to the strength of individual armies which can be confirmed from other sources, as when Juvaini says that the force sent to pursue Shah Muhammad of Khwarizmia in 1220, commanded by three named officers, totalled 30,000 men – the equivalent of three full-strength toumans. More frequently the sources fail to give us an indication of the size of the Mongol armies, but in the light of the above figures we can at least be certain that some of the higher estimates cannot be correct. For example Juzjani claims that the army which invaded Khwarizmia in 1219 was 800,000 strong, but even the Russian scholar Barthold, who reduced this enormous number by three-quarters, was still ascribing to Genghis far more than the total ration strength of his entire empire at the time.

An increasingly popular practice as time went on was for Mongol task forces to be formed by drafting men from other units to create new ones from a mixture of tribal origins, both Mongol and non-Mongol. This practice does not seem to have been common in Genghis' day, but became more so under his successors. Thus Juvaini says that Mongke Khan allocated two men out of every ten to Hulegu's army which was sent to invade Iraq in 1256. These *ad hoc* forces were known as 'tamma' armies, and were often employed on campaigns which would require them to be stationed on the frontiers of the empire for extended periods. One of their advantages may have been that, as the men were from different tribes and at first strangers to one another, they would be more amenable to discipline and less likely to revolt. Some of these forces remained at their posts for generations, until they eventually lost contact with the government in Mongolia, intermarried with local women and evolved into what might be thought of as new 'synthetic tribes'. For example, Professor Jean Aubin proved that the Qaraunas of Afghanistan, a tribe of mysterious origin whom Marco Polo met in 1272, had originally been a 'tamma' army despatched there by Genghis' successor Ogodei three or four decades earlier.

The Mongol Soldier
It is difficult from the surviving sources to tell which of the organisational features of the new Mongol army were introduced by Genghis, and which had their origins in tribal tradition. A system of grouping warriors in tens and multiples of ten, for example, had long been a feature of Turkish and other steppe forces. In any case the technical details of military organisation are only ever part of the story. The real secret of Mongol military success was surely the qualities of the ordinary trooper, brought up in a harsh environment, learning from an early age to survive the perils of famine, bad weather and hostile neighbours, his skills honed by several decades of internecine war. Juvaini states that 'it is recorded in no book that any of the kings that were lords of the nations ever attained an army like the army of the Tartars, so patient of hardship, so grateful for comforts, so obedient to its commanders both in prosperity and adversity'. ('Tartar' was a term commonly used in the west at the time for the Mongols and other peoples of the eastern steppes. It may have gained currency from an understandable confusion between Genghis' old enemies the Tatars, many of whom were now incorporated into the Mongol armies, and the inhabitants of Tartarus, the Classical hell.) Juvaini goes on to compare the Mongol soldiers to hungry dogs, which make the best hunters. They were used to obeying orders, totally familiar with their weapons, which they

carried with them in peace as well as in war; they willingly paid their taxes, and performed labour service as well as military service as a due to their rulers without having to be paid. Discipline was draconian. According to John de Plano Carpini, 'unless they retreat in a body, all who take flight are put to death'. The death penalty could also be imposed for leaving wounded comrades behind on the battlefield, or even for losing equipment. Unlike the settled farmers, whose crops would fail if left unattended, nomads could leave their livestock to graze and multiply in the custody of the women, children and old men. So while other kings could raise an army only at enormous expense, and usually took months to do so, those of the Mongol khans were ready for action at all times. Meng Hung says that every Mongol male between the ages of fifteen and sixty-one was liable to serve in the army when summoned. In fact in Juvaini's view they asked nothing more than that they should be sent to war, as plunder was their main source of income. As their commanders led them to victory after victory, their courage and confidence increased to the point where even overwhelming odds did not daunt them. Martin quotes the response of a general named Baiju to the concerns of a Georgian officer who, before a battle against the Seljuq Turks at Kuzadagh in 1243, pointed out that the Mongols were vastly outnumbered: 'You know not our Mongol people. God has given us the victory and we count as nothing the number of our enemies; the more they are the more glorious it is to win, and the more plunder we shall secure.'

The ability of Mongol troops to cope with forbidding terrain and harsh winter conditions was equally proverbial. In Mongolia itself winter temperatures can fall to -42°C or lower, and even in summer snow is not unknown, while violent winds can arise at any time. The steppe environment also required its inhabitants to be prepared to undertake long journeys on horseback with minimal preparation. Hence feats which outsiders considered miraculous, such as the passage of the Gobi or Kyzyl Kum Deserts, or the crossing of the frozen Yellow River in January, were routine to the Mongols. Even high mountain ranges seem to have presented no serious obstacle. Much of eastern Mongolia lies at an altitude of around 4,000 feet above sea level, and in summer the herds were moved to even higher pastures to escape the heat and the insects. This must have helped to acclimatise the men and horses to the conditions they would face when crossing the high passes. Martin cites several instances of Mongol armies using passes between 9,000 and 10,000 feet high in the Altai Mountains, and in the summer of 1218, while pursuing the Naiman Kuchluq, Jebei took his men over the Bedel Pass in the Tien Shan at an altitude of 12,600 feet. According to both Carpini and Marco Polo, rivers too deep to ford were crossed with the aid of large leather sacks which were filled with the troopers' possessions, tied up so that they were watertight and used as floats. The horses were driven into the water and guided across by a few scouts. Each man would then put his saddle on top of his sack and sit on it while holding onto the tail of a horse, or alternatively propelling himself with improvised oars. As described in Chapter 2, the *Secret History* also mentions river crossings made with the aid of improvised rafts.

Juvaini is our main source for the great hunting expeditions which took place every autumn on the steppe, and which – apart from their traditional role in providing meat for the winter – were consciously used as an opportunity to train the men for war. It is unlikely that Genghis was the first leader to do this, but from Juvaini's account it is clear that his hunts must have been on a far bigger scale than had previously been seen. Military units up to the strength of whole toumans were deployed around the area selected, sometimes starting many miles apart. They would then form an enormous ring which gradually contracted, trapping the wild game inside. It was strictly forbidden either to kill any animal before the Khan gave his permission, or to let it escape. This required careful cooperation between units as well as strict discipline, especially when it is considered that the creatures swept up in these hunts would include not only deer, horses and similar harmless species, but dangerous ones like wolves, bears, and even lions or tigers. When the ring was small enough the killing ground would be surrounded by ropes decorated with pieces of cloth to deter the quarry from escaping, and the Khan would personally begin the slaughter. Eventually the few surviving animals were released, and the carcasses were divided up among the hunters. This annual event was obviously a precursor of the large-scale annual manoeuvres used by modern armies to improve their techniques for handling large forces, and it may have given the Mongol generals a significant advantage in this respect over their settled opponents, who generally lacked the necessary space for such exercises, as well as the ready-made opponent in the great herds of wild game.

Clothing, Weapons and Armour

The Mongol soldier was equipped in a simple but practical fashion for the harsh climate of his homeland, though there does not seem to have been anything that we would recognise as a uniform. According to John de Plano Carpini, he usually wore a long fur or sheepskin coat, a fur cap with earflaps, and felt boots. Chinese paintings show that in hot weather he might discard the coat and replace the cap with a sort of low turban. He was armed with a bow as well as a selection of weapons for hand-to-hand combat, and in battle he donned an iron helmet and – if he could afford it – a suit of iron or leather armour. Men probably supplied most of their own equipment, and so the quality and quantity of weapons and armour might vary significantly within a unit. Modern writers often refer to Mongol 'light' and 'heavy' cavalry, implying the sort of distinction which existed between the hussars and cuirassiers of nineteenth-century European armies, for instance. However, in the great majority of contemporary accounts there is no suggestion that the members of the 'minghans' or 'toumans' were differentiated in any way according to their equipment or their function on the battlefield. It is true that Carpini says that within each unit the best-armoured men were placed in the front rank, but that is no more than one would expect of any military formation, and it need not mean that their tactical role was any different. A few units – the guards, and the Uru'uts and Mangquts during the wars of unification, for example – seem to have been regarded as especially effective, but the distinctions between the better armed and equipped aristocratic 'knights' and the lighter 'skirmishers' that we see in descriptions of the Khitan, Jurchen and other contemporary armies do not appear to have existed in the Mongol 'toumans'. Juvaini, emphasising the '*levée en masse*' nature of the Mongol army, describes it 'a peasantry in the dress of an army, of which, in time of need, all, from small to great, from those of high rank to those of low estate, are swordsmen, archers or spearmen'. But this writer is not very precise in his use of military terminology, and we cannot necessarily conclude from this one remark that the men with swords, bows and spears were not the same people. Nowhere else, in fact, is there any suggestion that there were Mongol soldiers who were not equipped with the bow, a weapon so characteristic of them that they were often referred to as 'the nation of the archers'.

The Mongol bow

Mongol sources seldom give much tactical detail, but the impression gained from the *Secret History* tends to confirm this reliance on archery. Genghis' mother, praising the strength of his brother Qasar, recalls how he forced his enemies to submit in long-range archery duels. Jamuqa, attempting to demoralise Tayang Khan before the Battle of Mount Naqu-kun in 1204, describes Qasar as a giant, who can shoot his arrows to an immense distance and slay ten or twenty men with each shot. Arrow wounds also predominate in actual battle accounts. It is recorded that several of Genghis' leading opponents, including Senggum of the Keraits and the Merkit Toqto'a, were killed or wounded by arrows on the battlefield, while others, like the Ong Khan's officer Iturgen, were captured when their horses were shot. Genghis himself famously had a horse killed under him by Jebei 'the Arrow', who brought the animal down with a single shot in the vertebrae of the neck. The other tribes of Mongolia, most of whom were eventually incorporated into the Mongol Empire, apparently depended on archery to a similar extent; for example the *Secret History* mentions three stragglers who returned to the Mongol camp after the battle against the Ong Khan's confederation at Qalaqaljit in 1203. One of these men had lost his horse to an arrow, while another had been shot in the neck.

The bow used by the Mongols and their nomadic neighbours was the composite type common in Central Asia and the Middle East, made from layers of horn, animal sinew and glue built around a wooden core. The all-wooden 'self bow' which was widespread elsewhere was much simpler to manufacture, but was less suitable for the steppe environment. Most importantly, wood was hard to obtain on the open grassland, and although much of northern Mongolia is forested, it does not provide wood of the quality needed to make powerful bows; in particular the yew, regarded in Europe as the best wood for longbows, does not grow so far east. So as early as the third millennium BC steppe craftsmen had been experimenting with bows reinforced with other materials, and some time in the second millennium BC the composite bow had appeared in an almost fully-developed form, probably in the Lake Baikal region. Making such a bow is a skilled and time-consuming task, but the end result is a weapon that is not just a substitute for a wooden bow, but actually has several advantages over it. The greater elasticity of the materials improves the cast, which is the speed at which the limbs will straighten after being bent, and hence increases the velocity of the arrow. A composite bow can also be designed so that it is only certain sections which bend, in contrast to the traditional yew bow which was made to come 'round compass', or in other words to bend evenly along its whole length to form a semi-circle. So the steppe weapon can be bent much further than its wooden equivalent without risk of breakage, and illustrations of steppe archers often show them drawing their bows to well behind the ear. Furthermore, by the first millennium AD these bows were frequently fitted with forward-angled rigid end sections known as 'siha', which acted as levers, making it easier to draw a heavy bow as well as further increasing the cast. Strickland and Hardy quote a modern test in which a composite bow with a draw weight of 59.5lbs shot an arrow at the same velocity as a yew longbow drawing 74lbs. Hence the Mongol bows could be made shorter without loss of power, making them more convenient for use on horseback. Excavated Central Asian weapons average between three and five feet long (with those from Mongolia being at the upper end of this size range), whereas self bows are normally about the same length as the shooter's height. A longer bow can be shot from the back of a horse, but it is difficult to manoeuvre it quickly, and in particular to swing it round to shoot backwards over the animal's tail – a favourite tactic of Central Asian horse archers, which became known as the 'Parthian shot' after the Parthian horse archers of Iran.

The actual method of drawing the composite bow is also different. Most archers around the world pull back the bowstring with two or more fingers, either gripping the arrow at the same time or, in the 'Mediterranean release' favoured in Europe, placing the fingers either side of the arrow without actually touching it. The latter was an improvement on more primitive methods as it enabled the full strength of the fingers to be devoted to pulling the string, but with the short composite bow, combined with the extreme length of draw, the string is at such an acute angle that it pinches the fingers, interfering with the release. So the steppe weapon is instead drawn with the thumb, which is locked in place by the index finger and usually protected from the concentrated pressure by a ring made of leather, horn or metal. Requiring the movement of only one digit, the thumb release is slightly faster and 'cleaner' than any of the various styles of finger release. Another factor is that with the thumb release, the position of the archer's wrist is roughly horizontal, and its natural rotation tends to push the arrow gently to the left (assuming a right-handed archer); the arrow is therefore placed on the right side of the bow, so that the pressure will tend to hold it in place. Exactly the opposite is the case with the Mediterranean release, in which the wrist is held vertical and the pressure is towards the right, encouraging the placing of the arrow on the left of the bow. The different archery styles are not therefore simply a matter of fashion or habit as is often thought, but are precisely tailored to the characteristics of the weapons in use. The author's own experiments suggest that with arrows kept in a quiver on the right hip, as the Mongols did, and the arrows placed on the right side of the bow, nocking and shooting is marginally faster (again, for a right-handed archer) than with any other arrangement. It is also worth noting that if an arrow is designed to be used with the thumb draw, the fletchings can be placed closer to the nock, where the shaft is fitted to the string, than is the case for the Mediterranean draw, where room must be left for the knuckles of the drawing fingers. It has been argued that the Mongolian design gives greater control for the equivalent surface area of fletching, so that the arrow will travel further and fly more steadily. How much difference these factors make in practice is difficult to quantify, as so much depends on the skill of the individual archer, but even a very slight 'edge' in speed or accuracy of shooting might be significant when there are tens of thousands of men involved, as there could be in a major battle. It may be significant that most of the exceptional feats of rapid shooting, both historical and contemporary, seem to have been achieved with bows of the composite type.

Discussion of methods of drawing the bow leads us to the question of draw weight, which is the amount of pull applied by the archer to bring the weapon to full draw, usually expressed in terms of lifting an equivalent weight. So for example a bow described as 'weighing' 100lbs, if held parallel to the ground, can be bent fully by attaching that amount of weight to the string. Clearly there are advantages in using bows of higher draw weight, as the energy required to draw them will be translated into greater velocity for the arrow, and hence greater range and penetrating power, but the mathematics are far from simple. There has been a great deal of controversy in recent years over the draw weights of English longbows, especially in view of the enormous figures quoted for the bows recovered from the wreck of Henry VIII's ship the *Mary Rose*. It may therefore be helpful to establish a few benchmarks. Modern target archers generally favour bows of around 30lbs draw weight, and would regard anything over 40lbs as 'heavy'. Field archers and medieval re-enactors, who generally shoot fewer arrows in a given time, often use weapons in the 50 to 70lb range, but very few of them seem to be able to manage the heavier ones consistently over several hours of shooting. It has been suggested that for a man of average build without a lifetime of training, the heaviest bow that can realistically be shot with is about 85lbs. Some of the *Mary Rose* bows are in the 170lb range, and there are a few archers who shoot bows of these weights today, but they are very much the exception.

We must also bear in mind that in a combat situation an archer would probably be required to repeat the performance dozens or even hundreds of times, in rapid succession. What can be achieved by a few picked athletes who practice continually is unlikely to be a guide to the average performance of a mass levy like the Mongol army. Nevertheless a figure of 166lbs (120 catties by Chinese measurement) for the draw weight of Mongol bows is often quoted; it appears to be derived from Meng Hung via H. D. Martin, who also cites H. G. Creel as saying that the 'Peking Guard' of the Ch'ing dynasty (presumably in the nineteenth century) used bows of 156lbs draw weight.

To put these claims into perspective it may be of interest to consider the archery regulations of those Chinese dynasties whose records are available. In the eighth century AD, officers of the T'ang army had to pass an archery test using composite bows of 120lbs draw weight. It was generally T'ang practice to promote men on the basis of physical strength as well as leadership ability, and the officer examinations also included weight-lifting competitions, so we can assume that the rank-and-file were not expected to wield bows of this power. The Manchus who established the Ch'ing dynasty in 1644, although not actually a nomadic steppe people, were neighbours of the Mongols, and had adopted a very similar tradition of archery based on the use of the composite bow from horseback. They were the last major power in Eurasia to rely mainly on mounted bowmen, and in the mid-eighteenth century they were still using these traditional weapons with great success against the Mongol tribes, who had by then largely adopted firearms. In 1760 imperial regulations laid down a minimum draw weight of 30 'jin' (18kg, or around 40lbs) for bows for use on horseback, and 50 'jin' (66lbs) for those used on foot (von Essen). Other Manchu sources described bows of between 92 and 152lbs, but it is implied that weapons of 80 'jin' (106lbs) and over were intended for displays and trials of strength only, and were not used in battle except perhaps by a few exceptional archers. The emperor and the imperial princes were supposed to be able to draw bows of up to 180 'jin' in military displays, but if this was actually done at all it must have been for an occasional one-off demonstration, and surely has no bearing on battlefield practice. More significant, perhaps, is the suggestion that the Manchu armies which defeated the Mongols and others in the 1750s may have done so with bows not much heavier than those wielded by today's sport archers. In earlier centuries, when armour was in more widespread use, there may have been a greater incentive to master heavier weapons to give a better chance of penetrating it, but this factor is hard to quantify. In modern tests a 144lb bow sent arrows of various types through both front and back of a mail coat fitted to a dummy, but in most cases armour must have provided adequate protection against commonly-encountered threats. If it had not, it would not have been worth the trouble to manufacture and wear. This is not to say that Mongol bows of 166lbs draw weight did not exist, only that they are unlikely to have been either universal or necessary for effective archery tactics.

Arrow quivers were made of birch bark and leather; they were so characteristic an item of equipment that in the *Secret History* 'taking away someone's quiver' is used as a euphemism for reducing them to subjection. Chinese illustrations show that the normal practice was to carry a bow in a case, strung ready for action, on the trooper's left side, and a separate quiver on the right. Several different types of arrow are mentioned in the *Secret History*, and although it is not always clear what the terms mean, it seems that some designs were optimised for long range, and others for inflicting maximum damage at shorter distances. For example Toqto'a the Merkit was killed by a 'shiba', which Urgunge Onon says was 'a particular type of arrow', adding that in the Orkhon Turkish language the term meant 'arrows that came raining down'. This might therefore refer to a projectile designed for high-angle shooting at long range. Senggum's wound at the Battle of Qalaqaljit Sands was caused by an 'uchuma', which according to the same writer had a short shaft and contained no iron or steel. Some arrows had horn or bone tips, though these would have been less effective than iron at penetrating armour, and may have been more popular for hunting than for battle. Elsewhere the same source mentions arrows called 'kebiyur', which were 'thin and dart-like', and 'angqu'a', which had forked heads, and may have been the type which Marco Polo describes as cutting the enemy's bowstrings. Others had heads designed to produce a whistling sound as they flew through the air, either for signalling or to intimidate an enemy. When Temujin and Jamuqa renewed their oath of brotherhood after their joint attack on the Merkits, Jamuqa gave his friend a whistling arrowhead made of cow horn with holes bored into it 'to make it sing'. Both Meng Hung and Marco Polo confirm that different arrowheads were employed for distance shooting and for penetrating armour at close range. The latter says that each Mongol soldier carried sixty arrows into battle, thirty heavy ones with broad heads for use at close quarters, and thirty lighter ones. Archaeological finds from Mongolia and the Altai mountains also include narrow, pointed iron arrowheads similar to the 'bodkins' used by English longbowmen – and like them presumably designed to pierce armour – as well as heavy triangular broadheads which could inflict lethal wounds on less well-protected targets. Surprisingly, all these designs appear to have been tanged rather than socketed; in other words the head was fixed to the arrow shaft by means of a pointed tang which was inserted into a hole or split in the shaft before being glued and bound in place. This tends to weaken the shaft and make it more liable to split on hitting a hard object than the alternative method, in which the solid wood is inserted into a hollow socket in the metal head. It has been argued that the tang fitting was a design weakness that seriously limited the effectiveness of early mounted archery. But it is unlikely that the Mongols would have persisted so long with a significantly inferior design. Socketed heads had been cast from bronze in the first millennium BC, but when iron came into widespread use the casting method was no longer appropriate. Forged tanged heads are far easier than socketed ones to manufacture in iron, which in view of the enormous numbers of arrows employed by the Mongol armies might have been considered to outweigh any slight disadvantages. Poplar, willow or reed were the most popular materials for the arrow shafts. The thirteenth-century Indian writer Fakhr-i Mudabbir says that poplar was too heavy for long-range arrows, and that the best all-round shafts were made from reed, but this was probably difficult to obtain in Mongolia. Jamuqa in the *Secret History* once refers to a 'peach-bark arrow'. Poisoned arrows are occasionally mentioned; the poison appears to have been made either from plants or from the venom of snakes (Nicolle and Shpakovsky). How routinely arrows were poisoned is not clear, though if it was known to be a risk it would explain the incidents in the *Secret History* in which the lives of Genghis and his son Ogodei were reportedly saved by companions who sucked the blood from their wounds.

Archery tactics

Despite the advantages of the composite bow, it may seem that they cannot have been decisive against other Central Asian nomads, or against the Jurchen cavalry of the Chin or the Turkish 'ghulams' who served in the Khwarizmian army, all of whom used weapons of very similar design. And yet there is evidence that the way in which the Mongols used their bows was different, and may have been better calculated to maximise those advantages. Frustratingly few contemporary sources give any details of exactly how the Mongols engaged their opponents, but a useful starting-point is a brief statement by John de Plano Carpini, who says that 'It should be known that when they come in sight of the enemy they attack at once, each one shooting three or four arrows at their adversaries; if they see that they are not going to be able to defeat them, they retire, going back to their own line'. Presumably these volleys were usually discharged on the move while closing with the enemy, though Turnbull argues that there would be no time to shoot three or four arrows from within effective range if charging at the gallop, and so Carpini must be describing a number of separate charges, each one resulting in the discharge of a single arrow. It is not, however, certain that the Mongols would necessarily be galloping, especially if they were advancing in the close, disciplined formations that some sources seem to imply. For example a passage in the *Secret History* referring to the Uru'uts and Mangquts in Genghis' army appears to be describing manoeuvres in formed bodies, rather than a wild charge at the gallop: 'every time they turn around, their battle order matches. Every time they turn about, their skill matches'. King Haithon of Armenia, who travelled to Mongolia in 1254, says that the Mongols often deployed in bodies so tightly packed that 'you would not take them for half their real numbers'. And according to one fourteenth-century Mamluk manual, one recognised Mongol tactic was for the whole army to attack in a single body, drawn up in close order with the aim of preventing any retreat: 'The Mongols . . . customarily form one squadron, in order to push one another against the enemy, to prevent all of them from retreating and withdrawing'. The experience of the Napoleonic period was that moving quickly in dense formations was very difficult and liable to result in accidents, even with experienced riders. Steppe mounted archers often trained their horses to stop dead, even from a gallop, to enable their riders to shoot, so perhaps we should imagine a Mongol unit closing at a slower pace – perhaps at a trot – and briefly stopping every so often so that the riders could dress their ranks and gain the advantages of shooting from a halt while still being able to manoeuvre. A devastating volley could then have been discharged from within a few yards of the enemy, before the troopers urged their horses into a gallop for the final charge against anyone who was still standing and prepared to face them. It would require a high degree of discipline and control over the horses for an entire unit to do this at the same time without falling into disorder, but these are exactly the qualities that the Mongols are described as possessing. Drawing a bow while controlling the horse with the legs alone – while at the same time aiming accurately, taking into account the movement of both shooter and target and the constantly changing range – required great skill, but according to Carpini the Mongols practiced this regularly from three or four years of age, so that the whole process eventually became instinctive.

Professor J. M. Smith is apparently relying on Carpini when he suggests that the usual Mongol tactics involved 'unit after unit galloping at the enemy as fast as could be with each man shooting one heavy arrow from as close as possible; each unit would then turn away and out of the path and line of fire of the next unit, which could follow almost on its heels.' Based on the comments of the fourteenth-century Mamluk writer Taybugha, Smith further deduces that a typical engagement range would be no more than thirty yards, which would be close enough for an arrow shot from a heavy bow to inflict serious damage. This sort of staged attack would have the effect of concentrating against one part of an enemy line, which would be pinned and then hit by a succession of charges until it broke. It would have the additional advantage that an arrow discharged while the shooter was moving towards the target would have greater velocity, and hence penetrative power, than if shot from the halt or while riding away. Amitai-Preiss, commenting on Smith's theory, considers that a manoeuvre of this type would have been too difficult to perform in practice, because of the risk of the units impeding and disordering each other as they advanced and then retraced their steps into the path of those coming up from behind. But – although it is obviously risky to attempt to reconstruct an entire tactical system from a few scattered hints in the sources – there is evidence that this problem had already been solved.

The Khitan Legacy

The Mongols were originally illiterate nomads, with few if any of the political institutions and administrative skills needed to run a large empire. Therefore it was inevitable that they were strongly influenced by neighbouring societies which did possess such skills. It has long been recognised that the two most influential of these peoples were the Uighurs and the Khitans. Both maintained mainly friendly relations with the Mongols; the Uighurs of the Tarim Basin joined them voluntarily in 1209, and although some Khitans fought for the Chin in China, others welcomed the Mongols as liberators from their hated Jurchen overlords. The Khitan successor state of Qara-Khitai, conquered in 1218, was probably another important conduit by which Khitan administrative methods were adopted into the Mongol Empire. Yeh-lu Ch'u-ts'ai, who eventually became Genghis' most trusted minister, was a Khitan captured after the fall of Chung-tu, and both Khitan and Uighur governors were employed in the former Khwarizmian Empire after the conquest. Their contributions were not limited to personnel. Genghis adopted the

Uighur script fo˙ the first attempts at writing the Mongol language, for example. A major contribution of the Khitans was apparently in the field of military organisation.

The Khitan people spoke a language related to Mongolian, but from at least the fifth century AD they had followed a more settled way of life in the forests of southern Manchuria. Manchuria seems to have been an important centre of military innovation in the early medieval period, perhaps encouraged by the interaction between the stock-rearing nomads of the north and west, the farmers of P'o-hai, which was situated near the gulf of that name in the northeastern sector of the Yellow Sea, and the nearby centralised states of China and Korea. Manchurian inventions may have included the first fully-armoured cavalry in the East, and perhaps also the stirrup. It is therefore reasonable to suppose that the organisation and tactics used by the Khitan army after the establishment of the Liao dynasty in 907 were indigenous developments. The Official History of the dynasty, the *Liao Shih*, provides some interesting details about these matters. The core of the army consisted of the regular 'ordo' cavalry regiments, which were between 500 and 700 strong; ten of these units made up a division, and ten divisions an army. Each soldier was supposed to bring with him two servants, a 'forager' and an 'orderly', to ride a fully-armoured horse, and to provide a selection of weapons including four bows, two spears – one long and one short – and a halberd. This arsenal would of course be too much for one man to handle, and Chinese paintings show Khitan armoured cavalrymen carrying just one spear, one bow, and a sword or mace as a sidearm. No doubt the other weapons were intended to equip the servants, and elsewhere the *Liao Shih* does state that the foragers at least were armed and wore body armour. This arrangement may have been reflected in the standard battlefield deployment, according to which the Khitans drew up in three lines, with the fully-armoured troopers at the rear, partially-armoured cavalrymen (presumably the foragers) in front of them, and mounted but unarmoured skirmishers in the front rank. The latter may have been drawn from among the orderlies, but were probably supplemented by various tribal irregulars.

More significant from the point of view of later developments were the tactics prescribed for the 'ordo' units. When on the offensive they were trained to attack in succession, with each regiment charging in turn, then retiring if it failed to break through, and being replaced by a following unit. Combined with the three-line deployment described above, this would have meant that the enemy were hit by a series of ever more dangerous charges, being pinned and worn down by the lighter troops before having to face the more formidable heavies. Then as soon as a gap was opened in the enemy line, the entire division would advance to exploit it, controlled by signals from the flags and drums which accompanied the commanders. Sometimes the horsemen would drag tree branches behind them to raise dust and confuse the enemy about their true numbers and dispositions. These charges could be repeated for days if necessary, until the exhausted enemy became vulnerable to a final push. But in order for this technique to work there must have been enough space for each unit to manoeuvre, and to retire if necessary, without obstructing its neighbours. The supports obviously could not be placed directly behind the advanced units, as it would then be impossible either to reach the enemy line to support them, or to allow them to pass if they fell back. The solution adopted in eighteenth- and nineteenth-century Europe was to deploy the cavalry 'in echelon', in a staggered line with each unit behind and to the side of the next. We are usually told that this was a Prussian invention of the Second Silesian War, but it seems that it may have been independently discovered in Manchuria many centuries before. The advantages of the echeloned attack were widely discussed during the Napoleonic period, and most of them would have applied equally well in earlier eras. The large gaps between units would have made it easier to manoeuvre and change direction to concentrate against a vulnerable spot; the enemy line could be effectively pinned by the threat of attack from the units to the rear without having to actually commit them until they could see how the situation was developing; and the most appropriate units could be sent into action at a time of the commander's choosing. This might involve committing the best troops first to achieve a quick breakthrough, with their flanks protected by their less well-equipped comrades, or, as the Khitans preferred, allowing the lighter troops to soften up the enemy before the decisive charge. Another advantage of this method of deployment was that an attacking unit could easily be withdrawn to rest and resupply, whereas the enemy, unsure of where or when the next blow would fall, would be forced to stand-to continuously. It was sometimes argued that each unit was more vulnerable in an echelon formation as an advancing enemy line could overlap and envelop its flanks, but the advocates of the system considered that that would only make the enemy himself vulnerable to a flank attack by the following units. On the other hand, if the enemy seized the initiative or the troops in echelon were irresolute, they could easily find themselves outnumbered at the point of contact and swept away by a massed charge. The tactic therefore worked best with steady and well-disciplined troops led by experienced officers – all qualities which the Khitans, like their Mongol successors, undoubtedly did possess.

Further evidence for a system of successive attacks can be found in a source closer to the Mongols themselves – the *Political and Military Institutes of Tamerlane*, recorded by Sharafuddin Ali Yezdi. The authenticity of these regulations is controversial, and they may date from considerably later than the Mongol period, but they nevertheless represent the tactics, even if idealised, of an army that consciously saw itself as the heir to the Mongol tradition. Timur-i-Leng, or Tamerlane, was a Turco-Mongol warlord who claimed descent from Genghis Khan (apparently falsely, though his wife was a genuine Genghisid), and established a powerful empire based in the Samarkand region at the end of the fourteenth century. According to Yezdi, he decreed that if the strength of an enemy exceeded 40,000, the army sent to attack it would be led by the 'emperor' in person. It would consist of forty units of cavalry (described as 'squadrons' in the translation by Major Davy quoted by Zaman), each presumably corresponding to a Mongol 'thousand'. They were organised into a 'Hurrauwul' or vanguard, a 'Burraunghaur' or right wing, and a left wing, 'Jurraunghaur', plus a reserve, or 'Koul', consisting of the ruler and his guards.

The vanguard and both wings were deployed in depth, with scouts in front, followed by two lines of six squadrons each. The troopers were to maintain their station and not attack without specific orders. When the action began, the prescribed sequence was for the first line of the 'Hurrauwul' to attack first, each of its six squadrons charging in succession. The second line would then follow suit, and if the enemy still remained unbroken the commanders of the two wings would similarly send in their units one after the other, following up themselves with their personal guards if necessary. 'Thus, by the power and assistance of Almighty God, when eighteen charges shall have been made on the line of the enemy, they will break and disperse.' It is interesting that, in contrast to this rather rigid system, the small-scale tactics to be used by each squadron seem to have been left to the discretion of its commander: 'he should accommodate his mode of attack to that of the enemy; and that he should observe in what manner the foe advanced into battle, and counteract his designs.' As with the Mongols of Genghis' day, this might have involved a choice between using close-range archery to disorder a steady opponent, for example, or an immediate charge with cold steel against one who was already wavering. If victory had still not been won by these means, Timur envisaged having to commit the royal guards, with himself at the head of the last reserve: 'And if at this period the victory be not decided, it is the duty of the emperor, with fortitude of heart and with exalted resolution, to put himself and the Koul of his army into motion.'

It is not suggested that this scheme represents exactly the organisation and tactics of the Mongol armies of Genghis Khan's era, but if the similarities between the practice of the tenth-century Khitans in Manchuria, and those of the fourteenth- or fifteenth-century Timurids in Samarkand, are more than coincidence, Genghis' armies are most likely to have been responsible for their transmission. The *Secret History*'s account of the Battle of Qalaqaljit Sands, discussed in Chapter 2, seems to be describing just this sort of deployment in depth, with successive units advancing to support those in front. Apart from this single example this tactic is never specifically described for the armies of Genghis, but according to their Egyptian opponents, the Mongols at the Battle of Hims in 1281 'were organised as squadrons . . . and followed one another as groups', which may be an attempt to describe the same thing.

Of course this need not imply that an army as successful as the Mongols knew only one way to deploy in battle. The massed close order charge described on page 49, for example, would have been particularly useful if an enemy was suddenly seen to be vulnerable to a rapid attack, and might account for the virtually instantaneous breakthroughs seen at battles such as Huan-erh-tsui in 1211 and the Kalka River in 1223. In any case a bow is a versatile weapon, and the theory of Mongol close-range archery doctrine need not preclude the possibility that other methods of shooting were employed when required. A carved stone found on the River Onon, now in St. Petersburg, commemorates the feat of Genghis' nephew Yisungge, who once shot an arrow to a distance of 335 'alds' (a Mongolian unit of measurement which translates to around five and a half feet), or over 600 yards. But the fact that this shot was remembered proves that it was exceptional, and no battle account suggests that anything like it was attempted in action. Carpini says that each trooper carried two bows, and although this would be a sensible precaution in case of breakage, it is also possible that the bows were designed for different tasks. One might have been heavier, intended for shooting armour-piercing arrows at close range, while a lighter weapon could be useful for rapid shooting from a distance, which could quickly tire a man drawing a heavy bow. The tactic of shooting at elevation against long-range targets is often regarded by modern writers as relatively ineffective, but earlier eyewitnesses were divided on the issue. Nicolaes Witsen, a seventeenth-century Dutch observer, reported that the Tartars of the Black Sea steppes could achieve a primitive 'time on target' effect with this method: 'they always shoot upwards so that the arrow falls straight from the top down so that it has the maximum power . . . he could count the time so precisely that when he shot the second arrow I could see a few times how the second almost touched the first and both arrows landed at the same time, close to each other'. Not everyone was so impressed. The

Baron de Marbot, who encountered bow-armed Bashkir horsemen during Napoleon's Russian campaign of 1812, recalled that 'the Bashkirs are totally undrilled, and have no more notion of any formation than a flock of sheep. Thus they cannot shoot horizontally in front of them without hitting their own comrades, and are obliged to shoot their arrows parabolically into the air so that nine-tenths of the arrows are lost, while the few that hit are pretty well spent . . .'. No doubt the Bashkirs had lost a great deal of the military knowledge of their Turko-Mongol ancestors, who understood very well the value of fighting in formation, and it is difficult for those of us who have not personally experienced this style of combat to be too critical, but it is not clear exactly what Marbot is describing. The performance of an arrow at long range is quite different from that of a musket ball or rifle bullet, because the arrow itself is a relatively heavy object, more of whose energy is retained in its mass, rather than its velocity. Unlike a bullet, an arrow falling to earth at the end of a parabolic trajectory is not 'spent', but retains (or rather has recovered as it falls) a greater proportion of its initial velocity, so that it is very nearly as dangerous as it would be if shot horizontally at point-blank range.

Archery among the Mongols' enemies

The closest parallels to the Mongolian style of mounted archery were probably to be found among the Jurchens and Khitans of Manchuria and northern China, whose methods are discussed on pages 92 to 93 and 50 to 53 respectively, and it is possible that in their heyday either of these armies would have been a match for the Mongols. However, the Khitans had been reduced to subjection by the Jurchens a century before, and most of those remaining in China eventually defected to the Mongols. The Jurchen cavalry had declined in numbers and probably in fighting spirit since they settled in China, and their armies were now heterogeneous collections of Jurchens and various allied cavalry together with large numbers of not always enthusiastic Chinese infantry, most of whom seem to have taken the field without armour and so were easily shot down by the Mongol archers. The campaigns in the west provided a more interesting test of the different archery techniques of the combatants. The tribal Turks and other inhabitants of the Central Asian steppes fought in a skirmishing style which is described fairly consistently by many sources from Classical times to the Crusades. They shot their arrows from a distance, using their speed to evade the attacks of their opponents, and only closing in for the kill when they were disorganised and weakened by volleys of arrows. As Ammianus Marcellinus said of the Huns who threatened the Roman Empire in the fourth century AD: 'As they are lightly equipped for swift motion, and unexpected in action, they purposely divide suddenly into scattered bands and attack, rushing about in disorder here and there, dealing terrific slaughter.' The Byzantine princess Anna Comnena described how the Turks whom her father the Emperor Alexius encountered in the early twelfth century 'do not fight with lances, but completely surround the enemy and shoot at him with arrows; they also defend themselves with arrows at a distance'. The Crusaders who encountered these tactics found them frustratingly difficult to deal with, as the Turks would not stand and fight in the Western knightly tradition, but would instead gallop away from a charge while turning in the saddle to shoot behind them. They could shoot their light arrows very rapidly, and could also engage an opponent at what were for the time very long ranges. At the Battle of Dorylaeum in 1097, says the author of the *Gesta Francorum*, the Seljuq Turks 'came upon us from all sides, skirmishing, throwing darts and javelins, and shooting arrows from an astonishing range'. Nicolle considers that the 'darts' were actually short arrows shot from a 'nawak' or arrow-guide, a length of wood with a groove for the arrow, like the tiller of a crossbow, which enabled missiles to be used which were shorter than the draw length of the bow. Because these were very light, they could attain much greater ranges than ordinary arrows: Strickland and Hardy suggest an extreme of 800 yards, and a more practical battlefield range of 400 yards.

However, the lightness of the Turkish missiles, as well as the ranges at which they were discharged, meant that they seldom did serious damage to an armoured opponent. This explains Beha ud-Din's often quoted observation about the Frankish infantry he saw on the Third Crusade, who were marching with 'from one to ten arrows sticking in them, and still advancing at their ordinary pace without leaving the ranks'. An even clearer statement is given by Anna Comnena, quoting her father's orders to his mounted archers (who on this occasion were fighting on his side against the Crusaders) to shoot at the horses rather than their riders: 'for he knew that cuirasses and coats of mail made them almost if not entirely invulnerable; to shoot at the riders, therefore, would in his opinion be a waste of arrows and entirely ridiculous'. Armies using these traditional mounted archery tactics could certainly be successful in battle, even against opponents who were better armoured than themselves, but they needed to take their time, wounding, tiring and weakening their enemies with arrows before they could finally close in to finish them off. Victories won by these attritional means, like those of the Parthians over the Romans at Carrhae in 53 BC and the Seljuks against the Byzantines at Manzikert in 1071, usually took a whole day or even longer to achieve, in stark contrast to the decisive charges which we see in accounts of Mongol battles. For example, at the Battle of the Kalka (discussed on pages 137 to 139) the Galician and Chernigov contingents in the Russian army were defeated so quickly by the Mongol charge that their allies had no time to react. Nicolle and Shpakovsky, in their book on the campaign, accept that Subotei, the commander of the attacking 'touman', did not wait for his archers to soften up the enemy before charging, but closed immediately with his heavy cavalry, and in support of this they quote a report that a Russian officer riding in the vanguard was killed with a spear. These authors seem to have seen this tactic as a departure from what they regard as the usual Mongol skirmishing methods, but if the analysis of Mongol tactics presented above is correct, Subotei's charge would in fact have been a standard manoeuvre. We can now perhaps see why the Turks and other steppe tribes performed so poorly against Mongol armies, which could match their archery and their speed of movement, so would not wait to be worn down by slow attrition, but were also effective in hand-to-hand combat by virtue of their denser formations.

A very different style of archery was associated with the heavier cavalrymen who formed the elite core of the armies of the Muslim states from Egypt in the west to Iran in the east. These were the 'ghulams' or 'mamluks' – both terms meaning 'slave soldiers'. In most, if not all, cases these were actual slaves, purchased as boys from the steppe tribes and trained as professional soldiers. They were valued not only because they were entirely devoted to the profession of arms, but also because they were thought less likely to become involved in internal power struggles than men recruited locally. They were equipped by their owners or employers, and so in comparison to their relatives on the steppe they had better armour and equipment, but they lacked access to the great horse herds reared on the grasslands. Because of the weight of their armour and the shortage of remounts, these 'mamluks' relied less on rapid manoeuvres than on shooting from the halt, in order not to tire their horses. A favourite tactic was to receive an enemy charge dismounted in line, disorder it with arrows, then remount and charge with sword and lance. Military training was studied scientifically in the Muslim armies, and a number of manuals of horsemanship, archery and other skills survive. One of these, by the Egyptian instructor Taybugha, describes their archery techniques in detail. He claims that a fully trained 'mamluk', shooting from the halt and holding his arrows in his left hand together with the bow, could discharge five arrows in two and a half seconds – a 'rate of fire' eight times faster that attained by a steppe archer shooting from the gallop, who had to wait until his mount had all four feet off the ground before he could shoot without his aim being disrupted by its vertical movement, and so could manage only one shot every four seconds at best, regardless of his personal skill. Furthermore the 'mamluk' could attain a range of seventy-five yards, whereas his opponent would have to shoot from thirty yards or less in order to have a chance of penetrating the mamluk's armour. Other writers made extravagant claims for the battlefield effectiveness of this tactic. For example al-Jahiz, writing of the army of the Abbasids, who ruled Egypt and Syria in the early thirteenth century, says that 'if a thousand Turkish [i.e. mamluk] horsemen are hard pressed they will loose all their arrows in a single volley and bring down a thousand enemy horsemen. No body of men can stand up against such a test.' Writing of the Mongol-Egyptian wars of the later thirteenth century, Professor Smith has argued that this rapid volley shooting, combined with the intensive training, heavier armour and bigger horses of the Mamluks, would have made them far superior soldiers to the Mongols.

The problem with this argument is that it is in danger of proving that what actually happened must have been impossible. The Mongols did repeatedly defeat armies using these tactics, in the Khwarizmian Empire, in Syria, and later against the Mamluk Sultans of Egypt. They were admittedly less successful against the latter after 1260, but by then they were at the end of very long supply lines and operating in the unsuitable terrain of the Syrian desert. Archery is in reality always a matter of reconciling conflicting requirements and striking a balance between range, speed of shooting, accuracy and hitting power. Long range can be achieved by using heavy bows and light arrows, but on arrival at the target such missiles will lack the energy to penetrate armour or inflict fatal injuries on horses. To achieve these results needs both a heavy bow and a heavy arrow, which will lose velocity more quickly and so will be ineffective beyond a moderate range. Reasonable accuracy can be combined with rapid shooting if the range is not too great and if the archer is aiming instinctively, as would be necessary in battle when targets were constantly moving or appearing at different ranges, but if a bow is too powerful for the shooter he will not be able to hold it steady and so accuracy will suffer. The result is that a skilled archer might be able to engage targets at 300 or 400 yards, to send an arrow through armour, or to shoot one every half a second, at least for a brief period, but he will not be able to do all these things simultaneously. In this writer's opinion, based on personal experiment, it is possible to shoot arrows very rapidly by 'snatching' at the string, drawing it part way back instead of to full draw, and releasing it as soon as possible, but this sacrifices range, power and accuracy. There were in fact three prescribed ways of releasing an arrow; one with the draw and release in one movement, another requiring the string to be held briefly before release, and a third described as 'twisted', in which the bow was drawn part of the way back, then there was a pause to aim, followed by a quick pull to full draw and an instantaneous release. Only the first of these could possibly have been compatible with Taybugha's 'five arrows in two and a half seconds'. It would be unwise to contradict an authority like Taybugha and state that the feats he records are impossible. Some exceptional men could perhaps shoot effectively at this rate in battle, but it seems likely that for most it would have been more of a circus trick than a realistic tactic. The Egyptian Mamluks did in fact stage displays of horsemanship and military exercises in the 'hippodromes', and many of the practices illustrated in their manuals seem more appropriate for this environment than for the battlefield. Of course this schematic discussion of tactics oversimplifies what must have been a far more complex situation on the battlefield, and no army need have been restricted to a single method of shooting. The steppe tribes usually maintained a small number of heavily-armoured men, perhaps riding larger horses obtained from the agricultural regions, who would charge and fight the enemy hand-to-hand once he had been weakened and disorganised by the shooting of their comrades. Mamluks were also trained to shoot on the move, and exercises involving shooting downwards, at ranges of twenty feet or less, at targets on the ground prepared them for the use of archery in conjunction with a charge to contact.

Similarly, the Mongols would have been just as capable as the tribal Turks of turning in the saddle to shoot while retiring, and some well-known Chinese paintings illustrate the practice. But battle accounts do not give the impression that the Mongols made much use of such tactics, or needed to. In the attack they tended to concentrate against one section of an enemy line and smash through it, as they did against the Jurchen at Huan-erh-tsui. Feigned flights were used as preplanned manoeuvres to draw an opponent out of position, as happened to the garrisons of the Tangut and Chin forts on the Chinese frontier, but if charged on the battlefield the Mongols generally stood and fought, sometimes dismounting to do so.

Nasawi describes how in 1216 a Khwarizmian army attacked a smaller Mongol expeditionary force passing their borders, but the latter seem never to have considered resorting to skirmishing. Instead the Khwarizmians were shocked by the ferocity with which their victims resisted, 'giving blows with the point and edge of the sword'. Marco Polo, it is true, gives a classic description of Central Asian skirmishing tactics in his account of the 'Tartar' armies: 'They are never ashamed to have recourse to flight. They manoeuvre freely, shooting at the enemy, now from this quarter, now from that . . . When they are fleeing at top speed, they twist round with their bows and let fly their arrows . . .' But – even apart from the fact that he was writing seventy years after Genghis' death – it is unwise to place too much reliance on Marco Polo's battle descriptions. Most are very formulaic, and it is by no means certain that he was an eyewitness to any of them. It is now accepted that his editor Rustichello, a popular romance writer, was responsible for most of the more dramatic passages in Polo's *Travels*, and Rustichello would certainly have been more familiar with the Huns and similar mounted archers described in Classical texts than with contemporary Mongol practice. King Haithon of Armenia, who did see the Mongols in action, gives a slightly different account. They are, he says, 'for the most part victorious over their enemies, yet they are not afraid to turn their backs in a fight if it is to their advantage . . . and if they happen to be routed they flee in troops and bands so well ordered that it is very dangerous to follow or pursue them, because they shoot arrows backwards in their flight, often wounding both men and horses that pursue them'. In other words, they could employ these tribal Turkish-style tactics very effectively, but they did not often need to unless things went wrong.

Marco Polo's famous description of one of Kubilai Khan's battles against his Mongol rivals no doubt owes a lot to the imagination of his editor, but it may also preserve a genuine impression of what an encounter between two armies using these tactics was like. He describes their weapons as 'bow and sword and club', plus a few lances, and describes how they would wait calmly until the signal was given before commencing the fight: 'For the Tartars do not dare to start a battle until their lord's drums begin to beat; and while they are waiting it is their custom to sing and to play very sweetly on their two-stringed instruments and to make very merry in expectation of battle'. This apparent nonchalance might have frightened the enemy more than any amount of shouting and threatening, and helps to give substance to Juvaini's poetic description of the Mongols as fearless warriors who were so eager for the fray that they 'considered the pricks of lances the kisses of fair maidens'. Polo continues: 'now you might see arrows flying like pelting rain, for the whole air was full of them. Now you might see horsemen and horses tumbling dead upon the ground. So loud was the shouting and the clash of arms that you could not have heard the thunder of heaven.' Haithon confirms, probably from personal experience, that 'Their method of fighting is very dangerous, so that in one Tartar battle or skirmish there are more slain or wounded than in any great conflict between other nations, which results from their archery, for they shoot strongly and surely, being indeed so skilful in the art of shooting that they commonly pierce all kinds of armour . . .'

Close-combat weapons

Despite the predominance of archery in their battles, the Mongols would also have needed to resort to 'cold steel' on occasion. Admittedly Carpini believed that they did so only as a last resort: 'if possible . . . [they] never engage in hand-to-hand fighting. They always first use arrows to kill the enemy and their horses.' In the *Secret History* Jamuqa describes the Uru'uts and Mangquts, fighting for Genghis at Mount Naqu-kun, in terms which suggest that they might have been accustomed to fighting enemies who were better equipped than they were for hand-to-hand combat: 'They chase men [armed] with spears, they pursue the bloody bandits and men [armed] with swords. They cut them down and kill them.' Nevertheless, the accounts of combat in the *Secret History* include numerous references to Mongols using weapons designed for hand-to-hand fighting, principally spears and swords. For example, when his father's people abandoned Temujin and his family after Yesugei's death, an old man who objected was stabbed in the back with a spear. Later on Belgutei was slashed on the shoulder with a sword in a fight with a Jurkin warrior. Other sources confirm the use of such weapons. At Bagh i-Khurram outside Gurganj, according to Juvaini, the Khwarizmians were killed with 'bow, sword and lance', and at the Battle of Huan-erh-tsui in 1211, T'u Chi says that Mukhali's men charged the Chin with lances.

According to Carpini Mongol spears or lances often had hooks below the head, designed to catch in a mounted opponent's clothing or equipment and pull him out of the saddle. This would have been especially useful against other steppe tribes, who habitually rode with much shorter stirrups than contemporary Europeans and so were less securely seated. One of the men who stole the young Temujin's horses chased him with a lasso on the end of a pole, normally used for catching horses, which might similarly have been intended to unhorse him so that he could be taken alive. The *Secret History* records that Genghis placed 'the banners, drums, pikes and spears' in the care of his night guards, so at least some of these weapons might have been stored centrally and issued to the troops as required, rather than being their personal possessions. On one occasion Genghis also seems to have given permission for some of his senior officers to wear swords, again suggesting that they might have been regarded as the Khan's property. Marco Polo refers to 'clubs', which were probably metal-headed maces of the sort which are known from archaeological contexts, and Carpini says that every warrior carried an axe; these are not mentioned in battle accounts and may have been primarily tools rather than weapons, although they could of course have been used for self-defence in emergencies by men who lacked swords.

Archaeological finds from Russia and Mongolia suggest that Mongol swords could be of a variety of types, some of them broad and straight like contemporary European blades, but by far the most common were slightly curved, single-edged sabres, with blades around a metre long. These were lighter than the swords typically used in medieval Europe, and as we might expect from the written sources they were optimised for cutting. On several occasions Genghis gives his followers instructions to slice through the necks or shoulders of his enemies, implying that swords were normally employed as cutting rather than stabbing weapons. The curvature of a sabre makes it more effective for this purpose than a straight sword, for two reasons. One is that a shorter section of the edge comes into contact with the target, so that the force of the blow is more concentrated. More importantly it facilitates a 'drawing cut', in which the swordsman draws his hand either backwards or forwards as the blade hits, slicing more deeply and inflicting more damage than can be achieved by a simple chopping motion. With a straight blade the initial blow and the subsequent cut require the sword arm to move in two different directions, while a curved weapon allows the whole sequence to be completed in one smooth movement. More of the blade can also be brought into play without having to extend the arm, simply by slicing backwards and downwards, which could have been an advantage in a tightly-packed melee (see Nosworthy for an interesting discussion of this factor in a Napoleonic context). A single-edged sword might seem to be less versatile than one sharpened on both sides, but it has the advantage that the back, being left unsharpened apart from a short section near the tip, can be wide enough to provide extra rigidity, and can also be used to parry an opponent's weapon without risking damage to the cutting edge. So while the Mongol sabre might have been less effective than the heavy, straight swords used by Europeans and Arabs at smashing through metal armour, it could probably have been wielded more dexterously in the press of a fight, and would have done more damage to less well-protected parts of an opponent's body. The very best sword blades were said to come from India and Syria, but although these could have been traded along the Silk Road, it is unlikely that any but the wealthiest Mongols would have been able to obtain them.

Armour and shields
Illustrations in fourteenth-century editions of Rashid ud-Din's work show most of the Mongol subjects wearing long coats of metal armour, and virtually identical items appear in Chinese paintings from the Yuan dynasty. These are of a type known as lamellar,

widespread in Central Asia since at least the sixth century AD, which was made of small iron, bronze or leather plates laced together. This produced a defence which was tough but flexible, and provided better protection against arrows than European mail, which had gaps in the rings through which a sharp point could penetrate. Normally, of course, armour would be worn over a padded fabric coat which would further cushion an impact and reduce injuries due to the hard armour plates or rings being driven into the flesh. In the Mongol army a silk undershirt was another popular item, as it would not tear when struck by an arrow but would be pushed into the wound, making it easier to extract the missile by pulling on the shirt. It is unlikely, however, that silk would have been generally available to the rank and file before the conquest of northern China.

The question of how widely armour was worn by Mongol soldiers has been the subject of considerable discussion. We can be certain from archaeological finds as well as contemporary illustrations and written accounts that some men had metal or leather armour for themselves or their horses, but we do not know how many of these armoured men there were or how they were organised. They could have formed a front rank or ranks over which their comrades would shoot, as was once widely believed, but this idea is derived from H. D. Martin's theory that the Mongols might have adopted the same deployment as the Jurchen troops of the Chin dynasty, and there is no hard evidence for this. Nicolle and Shpakovsky, in their discussion of the Kalka River campaign of 1223, argue that Jebei and Subotei's 'toumans' started off with about two-fifths of their men as armoured swordsmen and lancers, and that this proportion would have increased as they acquired equipment from their defeated enemies on their ride across Iran. However, they do not produce any evidence for this conclusion, and the two-fifths proportion seems to derive from Martin's suggestion, while the idea that the number of armoured troopers must have increased by the time of the Kalka battle is apparently based on the erroneous belief, discussed above, that Subotei's tactics on that occasion were something new. The same authors do discuss excavated examples of armour, but these are an unreliable guide to its prevalence simply because any negative archaeological evidence, for men not possessing armour, is by its nature unavailable.

It is often argued that the prevalence of metallic protection indicated by later illustrations would not necessarily be typical of the time of Genghis, before the great arsenals and workshops of China and Iran had fallen into Mongol hands. Numerous other Chinese pictures, as well as those on the Japanese *Mongol Invasion Scroll*, which depicts events of the later thirteenth century, show troopers apparently wearing only helmets for protection, although body armour of some sort could be concealed underneath their long coats. Some evidence for the widespread use of armour from the very beginning of the Mongol conquests, however, comes from references in the *Secret History*. Jamuqa, responding to Temujin's plea for help in rescuing Borte from the Merkits, tells him that he has taken up his lance, bow and sword, and 'put on my leather-thonged armour'. The reference to leather thongs refers to the lacing which held the plates together, and if it is anything other than a poetic convention the phrase might imply that the plates themselves were not made of leather, and so were presumably metallic. Excavated pieces of lamellar armour of the Mongol period found in the Tuva region are said to be of high-quality steel, and Carpini describes metal plates so brightly polished that an observer could see his face in them. Marco Polo mentions armour made of buffalo hide. There is also indirect evidence for armour in the form of descriptions of the wounds suffered in battle, which were most commonly to the face and neck – areas usually left unprotected by armour. Genghis was hit in the neck by an arrow in a battle with the Tayichi'uts in 1201, and the same misfortune befell his son Ogodei at Qalaqaljit Sands. In the same engagement their opponent Senggum was brought down by an arrow through the cheek. By contrast, wounds to the torso seem to have occurred more frequently in contexts where armour is less likely to have been worn. Thus Jamuqa's brother was shot in the back while stealing horses with an arrow which broke his spine, and Belgutei received a sword cut on the shoulder during a brawl in camp.

Smith argues that the Mongols could not have worn large

amounts of armour because their horses were too small to carry the weight. He calculates that a typical Mongol pony would weigh only about 600lbs, and quotes a modern rule of thumb that an animal should carry no more than 17 per cent of its own body weight. This would mean that if carrying a man and all his equipment plus armour, a Mongol horse would have been very significantly overloaded. But this argument does not seem convincing in view of the contradictory evidence for Mongol armour. Troopers were normally accompanied by large numbers of spare horses, some of which would have carried the heavy equipment on the march, while a fresh horse could have been kept in reserve for battle. Furthermore, as we have seen, Mongol battle tactics would not necessarily have involved a great deal of manoeuvring at the gallop. In fact there is some evidence that horses were not only expected to carry armoured riders in battle, but may sometimes have worn armour themselves, as contemporary Khitan and Tibetan cavalry horses certainly did.

Shields are occasionally mentioned in contemporary sources. Meng Hung lists four types, but one seems actually to be a sort of visor worn over the face, and two of the others are very large and probably restricted to use by sentries or in sieges. One of these types is probably the same as the tall rectangular wicker shields shown carried by dismounted Mongol troops on the *Mongol Invasion Scroll*. Meng Hung's final variant is specifically said to be used as a protection against arrows when fighting on foot. However, illustrations from the fourteenth century show horsemen from the Golden Horde and Ilkhanid Persia – both Mongol successor states – carrying small round convex shields of the type known in Persia as 'khalkha', made of woven canes with a metal boss in the centre. These may already have been in use by the Mongols of Genghis' day, and would have been a light but effective means of defence against arrows, though they were probably not often used by cavalrymen while mounted, and it is difficult to see how they could be managed by an archer who requires both hands to draw his bow.

Horses
Even more important to a Mongol warrior than this armour and

weapons were his horses. As their economy was based mainly on grazing livestock, the Mongols possessed large numbers of horses, which were accustomed to living out of doors and finding their own food in all weathers. In the twentieth century the fitness of the Mongolian breed for its harsh environment was still being enhanced by deliberate crossing with wild 'Przewalski horses', and the practice was probably even more prevalent in earlier times, when the wild horses were more common. The result was an animal (variously described as a horse or a pony) which grew a thick coat to protect it in winter, could dig through snow to find grass, and had hooves so hard that it seldom needed to be shod. War-horses were usually geldings, which were relatively docile, and Marco Polo describes them as being as well trained and responsive as dogs, even allowing their riders to sleep on their backs while they grazed. Mongol horses could also cover great distances at high speed. Martin quotes Douglas Carruthers as saying that in the early twentieth century a Mongol riding a single pony would routinely travel 600 miles in nine days, and calculates that on a two-day march from Bamiyan to Ghazna in 1221 Genghis' army covered 130 miles. As would be expected of a stockbreeding people, the Mongols valued their horses highly and looked after them well, though as discussed above this need not have precluded burdening them with what by modern standards would be considered excessive loads. They did not use spurs but controlled their mounts with the aid of a small whip, or just by the pressure of the legs. According to the *Secret History*, when Genghis sent Subotei against the Merkits in 1216 he gave him detailed instructions for the care of the horses. He also decreed the death penalty for anyone who struck a horse and damaged its eyes. Meng Hung says that in order not to cause injury the animals were never ridden until they were three years old, and Carpini adds that a horse which had been ridden one day would if possible be rested for the next three or four.

The phenomenal endurance of these animals was an important factor in the success of the Mongol armies, but their adaptations came at a price. They were small, varying between about twelve and thirteen hands, and Professor J. M. Smith has argued that not only were they too light to carry a heavily-armoured warrior for long periods, but their small stature would have placed their riders at a disadvantage in hand-to-hand combat against a Muslim 'mamluk' mounted on a bigger animal. However, numerous battle accounts show that the Mongols were capable of carrying out decisive charges despite the small size of their mounts. A more serious problem in the long run, mentioned in several sources, was the inability of the breed to thrive in hot climates. Juvaini says that when Dorbei Doqshin was sent into India in the wake of the Battle of the Indus River in 1221, he was forced to retreat by 'the great heat of the climate'. The effect on the animals is confirmed by the traveller Ibn Battuta, writing in the fourteenth century, who states that large herds of horses were exported to India from the Mongol Khanate of the Golden Horde, and that when they reached the land of Sind the herdsmen had to collect forage for them as the local grazing was insufficient; even so, he continues, 'the greater part of the horses die or are stolen'.

Tactics

Onon, in an appendix to his edition of the *Secret History*, gives a list of sixteen battle tactics attributed to Genghis Khan. The source he cites is a modern work in Chinese, so it is difficult to evaluate it, but it ties in well with what we know from other sources. Several of the tactics mentioned are evidently derived from the work of Meng Hung. Included in the list are the 'bush clump' and 'chisel attack' used against the Naimans at Mount Naqu-kun. The former required the men to advance cautiously in small groups, maintaining contact with each other but keeping a low profile; it was useful in conditions of poor visibility, and so was undoubtedly intended to conceal either the movements or the numbers of the Mongol army, or both. The 'chisel attack' seems to describe exactly the sort of echeloned attack that we have proposed above – a succession of charges by up to three waves of cavalry, followed by a general advance once the enemy were disordered. The other tactics comprise a mix of march formations, battlefield manoeuvres and ruses designed to confuse the enemy. Outflanking manoeuvres could be either tactical, as when Dorbei Doqshin sent a detachment by a mountain path to take the

Tumads in the rear in the campaign of 1216, or strategic, like the 400-mile desert march by which Genghis took Bokhara in 1220 (for which see Chapter 5). In the 'crow soldiers and scattered stars' manoeuvre the men dispersed widely in small groups before a battle to avoid being outflanked, and to encourage the enemy to do the same. Meng Hung says that a thousand men could cover a front of a hundred 'li' (roughly thirty-five miles) in this way. When the enemy tried to regroup the Mongols would follow suit, but being all mounted and well drilled in such manoeuvres they could do so much more rapidly, concentrating against a weak point while he was still trying to gather his forces. This, says Carpini, was one reason why the Mongols' opponents tended to overestimate their numbers. A variant on this tactic was to advance in an arc or 'bow' formation, with the wings of the army curved forward like the tips of a bow. The enemy would then advance against the refused centre and find himself encircled. Alternatively an unprepared opponent could simply be surprised by a forced march and caught while still in his camp, as happened to the Keraits in 1203.

Once battle was joined, Mongol tactics would be tailored to the strengths and weaknesses of the enemy. If he exposed his flanks he could be surrounded. If he stood in a strong defensive position he could be observed and harassed by cavalry patrols until shortage of supplies forced him to move, when the main army would attack. The Mongols might dismount and shoot from behind the cover of their horses, concentrating enough arrows on a vulnerable point to create a gap in the line. Mukhali used this tactic in China on several occasions in order to concentrate the archery of his troopers against opposing infantry, who were too slow-moving for there to be much risk of the Mongols being caught on foot by a sudden charge. Incidentally, Professor Smith considers that the normal procedure when shooting dismounted was to do so from a sitting rather than a standing position. He quotes the Oghuz Turkish epic, the *Book of Dede Korkut*, which describes the heroine Princess Saljan as doing just this. This position would be natural for a man who customarily shot from the saddle, and with the short composite bow it would be a far more feasible tactic than with a European longbow. If the arrows were laid on the ground in front of the archer they could be taken up and shot more rapidly than if they had to be drawn from a quiver, and a sitting man would also make a smaller target for any incoming missiles. An alternative would be to kneel, as Timur-i-Leng's men are described as doing. Smith speculates that the need to engage an opponent sitting on the ground might explain the mamluk technique known as 'qighaj', which involved shooting downwards and to the left at a target below the shooter's left knee.

Mongol commanders could even drive herds of horses or cattle into an enemy strongpoint to cause confusion, under cover of which they would attack. Listed as a separate tactic, but obviously complementary to several of the others, was 'combining swords and arrows', first 'softening up' the enemy with archery before charging in to attack him hand-to-hand. Stratagems included provoking an enemy into a rash pursuit by pretending to retreat, or alternatively intimidating him by making the Mongol forces look stronger than they were. This could be done in various ways; for example by lighting large numbers of extra camp fires, as Genghis did before the Battle of Mount Naqu-kun, by sending detachments to drag branches behind their horses and raise dust, or by mounting non-combatants and even straw dummies on spare horses, a tactic employed by Shigi-qutuqu against Jalal ud-Din at the Battle of Parvan in 1221. It seems to have been standard practice in the medieval period to exaggerate the size of one's own army in the hope of intimidating an opponent. Fakhr-i Mudabbir, writing in the Delhi Sultanate, advises that 'Although the king or the commander of an army may know the numbers of horse and foot, he must say two or three times this number: for it may happen that spies and informers make known to the enemy the size of the army'. And yet Genghis' armies may have been equally easy for the uninitiated to underestimate. As we have seen they probably wore less armour than the soldiers of most of the settled empires, rode smaller horses, and were generally unimpressive in appearance. The expensively-costumed and lavishly-equipped Chinese and Muslim armies were especially prone to overconfidence in the presence of the Mongols. Ibn 'Abd al-Rahim, for example, tells us that during his campaign of 1277 the

Mamluk Sultan Baybars admitted that 'I had believed that if 10,000 horsemen of my army were to meet 30,000 Mongols, I would defeat them'. This may help to explain why the trick of luring a pursuer into an ambush by means of a feigned retreat succeeded so often against opponents as diverse as the Chinese, Khwarizmians, Georgians and Russians. A very similar tactic, not specifically mentioned by Onon, is referred to in the *Secret History* as 'a dog's fight'. This was the plan put forward by Taiyang Khan at Mount Naqu-kun (though not adopted on that occasion), and involved the entire army retreating before the enemy until they reached a favourable position, then suddenly turning and attacking unexpectedly. The idea was that the advancing enemy would have lost their order during the pursuit, with those on faster horses leaving their comrades behind, while the retreating army would be able to concentrate and collect any reserves which it might have behind it, thus securing superiority of numbers for long enough to turn the tables.

At the end of a battle, if the enemy seemed ready to fight to the death, the Mongols would deliberately leave an escape route open in the hope that they would retire through it and could be cut down with impunity as they fled. And finally, once the enemy was on the run, he would be pursued relentlessly to ensure that he did not rally. This is confirmed by the account of Carpini: 'If it happens that the enemy fight well, the Tartars make a way of escape for them, then as soon as they begin to take flight and are separated from each other they fall upon them and more are slaughtered in flight than could be killed in battle.' However, if the Mongols were defeated, they deliberately scattered in all directions to make such a pursuit more difficult. Psychological warfare must also have been important, and as we have seen in Chapter 2 the *Secret History* attributes Genghis' victory over the Naimans at Mount Naqu-kun solely to the demoralising effects of Jamuqa's stories. Enemy commanders seem to have lost their nerve on other occasions, most notably in the case of Shah Muhammad of Khwarizmia, discussed in Chapter 5. Not surprisingly the seemingly irresistible progress of Genghis' armies caused widespread panic and demoralisation. Referring to the final campaign against Hsi Hsia, a Chinese source lamented: 'People hide in vain among mountains and caves to escape the Mongol sword . . . Since the beginning of time no barbarians have been so powerful as the Mongols are today. They destroy kingdoms as one tears up grass. Why does Heaven permit it?'

Signals were given on the battlefield principally by large kettledrums carried on horses or camels – Jamuqa in the *Secret History* refers to his drum 'made of the black bull's hide'. Standards were also in use to mark the rallying points for the different units, and to augment the drum signals when necessary. Mongol standards consisted of yak tails, varying in number according to the rank of the officer whom they accompanied, fixed to a long pole. The Khan's own standard was believed to have fallen from heaven and to have supernatural powers, so that a bird flying over it would fall dead from the sky. It bore nine white yak tails, and in Genghis' time the only other man permitted to carry a similar emblem was Mukhali, when he was acting as the Khan's viceroy in China. The role of scouts, who skirmished ahead of the main armies and sometimes fought duels with their counterparts in the opposing army, is referred to several times in the *Secret History*, but despite the obvious importance of the role, there are hints that the job was unpopular. When Ogodei was Khan he threatened to punish his son Guyuk for insubordination by making him a scout, 'so that he must climb city walls like mountains, until his ten fingernails drop off'. Marco Polo, however, says that no Mongol army would move without protecting its flanks and rear with screens of mounted scouts, who also had the task of maintaining contact between the widely separated columns which were employed when the terrain was favourable.

Non-Mongol Troops
As Genghis' empire expanded, its armies incorporated more and more men of non-Mongol origin, fighting either as members of the regular Mongol 'toumans' or in separate units. The Keraits, Merkits, Ongguts and other eastern steppe tribes which became part of the Mongol 'nation' in the first decade of the thirteenth century either

were already part of the same military tradition – as the battle accounts in the *Secret History* suggest – or assimilated to it very quickly. In fact by the time of the Mongol invasions of China all of these contingents would have been indistinguishable from each other, fighting side by side in the same units. If the theory put forward above is correct, the Khitans who joined the Mongols during their wars in north China also fought in a very similar style, and would have fitted into the Mongol tactical system with little or no retraining. Other steppe peoples, such as the Turkomans who fought in Khwarizmia, and the Brodniki of the Don valley who joined Jebei and Subotei in 1223, probably fought in a skirmishing style similar to that of the tribal Turks discussed above. There seem to be few if any indications from Genghis' day that such auxiliaries actually fought in the line of battle alongside the Mongols, and he may have felt that their assistance was unnecessary and might even weaken the cohesion of his forces. After all, he already possessed the best cavalry in the world. The loyalty of some of these tribes was also suspect. For example, Juvaini describes how a detached force of 10,000 Turkomans, which had been sent on an independent mission during the invasion of Khwarizmia in 1219, then mutinied and killed its Mongol commander. A Mongol unit under Tainal Nayan, which was operating in the same area, had to be diverted to hunt the rebels down.

More significant was the role of those foreigners who could supply skills that the Mongols lacked, especially in infantry fighting and siege warfare. Later in the century, during the Yuan period in China, Kubilai Khan's ministers regarded the diversity of troops available to them as a source of strength, and consciously selected the units which were most suited to the terrain and climatic conditions to be encountered on each campaign. For example, Chinese infantry made up a high proportion of armies fighting in the marshes of the south, or those sent on seaborne expeditions to Japan and Java, while the Mongol cavalry were concentrated on the northern steppe frontier. But all of Genghis' battles in the open field were won by the cavalry, and when footsoldiers were deployed against him, as at Huan-erh-tsui, they had been if anything a liability to the enemy. So it is unlikely that he considered it worthwhile to develop a corps of infantry, especially as the Mongols themselves had proved adept at operating in difficult terrain usually thought of as the preserve of those operating on foot. In his 1216 campaign, for example, Dorbei Dokshin had surprised the forest-dwelling Tumads by taking mountain paths so narrow and overgrown that his men had had to cut a path for their horses. Also, unlike for example the Huns, whom Ammianus Marcellinus described as 'almost glued to their horses', the Mongols were happy to dismount to fight when the situation called for it.

Siege Techniques

The one type of operation for which the Mongol cavalry was entirely unsuited was siege warfare. Since the Mongolian tribes did not possess walled towns themselves, the long wars of unification had provided no experience in attacking them; they had never needed to develop the long-range catapults and other engines employed in the settled regions of Eurasia; and the construction and earth-moving skills which were second nature to farming peoples were entirely foreign to the nomads. Not surprisingly, the cities which were taken in Genghis' first campaigns in China fell either to a stratagem – such as the feigned retreats with which Jebei and Mukhali lured out the garrisons of the Chinese frontier forts, or, like the cities of Chung-hsing and Chung-tu, after long and tedious blockades (see Chapter 4).

But by the time of the Khwarizmian war in 1219, this situation had changed. The great cities of the Khwarizmian Empire fell one after the other to Mongol armies employing advanced siege techniques. Juvaini tells of large-scale engineering works, including the filling-in of ditches and the erection of siege towers, and of assaults launched under the cover of bombardments of stones, logs and incendiary naphtha bombs hurled from huge catapults. Soon afterwards in China we hear of Mongols using similar methods against places like K'aifeng, which was besieged in 1232. It seems that it was still the elite Mongol soldiers who led the assaults, but the preparatory work was done by others. In both China and Central Asia commanders made a habit of rounding up the able-bodied men from one captured city for use against the next – another tactic also attested for the Khitans – but these would mostly have been untrained – and no doubt unenthusiastic – levies, useful for labouring work and as human shields, but no better qualified than the Mongols themselves as siege engineers. What changed the Mongol army from a brilliant but limited cavalry force into an unstoppable juggernaut was the influx of Chinese deserters from the Chin during the years after 1211. Just as China's cities were the best fortified in the world, so the men whose job it was to take them were the acknowledged experts in siege warfare. We are nowhere specifically told that Chinese engineers accompanied Genghis in his invasion of the Khwarizmian Empire, though we do know that when in 1256 his grandson Hulegu marched against the castles of the Assassins in northern Iran he was accompanied by a thousand Chinese artillerymen borrowed from his brother Kubilai. Surprisingly, Martin quotes the Sung writer Hsu Ting, who visited the Mongol court in 1235, as saying that most of the Mongol siege equipment had been taken from the Muslims. This could only have occurred after the invasion of the Khwarizmian Empire, but it was true that the most advanced type of machine, the counterweighted catapult or trebuchet, was unknown in China at that time. It was operated by releasing a heavy counterweight – which could be a solid piece of wood or a container filled with stones – and was capable of throwing a heavier missile to a longer range than the older versions worked by teams of men pulling on ropes. It has been claimed that it was also more accurate, as it avoided the problem of having to co-ordinate the movements of a gang of men to achieve an instantaneous release of the throwing arm. Counterweight trebuchets were probably invented in Europe early in the Middle Ages, and are first recorded in China at the siege of Hsiang-yang and Fan Ch'eng by Kubilai Khan in 1268 to 1273. Marco Polo claims to have been responsible for this innovation, but Chinese records attribute it to two engineers from Iraq. There is no reason, however, why these machines should not have been adopted in the west of the Mongol empire as early as Genghis' day.

It would be of great interest to know whether some of the most up-to-date Chinese inventions were also available to Genghis' armies, but direct information is lacking. The world's first documented use of explosive (as opposed to merely incendiary) gunpowder weapons dates from 1221, when Chin forces used iron-cased bombs, thrown from catapults, at the siege of the Sung city of Ch'i-chou. Ten years later a Chin fleet on the Yellow River shot similar bombs, known as 'chien-t'ien-lei' or 'heaven-shaking thunder', at a Mongol force which was pursuing it along the shore, and in 1232, according to the Chin dynasty's Official History, they saw extensive use at the siege of K'aifeng. On the latter occasion the Mongols were so frightened by these missiles that they provided their siege works with overhead cover made from cow hides, but the defenders countered this by letting the bombs down from the walls on chains, then detonating them directly on top of the hides, 'with the result that the cowhide and the attacking soldiers were all blown to bits, not even a trace being left behind'. In all these instances only the Chinese are described as possessing such missiles, but it would be surprising if the Mongols had not obtained some captured examples, along with men who knew how to use them. Certainly by the 1270s Kubilai Khan was employing not only explosive bombs, as depicted on the Japanese 'Mongol Invasion Scroll', but even a device known as a 'huo p'ao', which may have been a primitive handgun. On the other hand this new technology was by no means decisive, as is shown by the fact that K'ai-feng fell to the Mongols despite the 'chien-t'ien-lei', and Genghis and his immediate successors may have felt that it was too unpredictable to be relied upon. The logistic difficulties of transporting large quantities of gunpowder across the steppe could also have precluded its use in theatres of war outside China.

The Logistics of the Mongol Conquests

It seems to have been the practice of the tribal Mongols to fight only when their horses were well fed. The *Secret History* tells of the consternation of Genghis' men when they learned of an impending Naiman attack while they were out hunting. 'Many of them said:

"Our geldings are lean, what can we do now?"' Clearly, horses which were in good enough condition for the hunt were not necessarily considered fit for war. But the quantities of grass needed to keep an army's mounts in prime condition were enormous. This question has been studied by several modern scholars in pursuit of a lively debate about the role of logistics in setting limits to the Mongol conquests. Morgan has been among those who argue that it was shortage of pasture rather than the military resistance encountered that prevented the Mongols overrunning Syria, and the same argument has been applied to Subotei and Jebei's Black Sea campaign, and to Genghis' own abortive incursion into India. Professor Smith has produced some detailed calculations in support of this thesis. Starting with an estimate for a large Mongol army of 60,000 men and allowing five horses per man, it would have been necessary to find pasture for 300,000 horses. This does not allow for the herds of sheep and goats that also accompanied Mongol armies, of which the fourteenth-century Mamluk source al-Umari says that there could be as many as thirty per man. These would eventually be slaughtered and eaten during the course of a campaign, but without its horses a Mongol army was effectively helpless. Smith calculates that each horse would have required on average 9.33lbs of grass a day, which – taking the productivity of good Central Asian pasture land as 534lbs per acre per year – would mean that 300,000 horses would consume the grass over an area of about eight square miles every day. Water could also be a problem; assuming that a horse needs five gallons a day, of which half might be obtained from fresh grass, the theoretical 60,000-man army would consume at least three-quarters of a million gallons per day. A major river could cope with this demand, but the flow of most Central Asian and Middle Eastern rivers varies dramatically with the seasons, and would probably fall to inadequate levels during the summer and autumn. On this basis it would clearly be impossible for a Mongol army to remain very long in one place, even in well-watered grazing country, while the lower productivity of more arid regions might prevent campaigning by large armies altogether.

It is certainly important to bear these constraints in mind when considering the movements of Mongol armies, and especially those inexplicable withdrawals which often confused contemporaries. For example, the Egyptians appear to have thought that Hulegu's withdrawal from Baghdad to Azerbaijan in 1261 was permanent, encouraging their puppet Caliph to risk a counter-attack, when in fact he was simply migrating in search of grazing just as a Mongolian community would do in peacetime. Marco Polo, writing forty years later, says that the Mongols in the Middle East were still following the same route, concentrating in Azerbaijan for the summer grazing, then moving to the warmer lowlands of Iraq in winter. In the 1250s the Armenian King Haithon went so far as to reassure the Crusaders in Palestine that the Mongols were no threat to them, as they had only entered the region in search of grass for their horses. But Amitai-Preiss has argued convincingly that the problem of shortage of grazing has been exaggerated. One factor is that the Mongol expeditionary forces were often smaller than their enemies believed. We have seen that Genghis' entire army at its peak numbered around 129,000 men, and although non-Mongol auxiliaries are not included in this total, these units would not generally have had the great horse herds that consumed the bulk of the supplies. Most campaigns were probably conducted with a fraction of this total, and even where very large armies were required to cross unproductive regions – as during the crossing of the Gobi in 1211 – they could have moved in separate columns, only concentrating when they reached more fertile country where opposition would be expected. The number of horses accompanying each trooper is also uncertain, and may well have varied according to the supply situation. One version of Marco Polo's *Travels* claims that there were as many as eighteen per man, but Sinor favours an average of three or four. More significantly, the conquered areas could usually be counted on to supply other fodder than grass. Genghis, when he entered Bokhara, scandalised the religious community by ordering the receptacles in the great mosque to be cleared of their sacred books and filled with grain for his horses. Amitai-Preiss cites the example of Aleppo in 1281, whose inhabitants fled on the approach of a Mongol column, and 'abandoned crops, granaries and foodstuffs', and also points out that the Mongols would have had no reservations about letting their beasts graze in standing crops, or encroach on the pastures of local nomads. The same writer goes on to estimate that in the early twentieth century northern Syria was home to around 80,000 Bedouin nomads, which implies that a force of that size should have been able to support itself in a similar area of rather poor pasture, at least for the duration of a campaign.

At times it may nevertheless have been necessary for Mongol armies to employ emergency measures to solve their supply problems. Horses will in fact eat a wide variety of foods if necessary, including tree branches and even meat, and slaughtering some of the remounts would certainly have been preferable to seeing the entire herd starve. John de Plano Carpini and Marco Polo both report that the men themselves could subsist for up to ten days without having to stop to cook food. They survived mainly on dried milk, which was mixed with water and reconstituted into a liquid as they rode by the constant motion. They would supplement this with blood drawn from the veins of their horses, and occasionally with meat boiled in the stomach of the animal it came from. Some hostile sources accused the Mongols of resorting to even more drastic expedients. Matthew Paris, writing long afterwards about the invasion of Europe in 1241, repeated rumours that they were cannibals, who feasted on human corpses 'as if they were bread', and saved the most succulent young women for their officers. Carpini relates an equally unlikely tale that in 1214, during the invasion of north China, Genghis' armies were so short of food that he had to order them to kill and eat one in every ten of their own number. Evidently the atmosphere of terror surrounding the Mongols was such that there were people prepared to believe them capable of anything.

As far as other military supplies were concerned, we have evidence for some sort of centralised network which could supply the troops with equipment for particular conditions likely to be encountered on campaign. For example, according to the *Secret History* Dorbei Doqshin's men, who had been ordered to cut their way through the forest to surprise the Tumads during the campaign of 1216, took with them 'axes, adzes, saws, chisels and other tools'. And Rashid ud-Din says that the men serving in Hsi Hsia in the unusually cold winter of 1225 to 1226 were provided with special sheepskin coats, and their horses with felt coverings. Unfortunately the details of the sophisticated supply department which must have been necessary to procure such items in the necessary quantities and ship them to where they were needed have not been recorded.

Grand Strategy

What might be called the grand strategy of the Mongol armies was as advanced as their battlefield tactics; in fact they were among the very few armed forces of the period which can be shown to have had the ability to co-ordinate the movements of separate armies across an extended front. The narrative of the campaigns outside Mongolia includes numerous examples of outflanking moves being carried out successfully over hundreds of miles – Genghis' attack on Bokhara in 1220 for example – and of widely-separated forces coming together at times and places previously specified in their orders. A favourite ploy when advancing into a hostile country was to send a subsidiary army to operate on a roughly parallel but independent axis to the main army, sometimes separated from it by many days' march, probably with the aim of confusing the enemy about the Mongols' objective as well as protecting the flank of the main attack. Genghis' sons were entrusted with such a mission during the crossing of the Gobi Desert in 1211, and Subotei similarly supported Jebei in Qara-Khitai in 1218. This sort of operation could only be successful if the Mongol armies remained in touch with each other via regular messengers, travelling at great speed using relays of horses, so that they could concentrate quickly if necessary to prevent an alert enemy from defeating them in detail. It also required precise timing. Discussing the expedition of Jebei and Subotei to the Black Sea steppes between in 1222 to 1223, Sinor remarks that 'The coordinated movements of Mongol troops separated by a thousand miles could only be achieved by rigid adherence to a timetable which obligated indivi lual commanders to appear at a given time and place, but which left to their initiative the actions to be undertaken in the meantime.'

Mongol grand strategy also required detailed knowledge of the geography of countries where they had never previously operated, and in an age long before the appearance of accurate maps. The details of how Genghis and his commanders acquired this knowledge are unclear, but they must have relied heavily on the reports of traders and other travellers. A few of these, like the Muslim merchant Ja'afar, are named in our sources. The impression given there is that they were consulted on an *ad hoc* basis when they happened to be available, but it seems more likely that many of these men were permanently on the Mongol payroll.

The Mongols were illiterate until the time of Genghis, and we know of no indigenous map-making tradition among them. Joseph Needham, in *Science and Civilisation in China*, refers to a 'Mongolian Style' of cartography in which named places were located relative to each other on a rectangular grid, but most other geographical features were omitted. This style, however, first appeared under the Yuan dynasty in fourteenth-century China, and its antecedents are obviously Chinese. Sophisticated surveying methods had been in use in China since the third century AD, and it is likely that Genghis' conquests in that country were facilitated by the use of Chinese maps. The Central Asian steppe was unmapped, but was crossed by a network of nomad trails leading between sources of water and pasture which would have made navigation possible over great distances, especially with the help of local guides. The Muslim merchants travelling on the Silk Road would also have had a good knowledge of long-distance routes, and we know that many of these men were sympathetic to the Mongols. The clear skies of this arid region must have made orientation by means of the stars fairly straightforward. There are suggestions in the sources that Genghis had a fairly clear idea of where the furthest provinces of his empire lay in relation to each other, even though he may never have visited them personally. For example he sent Jochi to link up with Jebei and Subotei north of the Caspian Sea, a feature of which he must have been aware, even though Jebei had last been seen travelling southwest through Iran. Genghis also appears to have known the direction in which the Tangut kingdom of Hsi Hsia lay when he was camped on the Indus River on the frontier of India, as he made enquiries about whether a road existed. These considerations help to explain how Mongol armies could move with such assurance across the expanse of the Eurasian continent, the full extent of which was still unknown to any of the civilisations on its periphery.

Chapter 4

The First Campaigns in the East

By 1209 the 'mopping up' campaigns against Genghis' surviving opponents in Mongolia had been mostly concluded, and the Khan found himself in command of a large and battle-hardened army which urgently required further employment. It should be remembered that the Mongol troopers were paid only in a share of the loot from their campaigns, but that so far they had been fighting against fellow steppe peoples, who might have yielded a supply of livestock and captives, but not of the coveted silks, precious metals and other products of settled civilisation. In order to ensure his soldiers' continued loyalty Genghis had little choice but to embark on another war, and there cannot have been much debate about where that war should be directed. Both politically and strategically, China was the obvious target. From a strategic point of view, the Mongols would be following in a long tradition of incursions by nomad armies from the steppe into the agricultural lands along the Yellow River. North of the river lay a long-standing ecological frontier, between the regions to the south, which were sufficiently warm and well-watered to support farming and the growth of towns, and the arid grasslands further north, fit only for grazing horses, cattle and sheep. Successive Chinese dynasties had attempted to fortify portions of this frontier, but on the whole it was not defensible from a military point of view. In some places – especially in the east – there were mountain barriers which could channel and divert invasions from the north, but further west the valley of the upper Yellow River, which flowed roughly west to east across north China, provided a relatively easy means of outflanking them. Here the river formed an enormous loop to the north, enclosing an expanse of steppe known as the Ordos – in effect an advanced grazing base for any nomad army that could occupy it, on the exposed flank of the Chinese front. The approach to the Ordos from the north was guarded by several hundred miles of the stony desert known as the Gobi, but this had never proved an insuperable obstacle to well-mounted nomad armies accustomed to travelling long distances in arid terrain. Earlier Chinese regimes, notably the Ch'in and Han dynasties of the late first millennium BC and the early first millennium AD, had attempted to deny this base to invaders by occupying it with Chinese military-agricultural colonies, but these had never flourished for long. In fact by the beginning of the twelfth century AD the Ordos was no longer in Chinese hands at all.

For many centuries the balance of power between China and steppes had fluctuated in favour of one side or the other, but the situation had never been as encouraging for the latter as it was in 1209. When Genghis Khan turned his attention south, what had once been a strong and united Chinese empire was divided among three mutually-hostile regimes, Hsi Hsia, Chin and Sung, of which the first two – the ones closest to the northern frontier – were not actually Chinese at all. By the time of Genghis' rise to power the 'Altan Khans' or 'Golden Kings', as the Jurchen emperors of the Chin dynasty were known on the steppe, were universally hated among the Mongol tribes. Dissidents within the empire were well aware of this, and after 1206 Genghis began to receive a steady stream of refugees fleeing from punishment at the hands of the Chin. In that year he had been approached by a Jurchen prince named Ta-pien who was seeking support for a planned rebellion, but at that time Genghis had not considered his own position strong enough. At around the same time, however, Ala-qush Tagin, the ruler of the Ongguts, made it known that he would join the Mongols if they passed through his territory. The Ongguts were former vassals of the Chin who lived along the northern frontier and controlled the most direct approach to Chung-tu, the Chin capital, and so their support would be invaluable in the event of an invasion. In 1206 there were already 5,000 of them in Genghis' army, but it was not until the pro-

Mongol Ala-qush Tagin was firmly in control that he could be sure of the loyalty of the whole nation. Then in 1208 four Chinese officers arrived with valuable intelligence about the Chin army's dispositions, emphasising the weakness of their former employers and urging the Khan to strike as soon as possible.

The First Hsi Hsia Campaign

In the same year an embassy from the Chin also arrived in Genghis' camp. This was led by Yun-chi, the Prince of Wei, who was an uncle of the reigning emperor, and its purpose seems to have been to demand the resumption of the old tribute arrangements by which the Mongols had previously recognised the Chin as their overlords. Not surprisingly the Khan refused, and Yun-chi returned to China to argue for an immediate declaration of war. However, the old emperor died at this point, and according to the Yuan Official History the war plans were put on hold during the ensuing interregnum. But for this accident of history Genghis might have found himself in the role of a victim of Chinese aggression, rather than the aggressor himself, but by the spring of 1209 he had decided to strike first. His initial target, however, was not the Chin Empire but the neighbouring Tangut state of Hsi Hsia. From a military point of view this was logical, as Hsi Hsia was more easily accessible, and its cities were less formidable targets for an army still inexperienced in siege warfare. Furthermore, as explained above, it occupied a strategic position on the flank of the Chin frontier. But this was one of the few invasions launched by Genghis which appears to have been entirely unprovoked. Martin suggests that he may have been offended by the failure of the Tanguts to arrest Ilkha, the son of Toghrul of the Keraits, when he fled westwards after the defeat of his people in 1203. The Tanguts had once been allies of the Keraits, but this hardly seems a sufficient reason for war. More likely the exposed western towns of Hsi Hsia had been traditional targets for raids by the Mongolian tribes in search of livestock to augment their herds, and Genghis was simply following a well-travelled war trail. In fact in 1205 he had already sent two small raiding parties against the Tun-huang district, perhaps with the aim of gathering intelligence as well as loot. According to one well-known account, he captured a border town by demanding cats and swallows as tribute, then releasing them back into the town with burning rags tied to their tails to set the buildings alight. However, this story derives from a seventeenth-century Mongol chronicle, and is told of numerous conquerors in different parts of the world. It seems safest to regard it with scepticism, especially as more contemporary sources do not even record that the Khan accompanied this expedition in person.

But in April 1209, Genghis entered Hsi Hsia at the head of his main army. It may have seemed an easy opponent in comparison to the Chin, but the Tangut army was nevertheless a formidable force. Most of our information on it comes from the middle of the eleventh century, when Emperor Chao Yuan-hao had commanded a force of 158,000 men drawn from a population of four or five million, but Martin argues that there is no reason to believe that its strength had declined since then. Certainly it had continued to inflict defeats on the Sung until the 1120s, and since then had maintained Hsi Hsia's independence against the numerically stronger Jurchens, who paid grudging tribute to them as 'fiercely stubborn . . . and valiant in battle'. The population of Hsi Hsia was ethnically very mixed, and it is likely that troops drawn from the various peoples fought in their own traditional styles, but the core of the army was the Tangut cavalry, whose mobility had been decisive in the wars with the Sung. The Tanguts were probably heavily-armoured lancers like their Tibetan predecessors, as illustrated in tenth-century paintings from Tun-huang, which show men wearing long coats of lamellar armour and carrying bows and lances. They may also have been supplemented by more lightly-equipped mounted archers drawn from the local Turkish tribes. The cities along the Silk Road were inhabited by many Uighurs and Chinese, who probably fought as infantry with spears, bows or crossbows. The Tun-huang paintings also show men using what look like explosive grenades and Chinese-style fire-lances, suggesting that Chinese gunpowder technology had been imported (or possibly even developed independently) from an early date. The fire-lance was a primitive flame-thrower consisting essentially of a Roman candle on a stick, sometimes combined with a spear point. It had only a short range and burned out quickly, but was useful for keeping an opponent at a distance and was especially popular in siege warfare. Sung Chinese armies certainly employed fire-lances against the Mongols, though there seems to be no record of their use by the Tanguts or the Mongols themselves.

Martin, relying on the *Hsi Hsia Shu Shih*, has reconstructed Genghis' route from his starting point on the grazing grounds around Avraga in Mongolia, southwest down the Ongin Gol River and across the Gobi to the Gurban Saikhan Ula Mountains. These hills formed a sort of oasis in the desert where rich grass and abundant wildlife would have enabled the Mongols to rest and resupply. Then they moved southeastwards across a desolate expanse of sand dunes, and finally south, west of and parallel to the northward flowing stretch of the Yellow River. The total distance was about 650 miles across largely uninhabited desert, but the route was probably already well known to herdsmen and traders, and it seems to have presented few problems to the Mongol cavalry. It also enabled them to avoid detection by Tangut scouts until they struck the cultivated country at Wu-la-hai, northwest of the Hsi Hsia capital at Chung-hsing (modern Yinchuan). Here a Tangut army of 50,000 men under Li Tsun-hsiang and Kao Liang-hui came out to meet the invaders, only to be decisively defeated. This was Genghis' first battle against the main army of an organised state, but unfortunately we have no details of the events. We might speculate that the Tangut heavy cavalry, who had until then no experience of the fighting qualities of the Mongols, launched a headlong charge, and either rode into an ambush or were broken by flank attacks; certainly this is what happened on other occasions. The *Hsi Hsia Shu Shih* says only that Kao Liang-hui was captured, ordered to bow to the Khan, and then executed when he refused. The Mongols then pressed on towards the Ho-lan Mountains, which ran parallel to the river between Wu-la-hai and Chung-hsing.

There was only one road through the mountains, and that was blocked by the fort of K'e-i Men, held by Wei-ming Ling-kung with a force said to have numbered 70,000. Wei-ming did not wait to be besieged, but advanced to meet Genghis on the edge of the plain. Again the Tangut cavalry charged and this time the Mongols fell back, but Wei-ming did not follow up his success, instead returning to the fort and resuming his defensive position. It is likely that the Mongol retreat had been another feint, and the Tangut general may have realised just in time that he was being led into a trap, because he did not emerge from his defences for another two months, even when the Mongols returned and set up camp nearby. Then early in August Genghis struck his camp and moved off towards the steppe, leaving only a small rearguard to cover his retreat. Wei-ming immediately advanced with his entire force to destroy this rearguard, whereupon the main Mongol army, which had doubled back and waited in ambush, enveloped him from all sides. Wei-ming was captured and his army routed.

Martin suggests that the fort at K'e-i Men must have surrendered without further resistance, because the next we hear of Genghis he was outside the walls of Chung-hsing. The defence was conducted by the Tangut ruler Li An-ch'uan in person, and the city was protected not only by high walls but by a network of irrigation canals which hampered the Mongol deployment. What is more, at this stage the Mongols did not possess the siege train or the skilled Chinese engineers which they were later to use with such effect against fortified cities. So by October, when the autumn rains began, the siege had made no progress. Genghis then ordered his men to build a great earth dam to divert the rising Yellow River into the city, but although this caused a great deal of damage the defences continued to hold. It was at this point that Li An-ch'uan sent a messenger to the Chin emperor asking for help. The new emperor was the former Prince of Wei, Yun-chi, who had led the embassy to Mongolia during the reign of his predecessor, and was now ruling under the throne name of Wei Shao. Despite having been the leader of the anti-Mongol war party, he now threw away his best chance of eliminating the threat. Remarking that both Mongols and Tanguts were the enemies of the Chin, and that he was happy to see them destroy each other, he refused to intervene.

By January 1210 the Tanguts were demoralised and their walls were in a state of disrepair, having probably been damaged as much by the floods as by Mongol siege operations. There seems to have been no remaining Hsi Hsia field army available to relieve the city, which suggests that their losses in the two frontier battles had been extremely heavy. The defenders enjoyed a brief reprieve when the river broke through Genghis' dam and flooded his camp, but were eventually forced to negotiate. Li An-ch'uan swore allegiance to the Khan, gave him one of his daughters in marriage, and handed over an immense tribute in camels, woollen cloth, satin and trained falcons. He also promised to supply troops for the Mongol army if called upon in the future. The *Secret History* describes how the Hsi Hsia (whom it calls Qashin) accepted that their troops would be unable to keep up with the Mongols on campaign, but could serve with 'established camps and solidly built cities', which might imply that they were mainly valued for their skills in logistic support and siege engineering. Genghis then withdrew to Mongolia, well satisfied with his first foreign campaign of conquest. In fact the results of the war were even more in his favour than he realised, because the humiliated Tanguts then declared war on the Chin who had failed to support them. Hostilities between the two states continued for the next fifteen years, distracting the Chin from their main enemy in the north.

Genghis lost no time in initiating the next campaign. On his return to Mongolia he encountered an embassy from the Chin, informing him that Wei Shao had become the new emperor. According to protocol he was supposed to bow in the direction of the Chin capital as a token of submission, but the Yuan Official History describes how instead he spat on the ground and asked why he should kowtow to such a weakling as the Prince of Wei. This was no doubt intended as a declaration of war, but the same source records that Wei Shao stubbornly refused to accept that Genghis would dare to challenge him. He imprisoned one of his own officers for provoking trouble when he dared to report the Mongol preparations for war, and seems to have thought that the Khan was actually planning to lead a tribute mission. He even hatched a plot to murder

Genghis when he arrived at the court with his presents. But it was no peaceful embassy that Genghis was intending to lead south.

War with the Chin

Rashid ud-Din tells how the Khan climbed the sacred mountain of Burkhan Khaldun and prayed to the Eternal Heaven for victory, presenting the war as revenge for the murder of his predecessors Ambakai and Okin Barkhak by the Jurchens. Equally revealingly, the *Secret History* gives no reason for the invasion at all, no doubt assuming that to the Mongols it was obviously a just cause. And in contrast to the uncertainty at the Chin court, Genghis seems to have possessed detailed intelligence about the capabilities and intentions of his opponent. Some of this came from defectors from the Jurchen army, and some from the Ongguts, but it is the role of Muslim merchants like Ja'afar in gathering intelligence for the Mongols that is constantly emphasised in our sources. These men were mostly Uighurs and Sogdians, who controlled the trade along the Silk Road to the west and between China and the steppes to the north. It was in their interests to have the trade routes under the control of a single power which could guarantee the security of their caravans, and they seem already to have decided to throw in their lot with Genghis.

Even with these advantages, the task facing the Mongols was formidable. The population of the Chin Empire was assessed in a census of 1195 at 48,490,000, of which 6,158,636 belonged to the hereditary military families who supported a standing army perhaps half a million strong. Martin describes it as not only the largest army in the world at that time, but 'also the most powerful'. Before they overthrew the Khitans and seized power in north China the Jurchens had fought exclusively as cavalry, organised according to a traditional system known as 'meng-an mou-k'o', or 'thousands and hundreds'. Their principal weapon was the composite bow, with which they were highly skilled; the Chin founder Wan-yen Akuta is said to have demonstrated his ability to hit a target at a range of 320 paces. The standard unit was known as the 'kuai-tzu ma', or 'horse team'. This was formed of five ranks, of which the first two wore armour and carried halberds and lances as well as bows, while the rear three ranks were more lightly equipped and would provide support by shooting over the heads of the men in front, while being themselves protected from enemy shooting. One tradition states that they actually fought chained together; this is obviously unlikely as it would sacrifice the manoeuvrability which was the main strength of cavalry, but it may derive from the fact that they operated in disciplined, close-order formations. It is interesting that this system of deployment was the reverse of that used by the Jurchens' predecessors the Khitans, who screened their heavy cavalry with light troops rather than the other way around (see pages 50–3). By the thirteenth century, however, the Jurchens were declining in numbers and being increasingly supplemented by Khitans, Ongguts and other allied cavalrymen. The army had also come to rely heavily on local Chinese troops, who served mainly as infantry. An indication of the relative proportions is given in an account of a campaign in 1161, when Hai-ling Wang deployed 120,000 Jurchens and 150,000 Chinese for an attack on the Sung in the south.

Even more formidable than the field forces of the Chin were their fortifications and walled cities. After the establishment of the empire the Jurchens had become enthusiastic followers of the age-old Chinese tradition of building frontier walls. Although the Great Wall as we know it today is a construction of the sixteenth and seventeenth centuries, there was in the Chin period a network of rammed-earth walls north of the capital Chung-tu extending nearly 300 miles into the steppe, and sheltered behind a single outer rampart stretching more than 500 miles westwards from the Gulf of Po-hai. However, this elaborate defensive system seems to have presented no obstacle to the invading Mongols. It was relatively easy to outflank from the west, and our sources give no indication that it was even manned at the time of Genghis' campaigns. This failure may have been due to the fact that the garrisons were originally the responsibility of the Ongguts, who had now defected to the Mongols. The Chin walls were in any case poorly sited and not very solidly constructed, and even at the time of their construction one minister argued that they were a waste of money, since they were flattened by sand-storms as soon as they were built. Today few visible traces of them remain. The only effective border defences were the forts erected to control movement through the mountain passes, and as we shall see even these could often be bypassed. The empire's main defence consisted of the walls surrounding its great cities. These were built in the traditional Chinese style of rammed earth, faced where possible with stone, and were often on an enormous scale. The walls of Chung-tu, for example, were ten miles in circumference, forty feet high and forty-five feet thick. They were well provided with battlements and watchtowers, and protected by three concentric water-filled moats. Such fortifications were also defended by an array of weaponry including rope-powered catapults and heavy crossbows, and possibly even primitive gunpowder weapons (for which see the discussion in Chapter 3).

The history of Chinese dynasties is often seen as a cycle of rise and decline, with each regime falling victim to corruption and dissent once it passed the peak of its power. There are indications that by 1211 the Chin Empire was entering the downwards phase of such a cycle; Martin, for example, points to official corruption, lack of confidence in the currency, a disaffected landless peasantry, and a disastrous alteration of the course of the Yellow River in 1194 which had caused widespread damage and loss of life. Nevertheless, the regime was to show great resilience in the struggle against the Mongols, and if its armies were often outmanoeuvred they continued to fight with great determination. The war with Chin was to be Genghis' greatest test, and would absorb the greater part of his armies until the end of his life and beyond.

'In the Year of the Sheep [1211]', the *Secret History* tells us, Genghis Khan 'rode out against the Kitad people' (i.e. the Khitans, whose name was still widely associated with North China). As in the case of the Hsi Hsia campaign of 1209 this must have involved the crossing of several hundred miles of desert, but the Mongol account has no more to say about it, implying that such marches were already regarded as routine. Martin believed that the advance was made in two separate columns, which set out from the Kerulen Valley in March or April 1211, as soon as the spring grass had grown enough to support the horses, and before the heat of summer had dried up the streams flowing into the desert from the surrounding mountains. Genghis himself, in command of the Army of the Centre, was accompanied by the left wing army under Mukhali, while the Khan's sons Jochi, Chagatai and Ogodei took the right wing army on a roughly parallel route further west. Reaching Onggut territory in May, Genghis rested his animals over the summer, while the Jurchens hurriedly mustered their own forces behind the Yeh-lu Mountains to the south. If, as Martin believed, the right wing army under the three princes was intended as a diversion, it seems to have failed, because the Chin forces were concentrating facing Genghis around Wu-sha Pao, on the northern side of the range, in two corps deployed to block the only two practicable routes to the plain around Chung-tu. Various attempts have been made to estimate the size of the armies fielded in this campaign. Martin argued that the Mongols might have numbered 110,000 altogether, 70,000 of them with Genghis and Mukhali and the remainder with the princes in the west. However this was based purely on an estimate of the total forces available to the Khan, with a deduction of 20,000 or 25,000 left behind to protect his base in Mongolia, and the real numbers may have been considerably lower. Chinese sources give improbably high totals of 300,000 to 500,000 for the Chin, but it does seem likely that, whatever the actual figures, the Mongols were outnumbered.

Martin points out that although the main horse-breeding region of the Chin empire, in southern Manchuria, lay on Genghis' left flank behind the shelter of the Khingan Mountains, no attempt was made to threaten him from that direction. He suggests that this was because the Jurchens already recognised the Mongol superiority in a war of manoeuvre on the open steppes, and certainly they seem to have suffered from a defensive mentality. They advanced into the mountains in two bodies, the first of which reached Wu-sha Pao in August and began to build fortifications. Genghis sent Jebei on an outflanking move through the mountains which took the Chin troops by surprise and scattered them, then followed up by capturing the small towns of Wei-ning and Fu Chou. At the former they encountered an encouraging omen for the future when one of the officers in charge of the defence defected by having himself lowered over the walls on a rope, and returned to persuade his colleagues to surrender. Another defector, Ke Pao-yu, changed sides after being captured at Wu-sha Pao, and proved to be an expert siege engineer whose assistance was to be invaluable in later campaigns. Then, while camped at Fu Chou, Genghis learned that the second and larger part of the Chin army had arrived on the scene and was fortifying a position north of the pass at Huan-erh-tsui, the 'Young Badger's Mouth'. This force was composed mainly of elite Jurchen and Khitan cavalry, but also contained many Chinese infantry. Its commander, Ke-shih-lieh Chih-chung, had so far advanced slowly so that the footsoldiers would not be left behind, rejecting the advice of two of his officers that he should launch a swift attack with his cavalry and catch the Mongols while they were still occupied in looting Fu Chou. He argued instead that the enemy was too strong to be routed by cavalry alone, and so the support of the infantry was essential. On the other hand, he also refused to wait for the reinforcements which were on their way to join him under the Jurchen prince Wan-yen Hu-sha.

The Battle of Huan-erh-tsui and the Collapse of the Frontier

As the opposing armies advanced towards each other, Chih-chung made a last-ditch attempt to negotiate, sending a Khitan officer named Shih-mo Ming-an to ask Genghis what grudge he bore against the Chin dynasty. One Chinese source says that this was simply a diversion, and that it backfired when Ming-an defected and gave the Mongols detailed information on the Chin plans and order of battle. Another says that Genghis did not trust his apparent change of sides and had him tied up, but released him after the battle. Either way it was an early indication of what was to become a serious problem for the Jurchens; many of their Khitan subjects regarded the Mongols not as enemies but as liberators. The spot where the armies met, north of Huan-erh-tsui, was very near to the boundary between the settled country of China and the steppe. We cannot be sure whether Genghis chose the battlefield, perhaps on the basis of Ming-an's report, but the terrain obviously favoured the Mongols. If they were defeated they would have an uninterrupted line of retreat back to Mongolia, while if the enemy was forced back he would be driven into a bottleneck in the pass behind him. Furthermore, it seems likely that the site was too narrow for the enormous Chin army to deploy properly, as – despite Chih-chung's preference for combined-arms tactics – he was caught with his cavalry in a long line in front, while the infantry were massed uselessly in the rear. The Mongols attacked at once, probably in the echeloned formation that they had learned from the Khitans. According to Martin, citing the *Meng-wu-erh Shih*, two Chinese biographies of Mukhali state that the general led the first attack with the Mongol left wing army, charging with lances. Genghis himself then led the centre army into action. Martin says that 'successive waves' of Mongol light troops were first sent forward to disorganise the enemy with arrows, but does not quote a source for this, and the biographies he cites imply that the charge was launched immediately after Genghis and Mukhali had observed the Chin deployment. In any case the Jurchen cavalry were driven back on their infantry, but instead of providing support the latter merely obstructed their movements, and soon the whole Chin army was in hopeless confusion. In the words of the *Yuan Sheng Wu Ch'in Cheng Lu*, 'the Chin sustained a terrible reverse, men and horses trampling each other down in the rout and the dead being without number'. Rashid ud-Din, writing a century later at the other end of the Mongol empire, said that the Mongols still remembered Huan-erh-tsui as among the greatest of their victories. This is understandable, for it was this battle that made possible the eventual conquest of the whole of China.

Our sources offer varying and often confused accounts of the aftermath, though all agree that the Chin suffered very heavy losses. The *Secret History* says that Genghis pursued them as they fled south, and left their dead 'piled like rotten logs' all the way back to the far side of the mountains. Ten years later, when Ch'ang Ch'un crossed the pass, he found thousands of skeletons still unburied. Ke-shih-lieh Chih-chung escaped, rallied the survivors and apparently reached a rendezvous with Wan-yen Hu-sha, but the latter fled with 7,000 picked cavalrymen when he heard the news of the defeat, leaving Chih-chung to be overtaken and routed again by Genghis at Ting-an. The headlong Mongol pursuit continued – no doubt, as Martin says, making use of fresh horses – and at Hui-ho Pao, thirty miles from Huan-erh-tsui, Hu-sha was also caught and his bodyguard scattered, though he himself continued his panic-stricken flight. Chih-chung made yet another stand, probably on the Sang-kan River, with the aid of 3,000 reinforcements, but was again forced to flee after a day of fighting. Requisitioning horses and cash as he went, he eventually found safety, together with Hu-sha, within the walls of Chung-tu.

During the following two months, October and November 1211, the passes through the mountains and the fortified frontier towns behind them all fell to the Mongols. It seems to be at this point that Jebei seized the formidable fort at Chu-kung Yuan – though the *Secret History*, not always reliable about events outside Mongolia, describes the action as a prelude to the Battle of Huan-erh-tsui. Finding the place too strong to assault, Jebei adopted the strategy that Genghis had used against the Tanguts at K'e-i Men. He pretended to retreat, and lured the garrison into pursuing him for thirty-five miles. Then, near a hill called Chi-ming Shan, he turned and routed his pursuers. The continuing success of this old trick is rather surprising, but the main role of the frontier garrisons was normally to protect the surrounding countryside from raids, and aggressive pursuit was no doubt the standard response to the appearance of what must have looked like a small raiding party. The defeated Jurchens fled back into the fort, where they spread such panic that its commander evacuated it and allowed Jebei to enter it unopposed.

So demoralised were the Jurchens by these reverses that the Emperor Wei Shao even contemplated abandoning Chung-tu, but was persuaded to stay and fight by his own Imperial Guards. However, Genghis knew that he was not yet strong enough to attack the city, and instead despatched several columns to plunder the surrounding country, taking advantage of the temporary absence of the enemy's field armies. A deserter named Liu Po-lin now appeared in the Mongol camp with a proposal for an attack on Tung Ching (formerly known as Mukden, now Shenyang) in the Jurchens' Manchurian heartland, 200 miles to the east. In January 1212 Jebei was sent to try and take the city by surprise, but found that the defenders had already been alerted. So once again he employed a typical Mongol trick, and again the enemy reacted exactly as expected. He ordered his men to retreat as if in panic, leaving their baggage and the loot they had collected behind in their deserted camp. The Mongols retired for six days' march (by Chinese calculation, so probably, as Martin says, based on infantry marching speed and equivalent to about a hundred miles). When their scouts reported this, the people of Tung Ching felt safe enough to open the gates and plunder the camp. They then proceeded to celebrate the New Year, leaving the gates unmanned. But for a Mongol army equipped with sufficient spare horses, as Jebei's was, a hundred miles could be covered in a forced march of twenty-four hours. They returned during the night and scattered the celebrating crowds, then rode into the city unopposed and looted it. However, Jebei did not attempt to occupy Tung Ching permanently at this stage, but returned to link up with Genghis. Meanwhile the Chin had once again mishandled the political situation. Suspecting the loyalty of the Khitans – many of whom had fought loyally for them at Huan-erh-tsui – they sent Jurchen settlers into their Manchurian homeland to keep them under control, thus provoking the very revolt they feared. Genghis had already sent two emissaries to the Khitan territory, but while still en route they met a large Khitan army under Yeh-lu Liu-ke, coming to join the Mongols.

Then in February 1212 the victorious Mongols began the long march home from China with their loot. But this was only intended to be a temporary withdrawal, as is shown by the fact that Genghis left garrisons among the Ongguts and in a number of border towns including T'ien Ch'eng, which was entrusted to the defector Liu Po-lin. During his absence in China one Onggut faction had overthrown Ala-qush Tagin and attempted to go over to the Chin, but now the rebels fled and the remainder of the people hastily reaffirmed their loyalty. Meanwhile a Chin army had been sent to destroy the Khitan rebel Yeh-lu Liu-ke, but Genghis sent 3,000 Mongols to reinforce his new ally, who was victorious at the Battle of Ti-chi Nor and sent the enemy's captured baggage to the Khan as a token of his loyalty. It is difficult to disagree with Martin that this Chinese campaign was Genghis' 'greatest feat of arms'. Later, against the Khwarizmian Empire, he led more troops and conquered a larger area, but there the opposition was much less formidable. If he had indeed attempted to distract the Chin with the thrust of the right wing army in the west, he had not succeeded, but he had adapted his plans to the changing situation and taken instant advantage of the piecemeal deployment of the enemy facing him – an ability which he was to demonstrate again in the Khwarizmian campaign (see Chapter 5). By attacking without hesitation he had smashed three Chin armies in succession as they arrived at the front, and forced open the fortified mountain barrier that had protected the Yellow River plain.

Closing in on Chung-tu
In the autumn Genghis returned and laid siege to the town of Hsi Ching. A Chin army under Ao Tun-hsiang advanced to relieve the town, but the Khan withdrew before him, luring him into an ambush in a valley known as Mi-ku K'ou and annihilating his army. Genghis then returned to the siege, but was severely wounded by an arrow shot from the wall. He broke off the campaign and his army escorted him back to Mongolia to recuperate. However, he was back by September 1213, when he encountered a newly-raised Chin army, said to be 100,000 strong, at Wei-ch'uan. According to the *Yuan Ch'ao Pi Shih* 'the whole army of Chin was present', but it was probably weaker in cavalry and far inferior in overall quality to the forces that had been destroyed two years earlier. Martin points out that the empire was now so short of manpower that it had been necessary to declare an amnesty for all criminals in several northern provinces, in the hope of recruiting them into the army. Genghis observed that the enemy were deployed across the valley at Wei-ch'uan with both flanks resting on hilly terrain, so he sent flanking forces through the hills on either side, while he attacked frontally. He succeeded in forcing the Chin line back to a point where the valley was wider, allowing the flanking detachments to descend on it from

both sides. The Chin broke, and the chronicles relate the usual stories of the line of retreat littered with bodies. The *Secret History* mentions the destruction of an elite Jurchen unit known as the 'Red Jackets' or 'Red Capes'. The fugitives fled to the great fortress at Chu-yung, which guarded the final mountain pass before the city of Chung-tu, now only twenty miles away. Genghis sent Jebei to take some of the neighbouring forts by surprise attack, while he bypassed Chu-yung by following a path shown to him by the merchant Ja'afar, who had no doubt used the route before on trading missions to China.

A new Chin army arrived at the front just in time to see the Mongols emerging from the supposedly impregnable pass, and dissolved in panic. Chu-yung was then attacked from the rear by Jebei and Subotei, and the starving garrison surrendered. While their frontier armies were thus disintegrating, the Chin were beginning to tear themselves apart. Ke-shih-lieh Chih-chung had been temporarily disgraced after his defeat at Huan-erh-tsui, but had then been pardoned and stationed at Chung-tu with a bodyguard of 5,000 men. However, he seems to have been blamed by one of the commanders at Wei-ch'uan, Wan-yen Kang, for the defeat – apparently because he had failed to block one of the mountain passes. Kang denounced him to Emperor Wei Shao, so Chih-chung, fearing punishment, staged a coup, murdered both Kang and the emperor, and set himself up as regent. A Jurchen prince called Utubu was proclaimed emperor under the throne name of Hsuan Tsung, but Chih-chung began issuing his own orders without reference to him. Thus Chung-tu came under the control of the man whose ineptitude had largely been responsible for the danger the city was now in. In November Chih-chung took the field against two small Mongol detachments which approached the city, but the engagements seem to have been inconclusive. The Chin general blamed the lack of success on another officer, Chu-hu Kao-ch'i, whom he ordered to redeem his reputation by leading a suicidal attack on the Mongols with only 5,000 men, threatening him with execution if he failed. Inevitably Kao-ch'i was defeated, so he raced back to the city ahead of the news and took Chih-chung by surprise, killing him when he tried to escape. Kao-ch'i then took his rival's severed head and presented it to the emperor, making a full confession. As he had no doubt calculated Hsuan Tsung was by no means displeased, but promoted Kao-ch'i to the rank of Vice Commander of the Empire.

'Smoke and Drums'

Meanwhile Mukhali was besieging the stronghold of Cho Chou, which fell after a siege variously reported as lasting one, twenty or forty days. Even more ominous for the Chin than this enemy success in siege warfare was the means by which it had been accomplished, for three native Chinese officers formerly in Chin service had joined Mukhali with their whole commands. It may have been this setback, as Martin suggests, that persuaded Hsuan Tsung to sue for peace. However, Genghis, realising that he was now in a position of strength, rejected his overtures. Leaving 5,000 men to blockade the demoralised garrison of Chung-tu, he divided the rest of his army into three columns and set out over the winter of 1213 to 1214 to ravage the countryside as far south as the Yellow River. Numerous small and medium-sized towns were also taken, mainly by assault, using the ruthless tactic of driving captured civilians in front of the attackers to build siege works and shield the Mongol troops from missiles. Chinese sources claim that the defenders often refused to fight for fear of killing their own relatives. The biography of Mukhali in the *Yuan Ch'ao Ming Ch'en Shih Liao* gives a vivid picture of the terror spread by the Mongol armies: 'Everywhere north of the Yellow River there could be seen dust and smoke', it laments, 'and the sound of drums rose to Heaven.'

Yeh-lu Liu-ke, whose defection had obviously provoked the special hatred of the Chin emperors, was the target of two more punitive expeditions during 1214, but his Khitan troops crushed them both, and in the aftermath he consolidated his hold over much of Manchuria. By the beginning of 1214 the Chin still held only seven towns north of the Yellow River, and Chung-tu was effectively cut off from resupply or reinforcements from the south. This no doubt was Genghis' intention, because the capital was far too strong to be taken by direct assault with the still rudimentary siege train available to the Mongols. When the columns reassembled outside the city in March they did in fact make two attempts to storm it, with the Khan's reluctant consent, but were driven back with heavy losses. It is not surprising that Genghis was pessimistic about his chances of storming Chung-tu, because this was perhaps the most strongly-fortified city in the world. It was surrounded by the usual wall of rammed earth behind three concentric moats, and defended by 900 watchtowers filled with catapults and huge crossbows. But during the previous century the governor, Nien Han, had decided that the city was still too vulnerable, and had ordered the construction of four huge outlying forts, each about a mile square and garrisoned by 4,000 men. These were provided with their own arsenals and granaries and were intended to be self-sufficient, but were connected to the city itself by a network of underground tunnels. It was from these forts that troops sallied out to attack the Mongols in the rear whenever they attempted to assault the main city walls. But if the fortifications of the city remained impregnable, the morale of the defenders was showing signs of crumbling. In March or April 1214 Genghis sent a messenger to propose peace terms. The *Yuan Sheng Wu Ch'in Cheng Lu* has preserved details of the subsequent discussion between the emperor and his generals. One of the latter suggested that the Mongols must be suffering from supply difficulties, and that both the men and their horses would now be weakened by exhaustion and sickness. The Chin should therefore sally out and give battle. On the other hand, Wan-yen Fu-hsing, the commander of the garrison, argued that their remaining troops were too unreliable. They had been conscripted from distant provinces and their loyalty was doubtful; if defeated they would simply scatter in all directions, while even if they were successful it would be impossible to prevent them returning home, leaving the city once again vulnerable once the Mongols had rallied.

Hsuan Tsung accepted this argument, and agreed to pay Genghis a huge tribute in hostages, horses, gold and silk in return for peace. It is likely that the Mongols really were suffering from shortages, as it is at this point that Carpini alleges that Genghis ordered one in ten of his soldiers to be killed and eaten by the rest. It is likely, however, that the horses were suffering worse than the men, because suitable pasture was scarce south of the frontier. A Chinese account states that the invaders retired as far as the Chu-yung Pass where they slaughtered all their prisoners, perhaps because they were unable to feed them, though Martin argued that they were unlikely to have jeopardised the peace so soon by such an 'outrageous piece of barbarity'. In any case they did not retire as far as Mongolia, camping instead by the Dohon Nor, one of a series of lakes in what is now Inner Mongolia, not far from the Chin frontier. Hsuan Tsung, no doubt well aware that they would return, decided to move the seat of government to safety in the south, and in June set out with his court for the city of K'aifeng, leaving Chung-tu under the command of Wan-yen Fu-hsing. Thirty miles south of the city, the emperor became worried about the loyalty of the 2,000 Khitans who formed part of his guard, and ordered them to be deprived of their horses. Instead they mutinied and rode back to Chung-tu, where they outmanoeuvred and defeated a Jurchen force and stole more horses, before continuing north to join the Mongols. Learning from these defectors of the emperor's withdrawal, Genghis seized on this as a pretext for renewing the war. He had also been annoyed by the refusal of the Chin to allow a Mongol embassy to the Sung in the south to pass through their territory, but of course it is probable that he had intended to return to China in any event, as soon as his men and horses had rested and recovered their strength.

The Capture of Chung-tu
So in July 1214 Genghis sent an army under Samukha and Shih-mo Ming-an to resume the blockade of Chung-tu. The inhabitants began to starve, and in April 1215 Hsuan Tsung sent two relief armies north, every man of which was said to have been burdened with 70lbs of food in addition to the supplies carried in wagons. Both armies were badly led and were easily defeated by small Mongol detachments, the commander of one, Li Ying, being captured while drunk. All the supplies fell into the hands of the Mongols, while the people of Chung-tu were beginning to resort to cannibalism. Wan-

yen Fu-hsing and his colleague Mo-jan Chin-chung quarrelled about whether to escape or die fighting, resulting in the former committing suicide while Mo-jan fled to K'aifeng, where he was executed for treason. In June the leaderless garrison opened the gates and surrendered. The triumphant Mongols plundered and set fire to the city, parts of which were said to have burned for a month. Genghis had apparently not been present when the surrender occurred, but now found himself master of the Chin imperial treasury, and of almost the whole of China north of the Yellow River. Considering the campaign successfully concluded, he returned to Mongolia, leaving Shih-mo Ming-an with a mixed Mongol and Chinese garrison in command of what remained of Chung-tu. Meanwhile the Chin Empire began to disintegrate. Their surviving troops in northern Manchuria declared independence, while in Shantung on the east coast the peasantry, infuriated by an attempt to distribute their lands to refugees from the north, rose in a revolt which lasted for a decade. In the east the Tanguts of Hsi Hsia, now at least nominally vassals of the Mongols, launched a series of invasions which, although repulsed, continued to occupy a large proportion of the Chin forces.

Meanwhile, a complicated series of events delivered still more of Manchuria, the original homeland of both the Jurchens and the Khitans, into Mongol hands. P'u-hsien Wan-nu, the Chin general who had been sent to deal with the pro-Mongol Khitan Yeh-lu Liu-ke, finally succeeded in surprising his opponent's camp and temporarily scattering his troops, but Wan-nu then antagonised the Chin emperor by himself declaring independence as 'King of Tung Chen'. A Chin expedition drove him east into Korea, and Liu-ke took advantage of the distraction to re-establish his position. However, he still felt vulnerable to another Chin attack, so he went in person to visit Genghis, who despatched two armies, under Mukhali and Qasar, to assist him and finally reduce Manchuria to submission. Mukhali's task was greatly aided by the local Khitans, who mostly went over to him. Early in 1215 the city of Pei Ching was delivered to him by a Khitan named Shi-mo Yesen, who ambushed and killed the Jurchen officer sent to take over the garrison, used his written orders and his inside knowledge to impersonate the new commander himself, and then ordered the gates to be opened. The garrison commander fought on for a while, and then surrendered. Mukhali intended to execute him, but Shih-mo Yesen persuaded him that he had more to gain by clemency, and the prisoner was instead retained as commander of Pei Ching under Mongol rule. This enlightened attitude seems to have persuaded other Chin or former Chin officers to surrender, including a rebel named Chang Ching, who handed over a province stretching as far east as the Gulf of P'o Hai.

Chin Resistance
Nevertheless despite these territorial losses the Chin regime remained surprisingly resilient. Angrily rejecting Genghis' demand that he renounce the title of emperor and accept vassal status as 'King of Honan', Hsuan Tsung offered huge rewards for any general who could defeat the Mongols and re-take Chung-tu. The Khan responded by sending four columns back south to keep up the pressure. One of these, consisting of 10,000 men led by Samukha, linked up with 30,000 Tangut cavalry in the west and advanced towards Yen-an in the Ordos Steppe. It is not clear whether Samukha's subsequent movements had been specifically ordered by Genghis or whether he was acting on his own initiative, but he now embarked on the most spectacular long-distance raid of the war. When he approached the fortress of T'ung Kuan on the Wei River the garrison commander came out to fight, but was defeated and the fort was taken by surprise. Samukha continued down the Yellow River east of the Ordos loop, crossing to the south bank and heading for K'aifeng, where the Chin now had their capital. Four Chin armies were now in the field against him, but he evaded them by crossing the mountains near Ju Chou by rough tracks, and emerged at Hsing-hua-ying, only six miles from K'aifeng. The city was heavily fortified and Samukha had no siege train, although forcibly-conscripted Chinese infantry had now swelled his force to 60,000 men, so he was obliged to turn back westwards, followed by the converging Chin armies. At Mien Chou one of these armies caught

The open grassland, or steppe, of central Mongolia. Here Genghis' people, the Borjigin Mongols, followed the classic nomadic stockbreeding lifestyle. (Fotolia)

The barren wastes of the Gobi Desert, which lies south of the steppe zone and separates Mongolia from China. Despite the lack of water and pasture, Genghis' armies successfully crossed the desert in the course of several campaigns. (Fotolia.)

The Mongol army owed much of its success to the immense herds of horses which were supported by the grasslands, just as their descendants are today. The typical Mongol pony was not the elegant animal represented in Rashid ud-Din's illustrations, but was stockily built, no more than 12 or 13 hands high, and grew a shaggy coat to protect it from the winter cold. (Fotolia)

These modern statues, outside the Genghis Khan Museum in the Mongolian capital, Ulaanbaatar, show how the better equipped Mongol warriors of the thirteenth century may have looked. (Fotolia)

The Battle of Huan-erh-tsui in 1211, as depicted in the *Jami al-tawarikh* of Rashid ud-Din. These widely-reproduced images are the earliest to show Mongol soldiers in action, but they date from nearly a century later than Genghis' campaigns, and may not be an accurate guide to the clothing and armour styles of the earlier period.

Mongol cavalry pursuing a routed enemy, also from Rashid ud-Din.

Lance-armed Egyptian Mamluks pursue Mongol mounted archers in this depiction of the Egyptian victory at the Battle of Hims in 1281. Two of the latter appear to be conducting a rearguard action while their comrades escape to safety. From the fourteenth-century *History of the Tartars* by the Armenian historian Hayton of Coricos.

The only near-contemporary portrait of Genghis dates from later in the thirteenth century, and is preserved in the National Palace Museum in Taipei. It may be a somewhat idealised image, but it certainly does not depict the bloodthirsty monster of Western legend.

Stages in the construction of a modern replica of a Mongolian composite bow (photos courtesy of Green Man Longbows). This photograph shows the wooden core of the bow, with separate plates of horn ready to be attached. Horn, which resists compression, is fixed to the belly, the side which is nearest the shooter when the bow is in use, while animal sinew, which tends to spring back after tension like a rubber band, forms the back, facing away from the archer.

Preparing the core for the attachment of the 'siha', the rigid end sections which act as levers to increase the length of the draw and improve the 'cast', the speed at which the bow returns to its original shape on the release of the string.

The core of the bow with the siha and central hand grip glued in place.

The horn is strapped tightly in place while the glue dries.

Bundles of shredded sinew, which will be soaked in glue and applied to the wooden core.

The finished weapon. Note that when unstrung it curves strongly in the opposite direction to the shape it will assume when drawn.

Drawing a composite bow. Unlike the contemporary English longbow, the Mongol weapon does not bend throughout its length, but only in the relatively short sections between the hand grip and the siha. It feels less smooth to draw than a longbow, but the release is faster and the initial velocity of the arrow greater for the same draw weight.

Another view of the draw. Medieval illustrations show that Mongol archers often drew the string back much further than is shown here, as far as or even beyond the ear. A composite bow was less likely to break than a wooden one, even when overdrawn in this way.

A variety of siege techniques, including the use of heavy stone-throwing engines, is illustrated in this picture of the siege of Baghdad, taken from Rashid ud-Din's history.

Mongol tents, or 'gers', could be transported with the army on huge wagons, as depicted in this illustration from Colonel Yule's edition of Marco Polo's Travels, 1876.

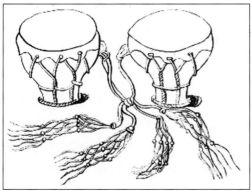

Mongol kettledrums, used for signalling in battle and carried on horses or camels. (Yule)

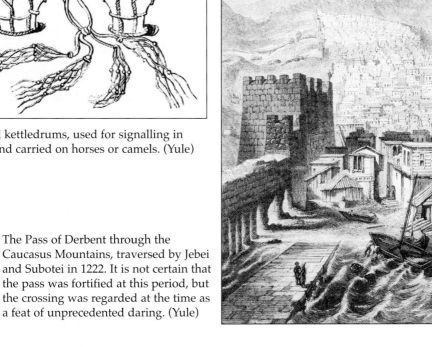

The Pass of Derbent through the Caucasus Mountains, traversed by Jebei and Subotei in 1222. It is not certain that the pass was fortified at this period, but the crossing was regarded at the time as a feat of unprecedented daring. (Yule)

A fortified pass through the mountains north of Chung-tu. Although dating from after the Mongol conquest, this archway may be similar to those encountered by Genghis during the invasion of 1211. (Yule)

Genghis' grandson Hulegu, founder of the Ilkhanid dynasty, and his queen Dokuz Khatun, as depicted by Rashid ud-Din.

Today Genghis Khan is revered as the founder of the Mongolian nation. This monument outside Ulaabaatar, completed in 2010, is said to be the world's largest equestrian statue – fittingly for the man who conquered the world's greatest empire on horseback. (Fotolia)

up with him, but Samukha defeated it in battle before crossing back to the north bank of the Yellow River, now frozen, in January 1216. The Mongol commander then laid siege to P'ing-yang, but was repulsed by the garrison and forced to retire before he was trapped by the pursuing field armies. At this point the Chin proclaimed an amnesty for anyone who had been forced to fight for the Mongols, which resulted in 13,000 of Samukha's infantry deserting. Then the Tangut contingent also went home, but Samukha was able to extricate his Mongols without further losses, even taking the town of Hsi Ching on his way back to join Genghis on the Mongolian steppes. Martin calculates that in his advance to the vicinity of K'aifeng he had travelled 700 miles in only fifty or sixty days. Unfortunately nothing more is heard of Samukha, who was clearly one of the most promising of Genghis' generals, and it is possible, as Martin suggests, that he died or was killed soon after his greatest feat of arms.

Manchuria was still not completely subdued. The defector Chang Ching had been ordered by Mukhali to take his troops south to join the war against the Chin in the Yellow River valley, but had refused, been arrested, and was killed while attempting to escape. His brother Chang Chih therefore raised the country in revolt. Mukhali knew that the towns which the rebels had seized would be extremely hard to retake, so he employed a stratagem to lure them into giving battle in the open field. He waited until the late summer of 1216, when all his forces were mustered, then sent part of his army to besiege the fortress of Liu-shih Shan, while another detachment advanced to keep Chang Chih's main army, based at Yung-te, under observation. When Chang Chih learned that the fort was being attacked by what seemed to be a small and isolated Mongol force, he sent his nephew Chang Tung-p'ing to relieve it with an army of 8,000 cavalry and 30,000 infantry. Its movements were reported to Mukhali, who made a forced march with his main body to intercept it, and brought Chang Tung-p'ing to battle at Shen-shui. According to the biographies of Mukhali cited by Martin, the Mongol commander realised that the enemy's Chinese infantry – who wore no armour – were vulnerable to archery, and so he ordered a section of his army to dismount and engage them with arrows. The remainder of the Mongols, who had remained mounted, then charged and completed the victory. Chang Tung-p'ing and 12,000 of his men were killed. Chang Chih then took refuge in the city of Chin Chou with his personal guard of 12,000 men, who were dressed in black uniforms and known as the Black Army. However, he antagonised his own officers by executing twenty of them whom he held responsible for the defeat at Shen-shui, and was himself murdered in his turn. The surviving rebels then opened the gates to Mukhali. The Black Army surrendered *en masse*, but it must have impressed the Mongols nevertheless, as it was incorporated into their forces under the command of Shih-mo Yesen. The willingness of Genghis and his generals to accept the surrender or defection of Chinese troops was in sharp contrast to their attitudes in other theatres, where turncoats were seldom trusted and units which surrendered were frequently massacred. They no doubt accepted the necessity of employing local allies if they were ever to subdue a country as large and populous as China, and it is likely that even at this early stage their armies included as many Chinese, Khitans and other auxiliaries as Mongols.

Early in 1217 Genghis appointed Mukhali to take overall command of operations in China, which now mainly took the form of sieges of isolated Chin garrisons north of the Yellow River, rather than the sweeping strategic manoeuvres of the previous six years. In the following year the Khan himself returned briefly to China when the Hsi Hsia ruler Li Tsun-hsiang, no doubt discouraged by the losses incurred in his campaigns against the Chin, refused to provide further troops. Genghis arrived outside Chung-hsing in January or February 1218, and Li quickly saw the error of his ways. In exchange for peace he agreed to renew his pledge of allegiance, but as soon as the Mongols retired his generals again forced him to change his mind, sending an insulting message to the effect that if the Khan could not deal with his enemies without Tangut help, he was not as powerful as he pretended to be. Genghis was by now too deeply involved in events in the west to be able to punish his vassal's insolence at once, so Hsi Hsia enjoyed a few years of respite before the inevitable retaliation. Further east, however, the war against the

Chin continued, with the Tanguts alternating between support for the Mongols and various degrees of defiance.

In January 1218 Genghis had sent Yeh-lu Liu-ke to finish off the last of the Khitan rebels who had taken refuge in Korea. By this time his old enemy P'u-hsien Wan-nu was fighting on the side of the Mongols, and contributed his Jurchen troops to the expedition. This campaign led to the submission of the king of the Koryo dynasty, formerly a vassal of the Chin, who cooperated with the Mongols in the capture of Kang-dong, where 50,000 rebels were reportedly taken prisoner. Liu-ke, presumably with the approval of the Khan, showed unexpected leniency on this occasion, merely executing a hundred of the ringleaders and deporting the rest. P'u-hsien Wan-nu was captured in 1233 and decapitated, his death finally bringing peace to Manchuria. The Koreans agreed to pay a tribute which included, apart from cotton, gauze and silk, 100,000 large sheets of paper. Yeh-lu Liu-ke then returned to China, but left behind forty Mongols with instructions to learn the Korean language. This was typical of the thoroughness of the Mongol intelligence system, and suggests that Genghis anticipated having to return at some time in the future to consolidate his authority. In fact this was not to happen until after his death. Wan-nu changed sides again after Mukhali's death in 1223 and managed to hold out in eastern Manchuria until 1231, when the new Khan, Genghis' son Ogodei, determined to suppress him once and for all. He requested help from the Koryo king, who – like the Tanguts in 1218 – was unwise enough to refuse. Ogodei therefore sent an army to invade Korea, beginning an intermittent conflict that lasted for four decades. The first invasion was repulsed, after a hard-fought siege at Kuju, when the Mongol general Sartaq was killed while attacking another defensive line. The invaders returned in 1235, but although the Koreans were repeatedly beaten in the field the war lasted until 1273, prolonged by their skill at defending their fortified towns and offshore islands, and by guerrilla warfare in the mountains.

Chapter 5

War in the West

The Conquest of Qara-Khitai

Genghis' unification of Mongolia in 1206 had brought him into contact with the kingdom of Qara-Khitai, a Khitan successor state which had been established west of the Altai Mountains after the Jurchen conquest of north China in 1125. It had been founded by a prince of the Liao royal house named Yeh-lu Ta-shih, who managed to lead a Khitan army across Mongolia and defeat the Seljuq and Qarakhanid Turks who controlled the region between the Tien Shan Mountains in the south and Lake Balkhash in the north, in what is now eastern Kazakhstan. Eventually the Qara-Khitai rulers, who came to be known by the grandiose title of 'Gur-khans' or 'Universal Rulers', extended their power as far south as the Silk Road cities of Khotan and Kashgar, in the Tarim Basin south of the Tien Shan, though their capital remained at Balasaghun, on the north side of the range. They were Buddhists, which made their rule unpopular with the Muslim majority in the region, and so their military power remained based on the dwindling descendants of the Khitan troops who had accompanied Yeh-lu Ta-shih. Further weakened by wars with their Khwarizmian and Ghurid neighbours in the first decade of the thirteenth century, the Qara-Khitai were prepared to welcome what at first seemed like a timely reinforcement from the east. As related in Chapter 2, Kuchluq, the son of the Naiman Tayang Khan, had escaped from the disaster which he had helped to bring on his people in 1205, and had taken refuge beyond the Altai Mountains in the west. In 1208, following another defeat by a Mongol expedition, he sought refuge with the reigning Gur-khan, Chiluku.

Kuchluq, like many of the Naimans, was a Nestorian Christian, but the Gur-khan probably thought of him as a useful ally against the Muslims, so he gave him his daughter's hand in marriage and allowed him to organise the Naiman and Merkit refugees in the country, numbering around 8,000 fighting men, into a private army. In 1209 Barchuk, the 'Idi-kut' or ruler of the Uighur Turks in the Tarim Basin, who had until then been a vassal of Qara-Khitai, revolted and transferred his allegiance voluntarily to Genghis Khan. At the same time war broke out between Chiluku and Shah Muhammad of Khwarizmia, his neighbour to the west. While dealing with these threats, the Gur-khan learned that Kuchluq had taken advantage of the chaos to loot the imperial treasury. He returned and defeated the rebellious Naimans on the River Chinbuje near Balasaghun, but was himself defeated by a Khwarizmian army before he had a chance to follow up his victory. What was worse, the Gur-khan's own troops had kept for themselves the booty which they had taken from the Naimans at the Chinbuje, which comprised most of the imperial treasure. When Chiluku ordered them to give it up so that he could continue to finance the war, they mutinied and handed him over to Kuchluq, who had by then been allowed to rally his troops. Kuchluq treated his father-in-law with outward respect, but from now on acted as if he himself was the rightful ruler of Qara-Khitai, although in practise this meant little as the state descended into chaos. He proved even less tolerant of Islam than his predecessor, and is accused by Juvaini and other Muslim chroniclers of numerous atrocities, including the crucifixion of the Imam of Khotan.

No doubt Genghis would eventually have sought the final destruction of his old enemy, but the immediate cause of war was a plea from Sugnaq Tegin, the son of Buzar, the ruler of the town of Almaligh, east of Balasaghun. Buzar had been arrested and held captive by Kuchluq, and his son besieged in the town. He appealed to Genghis for help, and in the early summer of 1218 Jebei was sent in response with an army of 20,000 men. At the same time another army under Subotei took a more northerly route, passing south of Lake Balkhash, in order to protect Jebei's flank from any hostile move by the Khwarizmians or the Turkish tribes of the steppes. Jebei crossed the Altai Mountains and marched to relieve Almaligh, being joined on the way by a contingent of Uighurs. Kuchluq retired before him, then tried to make a brief stand outside Balasaghun, but he must have realised that his subjects were not rallying to his support, especially after Jebei issued a proclamation promising full religious toleration. Balasaghun opened its gates to the Mongols, and Kuchluq fled south over the Tien Shan Mountains with Jebei in pursuit, chasing him, as Juvaini says, 'like a mad dog'. Everywhere the Mongols found themselves in the unfamiliar position of being welcomed as liberators. Kuchluq sought refuge in Kashgar, but the inhabitants refused to let him in, and instead surrendered to Jebei. The fugitive was finally cornered on the remote Badakhshan Plateau in the Pamir Mountains, where a band of hunters trapped him and handed him over to the Mongols. Jebei returned in triumph with Kuchluq's severed head, the sight of which was received with joy by his former subjects. His former Naiman and Merkit followers dispersed in all directions, some of them even finding refuge with the distant Kipchaq tribes of the Black Sea steppe, where they would encounter Jebei again four years later.

The Khwarizmian War
Of all Genghis' wars, the best known in the west is the invasion of the Khwarizmian Empire, which began soon after the conquest of Qara-Khitai, in 1219. In four years this campaign utterly destroyed what had been the greatest Muslim power in Central Asia and took the Mongol armies to the western perimeter of the continent, opening up an entire new world of which they had previously been unaware. Not only does the war mark the transition of Genghis' empire from an essentially East Asian to a global power, but it involved a catastrophe for the settled peoples of the region – those whom the *Secret History* calls the Sarta'ul – from which they appear never to have recovered. And yet this epic undertaking appeared to the Mongols themselves as of limited significance. The *Secret History*, for example, has very little to say about it, regarding it as no more than an appendix to the real story, of Genghis' rise to power

in Mongolia and his unification of the steppe tribes. From a military perspective at least, there is no doubt that the Mongols were right.

On paper the Khwarizmian Empire was indeed a formidable opponent, but it suffered from a number of fundamental weaknesses. It was a new creation, still ruled in 1219 by the man who had effectively founded it, the Khwarizm Shah Ala ud-Din Muhammad II. He had originally been a vassal of Qara-Khitai, but as the power of the latter faded he had emerged victorious from a long three-way struggle involving his former overlords in Qara-Khitai and the Ghurid Sultans of Afghanistan. This culminated in 1215 with the overthrow of the Ghurids, many of whom took refuge in their possessions in India, leaving Muhammad in control of the Afghan plateau. This region now formed the southeastern section of what was in effect a conglomeration of four separate and tenuously linked territories. North of the Afghan mountains, in the region known as Sogdia (now in Uzbekistan), were the great Silk Road cities of Samarkand and Bokhara, dominating the trade routes between China and the Mediterranean. It was originally at Bokhara that Muhammad established his capital. From Sogdia two rivers flowed northwestwards through the desert into the Aral Sea. The southernmost of these was the Amu Darya, the ancient Oxus, whose upper course flowed through the country known as Khurasan, and whose fertile lower reaches formed Khwarizmia proper. Some 300 miles to the northeast, and roughly parallel, flowed the Syr Darya, which was effectively the frontier between the settled Khwarizmian lands and the steppes which had been controlled by Qara-Khitai. A strategic weakness of this frontier was that most of the fortified towns were on the north bank of the river, and so were unprotected against an attack from that direction. Both river valleys were irrigated and densely inhabited, but between them lay an expanse of scrub-covered desert known in Turkish as the Kyzyl Kum or 'Red Sands', which made direct movement between them difficult. The communications hub of the empire was therefore the territory known as Zarafshan, between Samarkand and Bokhara. Zarafshan had been the site of conflict between Central and East Asian armies before, notably under the Chinese T'ang dynasty in the eighth century AD, but its eastern approaches had always been protected by the formidable barrier of the Pamir Mountains. This time, though, the threat came not from the east but from the northeast, and if an invader could cross the Syr Darya and operate in the arid country beyond, he would find the left flank of Zarafshan completely open.

Muhammad's empire was vulnerable not only geographically, but also politically. A large part of the army which had brought him to power was made up of mercenaries from the Qangli tribe, a Turkish-speaking steppe people related to the Kipchaqs of the Black Sea, but their loyalty was already suspect. In fact the Shah's mother, Terken Khatun, was a Qangli princess who seems to have controlled Khwarizmia proper as a personal fief, and had alienated many of the local aristocracy. When the Mongols captured the city of Gurganj on the Oxus, they found the prison full of Khwarizmian nobles incarcerated for their opposition to her rule. Throughout the empire Turks and Persians were on bad terms, a situation exacerbated by the Shah's religious policy. His attempts to extend his power into Iraq had been opposed by the Caliph al-Nasir in Baghdad, who was the head of the orthodox Sunni Muslim community. To counter the Caliph's influence Muhammad attempted to conciliate the Persian Shi'ites, but this only further upset the Sunnis in the rest of his empire.

The Khwarizmian army was said to number as many as 400,000 men. Its main striking force consisted of mercenary 'ghulam' heavy cavalry, armed in Turkish 'mamluk' style with swords, lances, maces and composite bows of similar design to those used by the Mongols. Troops of this type served in most Middle Eastern Muslim armies, but the Khwarizmians seem to have been more heavily armoured than their neighbours, and also had a higher proportion of men riding armoured horses. There were also lighter mounted archers supplied by the Qanglis and other Turkish tribes, as well as large contingents of infantry recruited from the former Ghurid realm. An unusual tactic recorded for the Ghurids was the use of a sort of moveable pavise called a 'karwah' made of oxhide stuffed with cotton, which could be rolled in front of the infantry to protect them from arrows. A number of these items could also be formed into a temporary barricade on the battlefield to surround an opponent or obstruct cavalry charges. The 'karwah' would seem to be an effective counter to many of the tactics used by the Mongols, but there is no record that it was actually used against them during the Khwarizmian campaign.

The first encounters between the Mongol and Khwarizmian Empires had in fact taken place as early as 1216. Juzjani says that around that time Muhammad sent an embassy to China under an official named Baha ad-Din Razi. Although ostensibly a trade mission, its real purpose was to investigate a rumour that Genghis had succeeded in capturing Chung-tu. The walls of the city were regarded at the time as the most formidable in the world, and the Shah was naturally anxious to know whether it was true that a new power had arisen capable of overcoming such an obstacle. The ambassadors had confirmed his worst fears. Not only had Chung-tu fallen, but it had been the scene of terrible destruction. They reported that they had walked for days over ground saturated with the fat from thousands of decomposed human corpses, and outside the walls they had seen a huge pile of bones which was all that remained of 60,000 young women, who had thrown themselves to their deaths rather than be violated by the invaders. Whether or not this was what Baha ad-Din Razi actually told the Shah, this account is clearly exaggerated, but Juzjani, who was serving in the Khwarizmian army at the time, may have recorded a story which was widely circulated. More encouragingly, the envoy added that he had been granted an audience with Genghis, who far from being hostile had expressed a desire for friendship and trade relations with Muhammad's empire. The Khan considered himself the ruler of the East, he added, and was happy to recognise the Shah as the ruler of the West.

It was probably shortly after this exchange that the first armed clash took place. As described in Chapter 2, in 1216 Jochi and Subotei had been sent to hunt down the Merkits led by Qultuqan Mergen, and had destroyed them in a battle in the vicinity of the Qaili and Qaimich Rivers. By chance Shah Muhammad was also in the area, having led an army, allegedly of 60,000 men, to punish a dissident Qangli chief. The subsequent events are related by Juvaini.

The Shah arrived on the field of the battle between the Mongols and the Merkits soon after it had been concluded, and learned from a wounded survivor that the Mongol army was still nearby. He followed its trail, and overtook it early the next morning. Jochi explained that he had been sent only against the Merkits and had no wish to fight the Khwarizmians, but Muhammad replied that all unbelievers were his enemies, and deployed for battle. Both sides then attacked, and the right wing of each drove back the enemy opposite. The Mongols then charged in the centre, nearly capturing the Shah, who was only saved by the intervention of his son Jalal ud-Din, commanding the victorious right wing. It seems that at some point Jochi was also in danger, as Genghis later rewarded Yeh-lu Hsieh-he, a Khitan recruit serving in the Mongol army, for saving his son's life. The battle, however, was a draw, and as night approached both armies withdrew to their camps. Muhammad was prepared to renew the fight on the following day, but he found that during the night the Mongols had retired, leaving their camp fires burning to deceive the enemy. In doing so Jochi was only obeying his orders and not necessarily acknowledging defeat, and it seems that the Shah was well aware of the poor performance of his army against an opponent a third of its size. In the words of Nasawi, 'A fear of these infidels was planted in the heart of the Sultan, and an estimation of their courage; if anyone spoke of them before him, he said that he had never seen men as daring nor as steadfast in the throes of battle, or as skilled in giving blows with the point and edge of the sword.'

So by the time the first Mongol embassy arrived in Samarkand early in 1218, the Shah had already had two experiences of his new neighbours and their fighting abilities, neither of which can have encouraged him to think that he could easily defeat them. This makes his subsequent conduct even harder to explain. Many writers have placed the blame for the disaster which was now to befall his empire on the character of Muhammad himself. 'No-one has a good word to say for this appalling creature' says John Man, '. . . a disaster in waiting.' In Denis Sinor's view the Shah's 'arrogant folly . . . was backed by neither statesmanship nor by adequate military abilities'.

Juvaini describes him as a drunkard, 'satisfying his desires in the company of fair songstresses and in the continual drinking of purple wine', and elsewhere as acting 'without thinking or reflecting'. But the Shah had previously acted with considerable energy in his wars with Qara-Khitai and the Ghurids, and it is hard to accept that a man so lacking in courage and judgement could ever have founded an empire, however short-lived. Perhaps the most charitable interpretation is that he was attempting the impossible task of pleasing all the various factions among his subjects. He might have turned increasingly to alcohol and self-indulgence as an antidote to the stress this caused, so that eventually his mental health gave way under the strain.

The first messenger to arrive from Genghis was a Muslim merchant named Mahmud Ali Khwajah, who presented extravagant gifts, including a lump of gold from China said to have been the size of a camel's hump. Along with these, according to Nasawi's account, came a message from the Khan, subtly drawing attention to the Mongol victories, of which the Shah must have heard, but assuring him that Genghis regarded him as 'on a level with the dearest of his sons'. Muhammad took offence at this, believing that the word 'son' implied vassal status, and interrogated Mahmud, asking once again if it was really true that the Mongols had taken Chung-tu from the Chin. The envoy replied that it was true, but attempted to calm the Shah by adding that Genghis' armies were in no way the equal of those of the Khwarizmian Empire. There has been much speculation about whether Genghis intended to provoke a war by using deliberately offensive language, but this is unlikely. For one thing, Juvaini does not record this conversation, which suggests that it was not public knowledge at the time he wrote. If it had been genuinely offensive, Muhammad would surely have publicised it to justify his response. In any case this sort of terminology was fairly routine in communications between Asian monarchs, all of whom were obliged to tolerate their neighbours' use of terms like 'Gur-khan', which implied some sort of authority over the lands beyond their borders.

Soon after the return of Mahmud's embassy, however, the

promised trade caravan from Mongolia arrived at the border town of
Otrar on the Syr Darya River. It consisted of 500 camels laden with
silk, fur, gold, silver and other luxury goods, and was accompanied
by a hundred Mongols and 450 merchants, all of whom, Juvaini
emphasises, were Muslims. But instead of sending this treasure on
to his master in Bokhara, the governor of Otrar, Khadir Khan, seized
it for himself and arrested, and later murdered, the escort. (Khadir
Khan is in fact not a name but a title, and means 'Great Lord'. Some
sources refer to him as 'Inalchik', a derisive nickname meaning
'Little Lord', which was presumably given to him by his enemies.)
Only one camel driver escaped to take the news of the massacre back
to Genghis. Juvaini says that Khadir was acting in pursuit of a
private feud, but that the deed was sanctioned in advance by the
Shah. In Nasawi's version the governor informed Muhammad that
the merchants were spies, and only then received the order to
execute them. The Shah may well have been implicated in the crime,
but in any case he was unwilling or unable to punish Khadir, who
had the support of the Qangli element in the army. So when another
embassy arrived from Genghis demanding that the governor should
be handed over to him, he executed the Muslim who led it as a
traitor, and sent his Mongol companions home with their heads
shaved.

The Invasion
Genghis obviously could not overlook such an insult, and
immediately made preparations for war. He was to lead the army in
person, leaving affairs in China under the control of his trusted
general Mukhali, and Mongolia itself in the hands of his younger
brother Temuge. Juvaini says that the Khan made no secret of his
plans, and even sent messengers to Muhammad to warn him that he
was coming, so determined was he to be seen to have justice on his
side. The Mongol army assembled on the Irtysh River in the summer
of 1219, and in the autumn crossed the Altai Mountains and
advanced across the steppe south of Lake Balkhash, formerly part of
the newly subjugated realm of Qara-Khitai. On the way Genghis was
joined by a number of allied contingents: 10,000 Uighurs, mainly

infantry, under the Idi-qut Barchuk, 6,000 Qarluq Turks led by their Khan Arslan, and a contingent of what Juvaini calls 'veteran warriors' drawn from the Muslim population of Qara-Khitai, under Signaq Tegin of Almaliq. None of our sources give plausible figures for the overall strength of the army. Martin suggests a total of around 150,000, but it has been argued that there were only 70,000 or 80,000 Mongol troops in the empire at that time, and that many of these were deployed in China or in reserve in Mongolia. As Genghis would hardly have taken the risk of forming an army in which the foreign auxiliaries greatly outnumbered the Mongols, he cannot have had many more than 50,000 men available for the western campaign. Juvaini describes many of the garrisons of the individual Khwarizmian cities as being larger than this. So although no precise figures are available for either side, it is reasonable to conclude that the Khwarizmian forces greatly outnumbered the invaders. The Shah's obvious strategy would therefore have been to concentrate his troops and attack the Mongols as they approached his frontier, and Genghis probably expected him to do this. An analysis of the situation published in 1933 by Squadron Leader C. C. Walker, and discussed by Martin, remains valid in many respects today. Walker pointed out that the line of the Syr Darya was strategically indefensible, but that it might have been possible, by advancing along the main route from Samarkand, to trap the Mongols between a mobile army and the garrison of Otrar. To counter this threat Genghis dispersed his forces, sending Chagatai and Ogodei to attack Otrar directly, while Jochi moved down the river northwestwards towards the Aral Sea, and a detachment of 5,000 men threatened Fanakat, where the road east from Samarkand crossed the Syr Darya. Meanwhile the Khan himself remained out on the steppe with the main army. The small Fanakat force was therefore the bait which would first lure Muhammad across the river, then fall back to Otrar. The Shah would believe that by advancing on the town from the southeast he had outmanoeuvred the Mongols and trapped their main army, at which point Genghis, so far undetected, would descend on his rear and surround him in his turn. If his analysis is correct it well illustrates the sophisticated planning of which Genghis' armies were capable, but the plan failed for the simple reason that Muhammad was afraid to take the bait.

His doubts about the allegiance of many of his subjects help to explain why he failed to concentrate his forces and take the offensive. Juvaini says that he was advised to do this as soon as news of the Mongol invasion arrived, but he was no doubt apprehensive that his predominantly Qangli Turkish and Sunni army might first decide to dispose of him before confronting the invaders. Instead he dispersed his army to reinforce the garrisons at Samarkand, Bokhara, and the towns along both river lines, thus permanently surrendering the initiative. Against an enemy who could both manoeuvre in the desert and take fortified cities, this deployment was disastrous. Of course, armies with this dual capability were exceptional, but the Mongols possessed it and by 1219 Muhammad must have known this. And although he was an experienced commander with a record of success on the battlefield, he now compounded his problems by losing his nerve completely.

If Genghis' original plan had been thwarted as suggested, he showed his versatility as soon as this became clear by adopting a new one, just as he had in China in 1211. Chagatai and Ogodei were left to besiege Otrar, where Khadir Khan, no doubt aware that he would receive no mercy, resisted for five months. Our main source for these events, as for the Khwarizmian war in general, is Juvaini. He says that the defenders of Otrar numbered 60,000, including both cavalry and footsoldiers – the former probably used for sorties against the Mongols beyond the walls, as their mobility would have been little use behind fortifications. The Mongol commanders may have led a 'touman' of 10,000 men each, so if Juvaini's figures are even approximately correct the defenders outnumbered them, but they seem to have made no attempt to engage them in a pitched battle. After the siege had been in progress for some time Khadir's second-in-command, Qaracha, surrendered with most of the Qangli troops. It may have been the fear of just such a defection that had prevented Khadir from taking the initiative, but the Mongols do not appear to have encouraged it. Instead they executed Qaracha and his men as traitors. We have seen that Genghis often treated those who betrayed their own lords in a similar way, even if their actions had ultimately been to his benefit, but the systematic refusal to accept Qangli defectors in this campaign contrasts with the welcome usually extended to those who joined the Mongol cause in China. We do not know whether this was official policy, but it is possible that the vacillating behaviour of the Shah and his soldiers, as well as the attacks on peaceful caravans, had encouraged the belief that the Qanglis were not to be trusted.

The surrender left Khadir Khan with only 20,000 men, with whom he now withdrew to the citadel, abandoning the city itself to the Mongols. These diehards held out for another month, sometimes sallying out, says Juvaini, to 'seek martyrdom' in groups of fifty at a time. When the citadel finally fell, Khadir retreated onto the roof with only two remaining bodyguards. The Mongols were under orders to take the governor alive, but he still fought on after his two companions were killed, throwing bricks which were handed to him by the women of his harem. At last he was captured and, in Juvaini's words, forced 'to drink the cup of annihilation', though he gives no further details of how he died. A story was later current that he was punished for his crimes by having molten silver poured into his eyes and ears, but this sort of elaborate torture was not typical of the Mongols, who usually put noble captives to death by suffocation in order to avoid shedding their blood. The walls of the town and citadel of Otrar were demolished and the surviving population deported as labourers or artisans, 'to practise their trade' for the benefit of the Mongols as Juvaini says, but no general massacre took place.

Meanwhile Jochi was taking the towns further down the Syr Darya one by one. At Suqnaq the people killed an ambassador sent to advise them to submit, so the Mongols stormed the walls, fighting in relays from dawn till dusk for seven days until the exhausted defenders could resist no longer. On this occasion Juvani says that the people were massacred, but the slaughter was clearly not total, as he adds that the son of the murdered envoy was installed as governor, 'that he might gather together the survivors that still remained in odd corners'. The next town, Barjligh-Kant, did not resist, and so was spared. The events at the city of Jand, further north, were almost farcical, and provide an all-too-rare episode of light relief in the narrative of the Mongol conquests. The garrison commander had fled with his men as Jochi approached, and again a Mongol envoy was sent into the town to negotiate surrender. Once again some of the citizens tried to incite the mob to murder him, but the quick-thinking messenger described to them what had happened at Suqnaq, and persuaded them to agree to submit. On 21 April 1219 Jochi arrived outside the walls, but found the gates still shut and the inhabitants lining the walls, though without any obvious preparations for battle. So he ordered his catapults, scaling ladders and battering rams to be brought up and prepared for action. While this was happening the people of Jand were seen setting up a catapult of their own on the walls, but in the absence of the military garrison they obviously lacked the expertise to operate it. They loaded it with a heavy stone and tried to shoot it at the Mongols, but it must have been discharged too near the vertical, because the stone fell back on the machine that had launched it and smashed it to pieces. In the ensuing confusion the Mongols climbed over the wall and opened the gates from inside. 'No one was hurt on either side' says Juvaini – a rather unexpected conclusion to an account of a Mongol siege. Jochi chose to overlook the botched attempt at resistance and spared the population, though he did allow his men to loot the city. The 5,000 Mongols sent to Fanakat were attacked by the local garrison and fought a pitched battle east of the river which lasted for three days, but were able to overcome the enemy without the help of the main army, and on the fourth day secured the surrender of the town. The surviving members of the garrison were put to death and the citizens once again drafted as a labour corps.

The Siege of Khojend
Juvaini describes the siege of Khojend at some length, and it is worth examining as an example of the siege techniques employed by the Mongols at this time, and the methods available to their enemies to counter them. The citadel was held by a famous warrior named Temur Malik, who commanded no more than 1,000 men. However.

it was exceptionally difficult to attack, being a 'tall stronghold' situated on an island in the middle of the Syr Darya, out of range of bows or catapults placed on either bank. Therefore the 20,000 besieging Mongols collected levies from the towns along the river – a total of 50,000 men according to Juvaini – and ordered them to carry stones to the river, where mounted Mongols rode into the water and dropped them to form a causeway. In response Temur Malik had twelve covered barges made, provided with loopholes through which men inside could shoot and protected with damp felt and a layer of clay mixed with vinegar to fireproof them. Each day and night these barges were rowed across from the island to harass the workmen and demolish the causeway, unaffected by the fire arrows and incendiary naphtha bombs which the Mongols shot at them. But they were unable to prevent the causeway extending further into the river, gradually bringing the citadel within range of the enemy artillery. Eventually Temur Malik and his men broke out and sailed downstream in seventy small boats, exchanging arrows with the Mongol cavalry who pursued them along the bank.

At Fanakat the Mongols stretched a chain across the river, but the fugitives broke through it and continued as far as Jand. There Jochi had built a bridge of boats carrying catapults to block their passage, and when he was warned of this Temur abandoned his vessels and fled west across the desert on horses, which had presumably been embarked with him. A Mongol army went in pursuit, and despite heroic rearguard actions Temur eventually lost his baggage and most of his men were scattered. At last he found himself alone and down to his last three arrows, with three Mongol troopers gaining on him from behind. He shot one arrow – which lacked a point, and so was unbalanced and harder to shoot accurately – and hit the leading Mongol in the eye, whereupon the other two backed off and allowed him to escape. Juvaini also recounts the unfortunate sequel. Temur fought with the Shah's son Jalal ud-Din until his death, carried on guerrilla warfare against the Mongols for a while longer, then sought asylum in Syria. Many years later, during the reign of Genghis' successor Ogodei, he returned and revealed his identity to his son, who had found favour at the Mongol court. But while attempting to recover his property Temur was recognised and arrested by Ogodei's son Qadaqan, who questioned him about his campaigns against the Mongols. In his replies the old warrior 'neglected the ceremonies of respect that are incumbent on those that speak in the presence of royalty', and an infuriated Qadaqan shot him fatally with an arrow. Elsewhere Juvaini praises the Mongol rulers for their lack of ceremony and 'excessive aloofness', but evidently, two generations after Genghis, this admirable trait was disappearing.

Bokhara and Samarkand

Genghis waited on the steppe until February 1220, when it must have been obvious that the Shah was not going to enter the trap that had been set for him. Instead he had taken refuge in Samarkand with a force which Juvaini puts at 110,000 men, including 60,000 elite Qangli Turks and twenty war elephants imported from India. Other writers give more conservative figures – Juzjani says there were 60,000 defenders, Nasawi only 40,000. Nevertheless the position was obviously far too strong to attack directly, so Genghis bypassed it, crossing the Syr Darya near Fanakat and then swinging north towards Bokhara via Zarnuq and Nur. This route took him through the Kyzyl Kum Desert, a stony wasteland dotted with low scrub, in a manoeuvre which has excited the admiration of many modern commentators. Legg calls it 'seemingly impossible . . . a march of nearly 300 miles through one of the most fearsome deserts in the world'. But neither Juvaini nor the *Secret History* bother to explain how it was done; the impression they give is that, like the crossing of the even more desolate Gobi, it was nothing out of the ordinary for the Mongols. In fact at least part of the route must have been well travelled, as Juvaini tells us that the citizens of Nur opened their gates to Genghis' army because they mistook it for a merchant caravan. But his descent on Bokhara in March 1220 does seem to have taken the Khwarizmians completely by surprise. Twenty thousand defenders sallied out and tried to give battle, but then abandoned the struggle and fled towards the Oxus River, where they were overtaken and destroyed. The people of the city then opened the gates and allowed the Mongols to enter.

Here Juvaini describes one of the best-known episodes of Genghis' career. He summoned the leading citizens, 280 in number, and proceeded to lecture them on the reasons for his coming. 'Know that you have committed great sins,' he told them, 'and that the great ones among you have committed these sins. If you ask me what proof I have for these words, I say it is because I am the punishment of God. If you had not committed great sins, God would not have sent a punishment like me upon you.' This extraordinary public statement is not of course a political manifesto. If he wanted the people to submit to him without further resistance it would be natural to exploit their religious beliefs in this way, so we cannot be certain that Genghis himself actually believed that he was the conscious agent of God's will. Some scholars have argued that the incident never happened, but reflects Juvaini's idea of Genghis' role in history rather than that of the Khan himself. But the chronicler's detailed account rings true, and when he wrote it forty years later there may have been eyewitnesses still living, so it is unlikely that the story is entirely fictional. Others seem also to have accepted the theory of divine punishment. The wooden receptacles that held the copies of the Koran in the great mosque were emptied and then filled with grain to feed the Mongol horses. Juvaini tells how when their hooves trampled the sacred books littering the floor, one of the clerics present protested to the great Imam Rukn ad-Din Imamzada, who replied, 'Be silent; it is the wind of God's omnipotence that bloweth, and we have no power to speak.' God's wrath had not yet run its course. The rich citizens were forced to pay a substantial fine, though Juvaini emphasises that no one was tortured or otherwise forced to pay beyond his means. But the garrison of Bokhara had retired into the citadel and continued to launch hit-and-run raids into the city, so Genghis ordered the town burned, and drafted the people to help fill in the moat around the stronghold. Juvaini also refers to 'fire hurled into the citadel', presumably naphtha bombs launched from catapults. Eventually the defenders surrendered, only to be massacred and their wives and children sold into slavery. The city was then temporarily abandoned, and the male population was marched away to serve as labourers at the next siege – that of Samarkand.

Genghis now closed in on the Shah's headquarters from the west, at the same time sending orders for his detached armies to rendezvous outside the city. But Muhammad abandoned his people and fled west with 30,000 soldiers, so three toumans under Jebei, Subotei and Toquchar, totalling 30,000 men, were diverted to hunt him down. When the rest of the Mongol army closed in on Samarkand, the garrison emerged and exchanged arrows with them until nightfall, when they were driven back within the walls with the loss of 1,000 dead, according to Juvaini. Juzjani says, more sensationally, that 50,000 of the citizens joined the attack, all of whom were killed. The next morning the Mongols advanced up to the walls to deprive the Khwarizmian cavalry of room to manoeuvre, so they sent out the elephants instead. It was well known in Classical and medieval times that horses which were unaccustomed to elephants were too afraid to face them, but the Mongols had the discipline to overcome this problem and shower the beasts with arrows until they turned back and trampled their own infantry. It is of course likely that Genghis' men faced the attack dismounted, as Marco Polo describes their successors under Kubilai Khan doing against Burmese elephants at the Battle of Vochan in 1277. On the third day of the siege the people opened the gates and the garrison retired as usual to the citadel, though 1,000 men under Alp Khan escaped, and the elephants with their drivers were captured. The Khan obviously did not think the animals were worth recruiting, because Juvaini says that when their keepers approached him to ask for food for their charges, he asked what they lived on in the wild. They replied 'the grass of the plains', so the Khan ordered them to be released to fend for themselves. Of course the arid region around Samarkand was not their natural habitat, and Juvaini adds that they all eventually died, perhaps in the cold of the following winter. The citadel of Samarkand was then surrounded and subjected to the usual barrage of arrows and flaming naphtha, after which the Mongols stormed the gates. There were now only 1,000 defenders left and the fighting was over in a few hours, or as Juvaini puts it, 'the space between two prayers'. The Qangli garrison suffered the usual massacre, but the population was allowed to return home after paying a fine. However, several contingents of forced labourers were later levied from the city, which Juvaini blamed for its temporary decline.

Massacre at Gurganj

With the fall of Jand, Bokhara and Samarkand, Khwarizmia itself was isolated, in Juvaini's words 'left in the middle like a tent whose ropes have been cut'. The flight of the Shah had left the armies stationed there leaderless, especially since the Queen Mother, Terken Khatun, had also escaped to the west. Muhammad's son Jalal ud-Din had tried to make a stand in the city of Gurganj (modern Urgench), but had left for the south after discovering an attempt to assassinate him. Juvaini says that although Jalal was by far the most able military commander in the empire, he was unpopular with many of his father's officials, as he was known to believe in appointing men on the basis of merit rather than political connections. So eventually the troops in Khwarizmia elected one of their own commanders, a relative of the royal house named Khumar Tegin, as their 'Sultan'. Khumar ensconced himself in Gurganj while Chagatai and Ogodei were sent to eliminate him. The Mongol brothers decided to reduce the odds against them by a stratagem, so they concealed their main force behind an ancient wall at Baghi-Khurram, outside the city, while a small raiding party ran off a herd of cattle that was grazing beneath the walls. What Juvaini describes as a disorderly mob of Khwarizmian soldiers, some on horseback and some on foot, poured out of the city in pursuit, and inevitably ran into an ambush. Emerging from behind the wall, the Mongols blocked the road in front and behind the enemy and slaughtered them; Juvaini gives the obviously exaggerated total of 100,000 killed. The survivors fled back to Gurganj through the Qabilan Gate and their pursuers poured in after them, but here both the garrison and the citizens were determined to fight. By nightfall the Mongols had been driven out, and the next morning Chagatai and Ogodei commenced formal siege operations. Here in the lower valley of the Oxus there were no large stones, so the Mongol siege engineers cut down mulberry trees and sawed the trunks into logs to use as ammunition for the catapults.

Under the cover of this bombardment, local conscripts were sent forward to fill in the moat. Khumar Tegin followed the example of his sovereign and fled, following which the attackers stormed the walls, but the people continued to resist, and ferocious street fighting broke out during which the town was deliberately or accidentally set on fire. On the second day of fighting 3,000 Mongols managed to reach the bridge across the Oxus which divided the city into two parts, but they were cut off and annihilated. The popular resistance enraged the Mongols, but eventually they were victorious, and the inhabitants were turned out into the countryside. Here, says Juvaini, skilled craftsmen were separated for deportation, the women and children were enslaved, and the remaining men were massacred. Each Mongol soldier was allocated twenty-four victims to kill, and the city was razed to the ground. Juvaini adds that in his day many places in the east were inhabited by refugees from Khwarizmia, but that 'I have heard of such a quantity of slain that I did not believe the report and so have not recorded it'.

Genghis Moves South

Genghis himself rested his men and horses in the region of Samarkand over the summer of 1220, then in the autumn he marched south to the fort of Tirmiz on the Oxus. Here, for reasons which are not entirely clear, the behaviour of the Mongols towards the local population seems to have become more brutal. Juvaini describes how the inhabitants were encouraged to resist by the natural strength of their fortress, which was well equipped and partially protected by the river, and that siege engines were used on both sides. But he does not explain why when Tirmiz fell, after a siege of eleven days, even the non-combatants were killed. Genghis then sent out patrols to subdue the people in the surrounding countryside, 'some by kindness, but most by severity'. He then crossed the Oxus and advanced on Balkh, which submitted at once. Nevertheless, the people were driven out onto the plain, ostensibly for a census, then slaughtered, while their city was burned to the ground. Juvaini says that this was done for fear of rebellion, as the Shah's son Jalal ad-Din was active in the region with an army. He describes how so many bodies were left unburied that lions, wolves, vultures and eagles could all feed together without quarrelling. Genghis' youngest son Tolui was then sent west into Khurasan, where he captured the great Silk Road city of Merv after a siege of only seven days, then broke a promise of clemency and slaughtered all but 400 of the population. In April Tolui carried out another massacre at Nishapur, allegedly in revenge for the death of Toquchar, his brother-in-law, who had been killed during an unsuccessful assault the previous autumn while he was pursuing Shah Muhammad. Juvaini describes the desperate resistance which the city now put up, employing 3,000 crossbows and 300 siege engines against the Mongols, who in response collected so many stones from the surrounding region for use as missiles that nine-tenths of them were never used, but remained where they were piled up on the plain. Once the attackers were on the walls the fighting continued for another day, with people being continually thrown down to their deaths, but at last the Mongols stormed into the streets. On this occasion the city was completely destroyed, even the cats and dogs being killed. At Herat there was no resistance, so Tolui left it under the joint control of a Mongol and a Muslim governor, and returned to join his father. From a military point of view this campaign had been a spectacular success, though marred by the apparently unnecessary destruction. Meanwhile Genghis was besieging a stronghold at Talaqan which was 'crammed full of warriors' and had so far resisted all assaults, but when Tolui's reinforcements arrived it was quickly captured.

At this point news arrived that Jalal ud-Din had attacked and defeated a Mongol detachment under Tekechuk which was besieging a castle at Valiyan in the Panjshir valley. Jalal had managed to join up with two other Khwarizmian generals, Amin Malik, commanding 50,000 Qanglis at Ghazna, and Saif ud-Din Ighraq, who brought 40,000 'valiant warriors' including Turkomans and ex-Ghurid soldiers, and had made a forced march to surprise Tekechuk, leaving his heavy baggage behind. In the first onslaught, says Juvaini, a thousand Mongols were killed, and the survivors retreated across the Panjshir River. Having raised the siege, Jalal then returned to his base at Parvan. Genghis responded by sending 30,000 men to Parvan under Shigi-qutuqu – a surprising choice for such a mission, as his previous experience seems to have been in the field of civil administration rather than military command. Jalal ud-Din led out his army to meet the Mongols, placing Amin Malik in command of the right wing and Ighraq on the left, while he remained in the centre. The entire Khwarizmian army was ordered to dismount, but to keep hold of their horses and be ready to mount and charge when an opportunity arose. An apparent exception was a unit of 10,000 cavalry under Amin Malik, who must presumably have remained mounted, since Juvaini describes them attacking the Mongol army and forcing it to fall back. Jalal then reinforced his right from the centre and left until it succeeded in pushing the Mongols all the way back to their starting point. A fierce fight continued until nightfall, when both sides returned to their camps. During the night Shigi-qutuqu attempted to deceive the enemy into thinking that reinforcements had arrived, by making every trooper set up a dummy on a spare horse. According to Juvaini, when morning came this ploy nearly succeeded, and Jalal's officers began to debate about the direction they should take in their retreat. But their commander persuaded them to stand fast, and they again deployed for battle. On the second day of the fight Shigi-qutuqu took the initiative and charged Ighraq's men, but they once again dismounted and drove off the Mongol charge with arrows. Then Jalal ordered his drums to be beaten, which was the signal for the entire army to mount up and advance. The outnumbered Mongols began to retreat. At one point they rallied and counter-attacked, striking down 500 of their pursuers, but Jalal 'rode up like a lion of the meadow or a leviathan of the raging sea', and the Mongol army finally fled the field.

When he learned of the defeat, Genghis at once marched to confront the enemy. Juvaini says that he 'in his haste reckoned night as day, and travelled two stages at a time, so that it was impossible to cook food'. No doubt he was aware that once the Mongols lost their reputation for invincibility it would be impossible for them to keep the people in subjection in the areas already conquered.

His army was held up by fierce resistance first at Gurzivan, which held out for a month, and then at Bamiyan, the site of the famous stone Buddhas, now destroyed, in northern Afghanistan. Here a son of Chagatai, Metiken, who Juvaini says was Genghis' favourite grandson, was killed by a stray missile, and in retaliation every living thing in the town was slaughtered, just as had happened at Nishapur. Juvaini adds that Bamiyan remained deserted 'to this very day'.

Meanwhile, in Jalal ud-Din's camp his subordinates were arguing over the plunder taken at Parvan. Amin Malik hit Ighraq over the head with a whip, but Jalal dared not punish him for fear that his Qanglis would mutiny, so Ighraq abandoned the army under cover of darkness and led his 40,000 men into the mountains. He was later killed in another pointless dispute with fellow Muslims. Jalal realised that this defection had left him too weak to confront Genghis, so he turned southeastward and rode for the Indus River, beyond which he hoped to find safety in the realm of the Sultan of Delhi. So when the Mongols reached Parvan they found that their quarry had already left. Genghis did not punish Shigi-qutuqu for his failure there, but instead rode over the battlefield with him, pointing out where his dispositions had been at fault. It is likely that the Khan also realised that the fault was partly his, as he had underestimated the enemy's strength and sent an inexperienced general into battle against a force perhaps three times the size of his own.

The Defeat of Jalal ud-Din

Jalal's pursuers caught up with him as he was preparing boats for the crossing of the Indus, and Genghis, now with the advantage of superior numbers, extended both his flanks and trapped the Khwarizmians with their backs to the water. In Juvaini's words, the Mongols 'stood behind one another in several rings in the shape of a bow and made the Indus like a bowstring'. Genghis began the battle with an attack on Amin Malik, on the Khwarizmian right, who was defeated and broke out with a group of survivors, aiming for Peshawar. On the way, however, he was intercepted by a Mongol patrol and killed. Jalal was left at the head of only 700 diehards, but he charged the Mongol battle line repeatedly, driving back the enemy in front of him. Genghis' men were under orders to take him alive, so he remained unharmed as his men fell one by one around him. Nevertheless, the Mongol line stood firm, and each time Jalal withdrew to regroup they moved forward, leaving the Khwarizmians with less room to manoeuvre. At last Jalal led one last charge, then he wheeled his horse and galloped over the steep river bank into the Indus. Genghis forbade pursuit and watched in admiration as his opponent swam his horse to safety on the far bank still carrying his weapons, exclaiming 'Such sons should a father have!' But his troopers shot at the other fugitives who tried to follow him, so that all but about fifty were killed or drowned.

At least temporarily Jalal ud-Din was removed as a threat to the Mongol occupiers of his father's empire, but this was by no means the end of his career. As Genghis made his way back through Ghazna he was informed that his enemy was attempting to raise troops in India. The Khan therefore sent Dorbei Doqshin, the victorious commander in the Tumad War, across the Indus with two toumans to finish him off. Juvaini says that Jalal had withdrawn towards Delhi, so Dorbei Doqshin sacked the fortress of Nandana and then besieged Multan, where he had to bring in stones for his catapults by raft down the river. He succeeded in bringing down a section of the walls, but the city was saved because the Indian summer was approaching and 'the great heat of the climate prevented his remaining longer'. So he raised the siege and returned to Ghazna to rejoin Genghis. The 'Slave Dynasty' of the Sultans of Delhi had been founded in 1206 by Qutb ud-Din Aybak, a former Ghurid officer, and at this time was still in the process of taking over most of northern India. The army of the Sultanate relied mainly on its Turkish 'ghulam' cavalry and its elephants, while the Hindu infantry were not always enthusiastic. It was later to become one of the most intractable opponents of Genghis' successors, but for the time being the Sultan wisely avoided a confrontation with the Mongols.

After Genghis' departure from the Khwarizmian Empire, Jalal ud-Din returned and raised yet another army. He was defeated by a Mongol expedition at the Battle of Isfahan in August 1228, but again escaped and continued the fight until he was murdered by bandits in 1231. His soldiers remained in the field and took part in the civil wars in Ayyubid Syria until 1246, when they picked the wrong side and were crushed by the Ayyubid Sultan. Their best-known feat during this period was the recapture of Jerusalem from the Crusaders in 1244. The Khwarizmians had shown that with effective leadership they could have been a formidable opponent for the Mongols, and it is interesting to speculate what would have happened if Jalal ud-Din had commanded the army from the beginning of the invasion. But by the time he was in a position to do so, his father had already undermined the empire by his ineptitude and cowardice, then abandoned its people to their fate.

Pursuit and Reconnaissance in the West
The three generals who had been sent in pursuit of Shah Muhammad after his escape from Samarkand followed separate routes across Iran, and the sources which mention their activities are often inconsistent. Toquchar had apparently been given the additional task of forming a cordon to prevent the Shah's sons escaping south from Gurganj to continue their resistance in Afghanistan. In this he was unsuccessful, allowing Jalal ud-Din to break through to Afghanistan, and Toquchar was eventually killed while attempting to storm the city of Nishapur. Jebei and Subotei first came to Balkh, where the people made no resistance but supplied them with food and guides. At Zava the inhabitants closed the gates, but as the Mongols were in a hurry they rode on. However, the people on the walls could not resist the temptation to shout insults at them as they departed, so Jebei and Subotei returned and attacked the place. They captured it after three days of fighting, killed everyone they could find within the walls, and burnt what they could not carry away. Elsewhere the city of Nishapur and most of the villages they passed submitted at once and were spared from destruction, temporarily at least. The two generals split up as they rode west, then met up again at Rayy, south of the Caspian Sea. But the Shah had left the town just ahead of them, and joined his son Rukn ud-Din and his 30,000 troops at nearby Qazvin. Although he was now strong enough to strike back at his pursuers, Muhammad once again hesitated. He first considered seeking asylum in Baghdad, then returned to Hamadan, where his

army clashed with Jebei's touman in the autumn of 1220. True to form, however, the Shah did not lead his troops into battle but left them to fight a rearguard action while he took flight again. The Mongols defeated them easily and resumed the pursuit, but Muhammad managed to cross the Elbruz Mountains to the Caspian, where he took a boat out to a remote island. There, in late 1220 or early 1221, he died, probably of pneumonia. Soon afterwards, it seems, Jebei's patrols captured the Shah's mother, Terken Khatun, and sent her back to Mongolia, where she remained a prisoner for the rest of her life.

Jebei also sent a messenger to Genghis, asking permission to remain in the west and reconnoitre the surrounding regions, till then entirely unknown to the Mongols. He and Subotei then established a base on the Murgan Steppe in Azerbaijan, where the pasture was plentiful and the local ruler, Ozbeg, the Atabeg of Tabriz, was friendly. Many of the Turkoman and Kurdish nomads of the region also arrived to join the Mongols, presumably in the hope of sharing in their plunder. From this base, and with the help of their new allies, Jebei and Subotei launched raids in all directions. First they advanced north into Georgia, where they were at first mistaken for fellow Christians since they were known to have been fighting against the Muslim Khwarizmians. When the mistake became apparent, the Mongols had to face an attack by an army of 10,000 men under King Georgi IV Lasha. The Georgians were formidable opponents, whose noblemen, although Christian, fought in similar style to the Turks as armoured cavalry with lance, sword and bow. However, they were unfamiliar with Mongol methods, and were defeated at the Battle of Khunan, in which Georgi received a wound in the chest from which he never recovered. Jebei then turned his attention back to northern Iran, where he sacked Rayy and Hamadan in retaliation for the support they had given to the Shah, before he and Subotei returned to Georgia in the autumn of 1222. A fresh army had been raised to confront them outside the capital city of Tbilisi, but the Georgian cavalry again fell into a typical Mongol trap when Subotei pretended to retreat and provoked them into a headlong pursuit. Just as he had done so often in China, Jebei then emerged from ambush and routed them. The survivors fled inside the walls of Tbilisi, but the Mongols did not follow up as expected by attacking the city. Instead they turned north again, and rode off towards the Derbent Pass through the Caucasus Mountains.

It appears that Jebei had never intended to conquer Georgia, only to neutralise any possible threat to his rear. Permission had now been received from Genghis to return home by the route around the northern end of the Caspian Sea, and guides had been obtained who could be persuaded to lead the army through the precipitous mountains, where Juvaini says that no one could remember an army passing before, to the open steppe on the far side. But as the Mongols descended from the Derbent Pass via the Daryalsk Ravine, the guides escaped and went ahead to give warning of their approach. So as they moved through the foothills overlooking the Terek River they found their way blocked by a huge army of mounted warriors. These were the men of the Kipchaqs and Alans, nomads who inhabited the steppes north of the Black Sea, reinforced by Lezgians and Cherkesses from the Caucasus. The Kipchaqs were close relatives of the Qangli Turks, and in fact turned out to include a number of refugees from the Khwarizmian army. The Alans and others were of a different ethnic origin, but most of them fought as mounted archers in a similar style to the Turkish tribes that the Mongols had encountered in Central Asia. The Mongol army attempted to ride through them, but their numbers were too great, and the broken terrain made it difficult for the invaders to deploy for battle. So the Arab historian Ibn al-Athir describes how Jebei and Subotei resorted to diplomacy, sending envoys to persuade the Kipchaqs that they and the Mongols were kindred peoples, whereas the other tribes were untrustworthy foreigners. This ploy may have been helped by the presence of large numbers of Turkomans, who were indeed related to the Kipchaqs, with the Mongol army. The Kipchaq Khan Koten fell for this and agreed to abandon his allies, who were quickly scattered. Jebei then overtook the Kipchaqs on their homeward march and destroyed their army in a series of battle near the River Don. Koten, however, escaped and fled for his life into the forested country that lay north of the steppes. There he canvassed the rulers of the various

Russian principalities for support, arguing that the invaders would soon be seizing Russian land as well.

In fact this was not their objective at all. Jebei and Subotei spent the winter of 1222 to 1223 on the steppes, mounting only limited expeditions to explore this new country. They seem to have established friendly relations with the Brodniki, Russian refugees who had settled on the steppe along the River Don, some of whom may have fought alongside the Mongols in the subsequent clash with the Russian princes. Early in the new year Subotei raided into the Crimean Peninsula and – possibly at the instigation of rival Venetian merchants – captured the town of Sudak, a trading port belonging to Genoa. Jebei advanced as far west as the River Dniester, on the border of present-day Moldova, which marked the westernmost point reached by Genghis' armies. It may also have made Jebei, who a few years before had been campaigning on the shores of the Yellow Sea in Manchuria, the best-travelled soldier in history up to that time. His campaigns had spanned ninety degrees of longitude, or a quarter of the way round the globe. Then he and Subotei turned back for home. But about the middle of May 1223, near the River Dnieper in what is now Ukraine, they were intercepted by Koten and his new Russian allies. Their army was led by the Princes of Kiev, Galicia and Chernigov (all three of whom were coincidentally named Mstislav), and was said to have a combined strength of 90,000 men. The core of the princes' armies consisted of the 'druzhina' or guard cavalry, who wore armour and fought with swords and spears, and Nicolle estimates their total numbers at between 15,000 and 20,000. The 'polk' or town militia, and the impressed peasants or 'smerdy', who formed the bulk of the army, were less well equipped and fought mainly as infantry with spears and shields. The Kievans also fielded bowmen, both on foot and mounted, including not only Kipchaq allies but mercenary horse archers known as 'Chernye Klobuki', or 'Black Caps'.

The Battle of the Kalka River
At first the Mongols sent messengers to explain that they did not want to fight the Russians, but the princes foolishly allowed the

Kipchaqs to kill these men. The 'Russian Chronicle' recorded Jebei's reply, which followed closely the formula attributed to Genghis by Juvaini: 'If you support the Polovtsians [this was the Russian name for the Kipchaqs], kill our ambassadors and are marching against us, then do what you will. We did not attack you and God will be our judge.' The Russians advanced down the west bank of the river Dnieper to meet up with a contingent of Galician infantry who were sailing upstream in boats, then sent an advance guard across to the eastern bank which attacked a Mongol detachment under an officer called Gemyabek, who had been observing them. Prince Mstislav of Galicia led the pursuit, and Gemyabek was captured when he tried to make a stand on an old Kipchaq burial mound. The next day another patrol encountered some Mongol herdsmen, who fled and left the animals to be rounded up by the Russians. These encounters were no doubt staged by Jebei and Subotei in order to convince the enemy that the Mongols were afraid of them, and in this they succeeded. The entire Russian army now crossed the river by a bridge of boats and marched eastwards into the steppe in search of their enemies.

The feigned retreat was of course a traditional stratagem, but on this occasion Jebei and Subotei elevated it from a battlefield tactic to a full-scale strategic manoeuvre. The Mongols retreated eastwards for nine days, luring the Russians into an increasingly reckless pursuit. They seem to have allowed their pursuers to capture whole herds of livestock on the way, to encourage their overconfidence and perhaps to slow them down, because the Russian chronicles tell us that 'the whole army was full of cattle and continued on its way'. Then on the tenth day (probably 31 May 1223), on the open plains along the Kalka River in present-day Ukraine, the Mongols struck back. The Galicians were in the van of the allied army, their commander, Mstislav Mstislavich 'the Daring', having pressed on across the river while the other princes argued about whether to abandon the pursuit. Ahead of the Galician division rode Prince Daniil Romanovich of Volhynia with the horsemen of his own 'druzhina'. The Chernigov forces had eventually followed the Galicians, but there was still a wide gap between the two contingents, covered only by Kipchaq scouts. The exact location of the battlefield is unknown, but it is likely that the Mongol commanders had carefully chosen it in advance. Nicolle and Shpakovsky reproduce several photographs of the general area, which show open, rolling steppe interrupted only by the valley of the Kalka and the scattered woods and rocky bluffs on both banks. The river itself was fairly narrow, certainly less than a bowshot across, and was by no means an impassable obstacle. But it would be enough to slow the Russian cavalry and prevent it from moving forward quickly to support their advanced units, as well as hampering any retreat. Meanwhile, on the open grasslands further east, the Mongol army could manoeuvre without hindrance.

Suddenly Subotei's 'touman' appeared out of a fold in the ground and swept away the Kipchaqs in a swift charge, then crashed into the Volhynian advance guard. The fighting must have been hand-to-hand, because one of Prince Daniil's officers, Vasilyok Gavrilovich, was killed with a spear, while the prince himself was wounded in the chest. Mstislav of Galicia tried to deploy his troops but they were thrown into disorder by the fleeing Kipchaqs. Subotei then attacked the Chernigov army, which was still crossing the river, and despite a heroic rearguard action by Prince Oleg of Kursk drove it back in confusion. He then wheeled to attack the Galicians from the rear. The latter cut their way out despite heavy losses, but although Mstislav Svyatoslavich of Chernigov managed to rally his troops, he did not return to assist his allies. Instead he abandoned them and retreated northwards. This did him no good, as the Mongols later caught up with his army and routed it, but it ensured the destruction of the third Russian force, under Mstislav Romanovich of Kiev. This was still encamped west of the Kalka when Jebei, who seems to have led the Mongol right wing on a wide outflanking move, surrounded it. The Kievans resisted for three days under a relentless barrage of arrows, but were eventually forced to surrender. Their prince and his leading vassals were then executed in retaliation for the murder of the Mongol ambassadors, by being crushed to death under a platform of wooden planks. This apparently sadistic method was no doubt employed because of the traditional prohibition on shedding the blood of royal and noble prisoners.

The Bulgars

Even by Mongol standards this was an extraordinary victory; one of the largest armies Europe had ever produced had not just been beaten by a much smaller opponent, but actually surrounded and crushed beyond recovery. It appears, however, that many of the Russian and Kipchaq troops played little part in the fighting; the latter were perhaps demoralised by their earlier defeats, while many of the Russian militia were on foot and must have been too slow-moving to influence the initial cavalry battle east of the river. The *Chronicle of Tver* describes the battle as a disaster 'such as has never been seen since the beginning of the Russian Land'. And yet the *Secret History* dismisses the whole campaign in a line or two, and Juvaini ignores it completely. From a Mongol perspective, it was just another sideshow.

Jebei and Subotei did not stay to exploit their success, but continued their march back to Mongolia. They reached the River Volga somewhere near modern Volgograd, then moved northeast up the western bank to attack the Volga Bulgars who lived on the edge of the forest zone around the Volga and Kama Rivers, near the present-day city of Ufa. It had originally been planned that they should rendezvous here with another Mongol army under Jochi, but the latter had apparently been ill and his army was still far to the east. Jebei and Subotei nevertheless proceeded without him, crossing the Volga near the Bulgar town of Suvar, but according to Ibn al-Athir they marched into an ambush and suffered an unprecedented defeat. The Mongols were forced to abandon the campaign after suffering heavy losses. Jebei disappears from the records after this, and it is generally supposed that he died from disease on the return journey to Mongolia. Martin, however, suggests that he may have been killed by the Bulgars, or died later of wounds received in the battle – a humiliating end to his career, which might explain why Mongol sources are silent on the matter.

The Volga Bulgars had originally been a steppe people, but now lived by farming and trading, and had begun to build castles of wood and stone. They had converted to Islam in the tenth century, and had apparently received engineers from Baghdad to help improve their fortifications. By the thirteenth century their noble cavalry was equipped in Russian style, but there were also many infantry – principally archers – provided by the local forest tribes. They were obviously better equipped than the Mongols for fighting in the dense Siberian forests, but we have seen Mongol armies operate successfully in such terrain before – for example against the Tumads in 1216. However, Jebei and Subotei's force had already been weakened by the attrition of a long campaign, and was a very long way away from any resupply or reinforcement. It may have been a sensible decision to retire rather than risk another assault, and there is no evidence that Genghis blamed his commanders for this failure. Subotei eventually obtained his revenge in 1237, when he conquered the Volga Bulgars during the second Mongol invasion of Europe under Batu Khan.

Chapter 6

The Fall of North China

Meanwhile, in China itself Mukhali had been carrying on the war as Genghis' viceroy under a banner of nine white yak tails, a distinction shared only by Genghis himself. Martin calculates the mounted contingent of Mukhali's army at between 65,000 and 70,000 men, but only 10,000 of these were sent direct from Mongolia, though no doubt other Mongols already stationed in China were also under his authority. The cavalry also included 10,000 Ongguts, as well as Khitans, Jurchens and Chinese. Despite the great size of this force, Martin believed that Mukhali's mission was a limited one, intended only to seize further territory which could be used as a springboard for an advance on K'aifeng when Genghis returned from the west. In the autumn of 1217 he divided his army into three columns which marched east, west and south from Chung-tu, taking many small towns but apparently avoiding the stronger cities. At this point the Chin were also involved in a war against the Sung to the south, who had previously paid them tribute but had discontinued it in 1212. Nevertheless, they managed to despatch a field army under Chang Jo which encountered a Mongol army at Lang-ya Ling in the late summer of 1218. The Chin were defeated, and Chang Jo was captured when his horse threw him. He refused to kneel before his captors, but was spared and persuaded to join the Mongols. Most of his surviving troops followed him, so he was permitted to lead them as an independent column which achieved several victories against his old comrades in Chin service. In September 1218 Mukhali himself laid siege to the city of T'ai-yuan, an operation which is of interest because of the contrast with previous Mongol siege attempts. By now they were no longer the amateurs that they had been as recently as 1215, but came to the town with a train of siege artillery which wrecked the northwestern bastion, breached the main walls and provided cover for a final assault with 'a rain of stones and arrows'. Three months later, the equally strong fortress of Chiang Chou was taken by mining operations which caused a tower to collapse. Apart from Chang Jo's expedition, no Chin field armies appear to have attempted to intervene as the cities fell one by one.

The Sung Intervene

The gradual mopping-up continued during 1219 and 1220, while a Sung army under Li Ch'uan pushed up from the south and received the submission of the Chin commanders in the province of Shantung on the east coast. However, a Chin officer named Meng Ku-kang decided to fight on, and eventually lured the Sung into an ambush and defeated them. The Sung army usually gets a bad press, but despite its lack of cavalry it had plenty of solid infantry and was backed up by state-of-the-art technology. Its tactics were not as defensive as is often supposed, and much emphasis was placed on the role of picked infantry assault detachments, personally led by high-ranking generals. The downside to this, of course, was that the quality of the rest of the infantry would often suffer from the removal of their natural leaders. Mukhali marched into the power vacuum resulting from the Sung intervention in November 1219. One of the Chin generals, Yen Shih, immediately changed sides again and joined the Mongols, giving them control of a population of 300,000 families without a fight. Then early in 1220 the Chin government sent a new army under Wu-ku-lun Shih-hu to recover Shantung. Shih-hu crossed the Yellow River from the south by the ford at Huang-ling-kang, and rather unwisely sent 20,000 infantry ahead to attempt a surprise attack on Mukhali. The latter was warned of their approach, and scattered them with a force which according to his biography in the Yuan Official History numbered only 500 cavalry. Martin regarded this as 'quite incredible' and suggested that Mukhali must have had at least ten times that number, but the Chin troops may well have been poorly trained, and it seems quite likely that they could have been demoralised by a sudden attack by a relatively small force of horsemen, especially if it came from behind a flank. Mukhali then advanced to Huang-ling-kang and engaged the main Chin army. Martin reasonably believed that this too must have consisted almost entirely of infantry, probably without armour, because they made no move to counter-attack, but stood on the defensive while the Mongols dismounted and shot them down with arrows. Mukhali then ordered a charge, and the demoralised Chinese were pushed into the river where many of them drowned. Some sources give a different account of this battle, claiming that the Chin position was on the south bank of the river, but Martin argues that the river was too wide for the Mongols to have engaged them from the opposite shore.

Soon afterwards, Mukhali received ambassadors from both the Chin and the Sung. He welcomed the latter hospitably, but sent the Chin envoy on to Genghis, who pointed out that his general had now conquered almost all the territory north of the Yellow River that he had demanded as the price of peace in 1214. Nevertheless, he would leave the Chin unmolested in the south if they agreed to surrender the last few cities in the district of Kuan-hsi in the far west, in what are now the provinces of Shensi and Kansu. This was refused, and Mukhali marched west in 1222 to take the cities by force. At first he met little opposition as the Chin garrisons either deserted or fled before him, but the stronghold of Yen-an resisted, and the Chin general Wan-yen Ho-ta even launched a counter-attack, falling on a Tangut force which was operating in conjunction with the Mongols and destroying it. Mukhali advanced on Yen-an and met Wan-yen Ho-ta about ten miles to the northeast. The 30,000 men of the Chin army were drawn up on a steep hill. A Mongol officer named Mongka Bukha reconnoitred the position with 3,000 cavalry, and returned to report to Mukhali that the enemy were in a strong position but, having apparently mistaken the scouting force for the main Mongol army, were overconfident and seemed eager to attack. So, on the following day Mongka Bukha was sent forward to make a feint attack, while Mukhali deployed the bulk of his army in ambush in two valleys seven or eight miles away. The Chin took the bait as usual and charged, so Mongka Bukha's men threw away their banners and drums and pretended to flee. Wan-yen Ho-ta rode straight into the ambush and was lucky to escape with his life, but left behind 7,000 of his men dead. Mukhali followed up by besieging Yen-an, but was still unable to take it, so instead he drove east down the Yellow River to Ching-chao (modern Xian), with the support of another Tangut army sent from Hsi Hsia. To his surprise he found the city defended by Wan-yen Ho-ta, who had been hurriedly transferred from Yen-an, with an army said to have been 200,000 strong. This time Ho-ta refused to come out from his defences and fight, but maintained a stubborn resistance even after Mukhali reduced all the surrounding towns and isolated the garrison. Then the commander of the Tangut army was killed by an arrow, and his troops – perhaps acting under orders from the new emperor Li Te Wang, who succeeded his father in 1223 and was known to be wavering in his allegiance to the Mongols – went home. Soon afterwards came news that a Sung army under P'eng I-pin had invaded Shantung. Then, in April 1223, Mukhali himself unexpectedly fell ill and died.

The Conquest Falters

The Chin took advantage of the resulting confusion to recapture several towns in the north, and Wu Hsien, a former defector to the Mongols, changed sides again and marched to join up with P'eng I-pin. At first it must have seemed that all of Mukhali's gains were likely to be lost. That this did not happen was largely thanks to a young Chinese officer named Shih T'ien-tse, whom Martin describes as 'one of the outstanding figures of Mongol military history'. He gathered a small army which at first consisted only of 1,700 Chinese troops and 3,000 Mongols, and defeated Wu Hsien at Chung-shan. He then advanced to attack the Sung, collecting reinforcements on the way. At Tsan-huang he encountered a much larger army under P'eng I-pin and Wu Hsien, deployed with the Wu-ma Hills in their rear. P'eng was apparently worried about being outflanked, which suggests that T'ien-tse was superior in cavalry, so the Sung set fire to the vegetation on the hills to deny them to the Mongols. Somehow, however, T'ien-tse managed to get archers onto the slopes, perhaps under cover of the smoke, and attacked from both sides. P'eng was captured and the Sung army destroyed. Nevertheless, P'eng's colleague Li Ch'uan continued to hold out in the city of I-tu, which was besieged by a Mongol army under Boru in October 1226. Learning that Li was planning a sortie, Boru lured him into another ambush by a feigned retreat to the Tzu River, where he turned and slaughtered 7,000 Sung troops. Li fought on until May 1227, when, with the garrison starving, he surrendered. Boru, with Genghis' agreement, spared him and appointed him governor of Shantung under Mongol authority. This brought to an end the first war with the Sung, and with the death of Genghis in August the attention of the Mongols was directed elsewhere. The conquests in China were not to resume in earnest until 1231, but Genghis and Mukhali between them had established a permanent bridgehead extending across Manchuria, Shantung and the Yellow River plain as far west as the Ordos. With the frontier defences gone, neither the Chin nor the Sung were ever able to regain the initiative. In 1234 K'aifeng itself fell and the Chin dynasty was extinguished. The Sung in the south, who had foolishly stabbed the Chin in the back instead of supporting them, were now left without protection against further Mongol expansion. Nevertheless, Sung China was still the richest and most populous state in the world, and it was another forty years before its capital at Hangchow finally fell to Genghis' grandson Kubilai, who became the first man in three and a half centuries to rule the whole of China.

The Destruction of Hsi Hsia

In 1223 Genghis began his journey back to Mongolia after the conclusion of the Khwarizmian campaign, but he travelled at a leisurely pace and did not arrive until two years later. In the meantime the Tanguts of Hsi Hsia, who must have known that the Khan intended to punish them on his return, had not waited passively to be attacked. After their army had withdrawn from the war with the Chin early in 1223, they had beaten off two limited Mongol invasions and even retaliated by launching raids northwards into Mongolia itself. In the early summer of 1224 a Mongol army besieged the city of Sha Chou, but an attempt to dig under the walls was frustrated by a Tangut countermine. Genghis, who was kept informed of events by messengers, then ordered Boru to stage a diversion by attacking Yin Chou, in the east of Hsi Hsia. This diversion was more successful than the main operation, as Boru defeated a Tangut army outside the town and then stormed it. Li Te Wang submitted again to Genghis and offered his son as a hostage, while at the same time secretly negotiating with the Chin, then changed his mind and informed a Mongol emissary that the hostage would not be given up. Then in October 1225 a treaty between Hsi Hsia and the Chin Empire was made public. Martin suggests that the Tanguts had received news of the clashes between the Mongols and the Sung, and decided to throw in their lot with what looked like an increasingly united anti-Mongol front. But, not surprisingly, Genghis' patience was exhausted. In the autumn of 1225 he gathered a large army and marched into Hsi Hsia at its head.

As usual our sources give various figures for the size of this army. Rashid ud-Din provides a detailed order of battle which adds up to 170,000 men. These included large numbers of foreign allies: 50,000 Khwarizmians, 30,000 Kipchaqs and other western steppe nomads, and 20,000 Indians. Unfortunately, as Martin points out, this list cannot be reliable since it includes among the generals Jebei, who by then had apparently been dead for three years, and Chaghatai, who we know from other sources had been left to look after affairs in Mongolia. The Khwarizmians and Kipchaqs, as very recent former enemies, also seem unlikely additions. The Hsi Hsia Official History says that the invaders numbered 100,000, and this figure may be closer to the truth, though probably still too high. In November 1225 Genghis stopped at Aburqa, on the upper reaches of the Ongin River, to hunt wild horses, and was thrown from his own startled horse when the animals stampeded past. It was obvious that he was seriously injured, and his generals advised him to abandon the campaign. The Tanguts, they pointed out, were not nomads and could not escape, so their punishment could wait until he had recovered. The *Secret History* says that negotiations were opened with the enemy and that Li Te Wang was prepared to be conciliatory, but his military commander Asha-gambu replied in provocative terms. 'By now', he said, 'you Mongols should have learned how to fight. If you say "Let us fight", I have a camp in the Alashai Mountains.' Genghis replied 'Even if I die, I have no choice other than to confront his boastful words'. First, says the *Secret History*, he cornered Asha-gambu in his mountain stronghold and destroyed his army. Chinese sources record the battle in the mountains as taking place later, in January 1227, but for whatever reason the Mongols were allowed to keep the initiative as they set about reducing the cities of western Hsi Hsia one by one. Li Te Wang had ordered the destruction of a bridge over the Sha-chi River – which was ineptly done, so that Subotei was able to repair the damage in a single night – but otherwise remained passive, perhaps in the hope that the western garrisons would hold out long enough to allow a Chin army to come to his assistance. But the Mongols were far more expert in siege warfare than they had been in their previous invasion, and were able to concentrate their full strength against each town in turn. None of them held out longer than two months, while Hsi-liang, described by Martin as the 'second city' of the kingdom, capitulated without resistance. Genghis spent the summer of 1226 in the mountains, controlling operations from a distance as he recovered from his injuries, but in September he once more took command of the army.

Throughout the autumn the Mongols laid siege to the fortress of Ying-li, controlling the Nine Fords across the Yellow River, but it was not until December that they succeeded in forcing a passage. They then marched through the Ordos Steppe and attacked Ling Chou from the north. This city was situated on the east bank of the north-flowing section of the Yellow River which forms the western boundary of the Ordos, and was at the centre of a productive region of irrigated fields. The irrigation ditches would normally have been an obstacle to the Mongol cavalry, but by this time the river and the surrounding waterways were frozen. Li Te Wang had now died, and his successor Li Hsien despatched a large army under Wei-ming Ling-kung to relieve Ling Chou. The Hsi Hsia Official History again gives the suspiciously round figure of 100,000 for this force, so we can assume that it was roughly comparable in numbers to Genghis' army, but the Tanguts had repeatedly shown their inability to match the enemy in open battle. On this occasion Genghis crossed the frozen river to the western bank to meet them, and inflicted another crushing defeat. Rashid ud-Din says that the battle actually took place on the frozen river, but no other sources mention this; the same writer also gives the incredible figure of 300,000 for the Tangut casualties. It was, however, certainly a decisive Mongol victory, and the garrison of Ling Chou, having no hope of relief, surrendered soon afterwards.

Pressing on southwards Genghis next approached the Hsi Hsia capital at Chung-hsing, provoking Li Hsien to bring another army from the east in person. He crossed the Alashai Mountains unopposed – perhaps because, as Martin suggests, Genghis allowed him to do so because it would be harder for him to retreat if defeated on the western side. The Tanguts were once again beaten, and Li Hsien was besieged in Chung-hsing while Mongol detachments were sent out to mop up resistance in the rest of the country. Subotei was sent east to prevent any attempt by the Chin to intervene; on another of the epic marches for which he was becoming famous, he captured several border towns as well as 5,000 horses which he sent back to Genghis, but no Chin field army materialised. By May 1227, the capital alone remained in Tangut hands, and in July Li Hsien finally agreed to surrender. He was given a month to collect presents to bring to Genghis, but by the time he arrived the Khan was dead. He had fallen ill again during August, and probably died on the 25th. The ultimate cause is usually supposed to be the accident he suffered in the autumn of 1225, but there were many other potential causes of death on campaign. Earlier in the year, for example, the Khitan minister Yeh-lu Ch'u-ts'ai had been busy collecting medicines to combat an outbreak of disease among the troops. Juvaini says that Genghis' dying words included an instruction to conceal his death from the Tanguts, which no doubt explains the bizarre account in the *Secret History*, in which Li Hsien arrived in the Mongol camp and had an audience with Genghis through the closed door of his tent, without ever being allowed to enter. The last king of Hsi Hsia was then killed, also in accordance with the last wishes of the Khan. Most popular accounts of this campaign conclude with the statement that the Hsi Hsia civilisation was completely destroyed. Martin calls this 'the most destructive war in the annals of Mongol history'. As discussed in Chapter 7, the destruction fell far short of genocide, and many Tanguts survived as Mongol subjects, but the cities do not seem ever to have been rebuilt. Hsi Hsia was the first of three Chinese regimes that Genghis and his successors were to extinguish. Genghis' body was returned to Mongolia to be buried, but despite countless theories and fruitless searches the location of his tomb remains a mystery (see Man, 2011, for an interesting if inconclusive discussion of the question). Marco Polo says that the soldiers escorting the funeral cortège killed everyone they met so that their spirits could serve the Khan in the next world, but though the story is still repeated, it is found in none of the more contemporary chronicles and is probably just one of the many legends that attached themselves to a man who had so drastically changed the world.

Chapter 7

A Mongol Empire?

Any attempt to evaluate Genghis' legacy encounters the difficulty that we cannot be sure what he was trying to achieve. From his order to keep his death a secret until the Tanguts had finally laid down their arms, we can deduce that he expected the news to encourage his enemies to resist. They may well have anticipated that the Mongol empire would collapse immediately as his leading generals fought among themselves over the spoils, just as the empires of other conquerors had often done. But this did not happen. Instead the succession passed peacefully to his son Ogodei, in accordance with his last wishes. Several versions of Genghis' last words are reported. The Yuan Official History, for instance, says that he devoted his last energies to devising a detailed strategic plan for the conclusion of the Chin war. But the more detailed account of Juvaini, if accurate, suggests that he foresaw a long-term future for the empire he had created. He sent for his sons Ogodei and Tolui, and told them: 'For you I have created this empire . . . My last will and testament are these. If you want to retain your possessions and conquer your enemies, you must make your subjects submit willingly and unite your energies to one end, as in that way you may continue to hold your power.' He then appointed Ogodei as his successor. The *Secret History* tells us that he had previously decided on Ogodei because the bitter personal rivalry between his two older sons, Jochi and Chagatai, made it impossible for either to submit to the other. They had almost come to blows in front of their father, with Chagatai calling his brother a 'Merkit bastard' (an allusion to his mother Borte's enforced residence with the Merkits before Jochi's birth), and the elder boy retorting that Chagatai was his superior 'only in stupidity'. Ogodei's main fault was that he drank too much, but he had a reputation for tact and generosity, as well as a sense of humour. According to Rashid ud-Din, Chagatai once persuaded him to limit the number of cups of wine he drank every day; Ogodei kept his word, but simply procured an extra-large cup. The *Secret History* says that Ogodei later regretted his one lapse into cruelty, when he had the unmarried girls of one Mongolian clan enslaved because their families had tried to marry them off without his permission – a lapse which he blamed on the influence of his womenfolk. By contrast Juvaini gives numerous examples of his open-handedness and his concern for the welfare of all his subjects, not just the Mongols. Genghis was an excellent judge of character, and his choice of such a man to continue his work gives us the clearest possible indication of the direction which he hoped it would take.

Professor Owen Lattimore has argued that Genghis' wars were all part of a great strategic plan, designed to build a state free from the main source of weakness that had bedevilled other steppe-based empires. This arose from the fact that previous nomadic conquerors, as soon as they had built up an army strong enough to invade one of their wealthy neighbours – usually China – had done so, establishing themselves and their followers as the overlords of the settled population. But this created a power vacuum on the steppes, which would inevitably be filled by a new conqueror who would follow the same route. So Genghis first neutralised the Chinese states of Hsi Hsia and Chin, then returned to Central Asia to consolidate his position over all the Mongolian peoples and the related Turks, at the same time securing his rear by eliminating the Khwarizmian Empire. Only then did he set out to permanently conquer and occupy his principal objective, China. This would have been a vision of extraordinary scope, but unfortunately, as Morgan points out, there is no evidence, apart from the actual sequence of campaigns, that such a plan existed. If Genghis had something of this sort in mind, our sources never mention him discussing it with members of his family or his army commanders. Apart from China, in fact, his most important foreign conquests happened more or less accidentally.

Even in Mongolia itself the *Secret History* casts him as the victim of aggression by the Merkits, Keraits and Naimans, rather than planning their downfall from the beginning. For example, it describes him sending Jochi and Subotei against the Merkits in 1216 not to fill any power vacuum, but explicitly for revenge for previous perceived wrongs. Similarly, Qara-Khitai was conquered not for its own sake, but in order to dispose of Kuchluq. And in Juvaini's account the Khwarizmian war occurred contrary to the wishes of the Khan, who would have been happy to maintain friendly trade relations. What is more, he did not defer territorial conquest in China after the fall of Chung-tu in 1215, but simply left it in the capable hands of Mukhali. This is not to suggest that Genghis was merely the peace-loving victim of a succession of aggressors. He pursued the unification of Mongolia ruthlessly, and having achieved this, like many of his predecessors on the steppe, he saw China as the obvious next target – though even the war with the Chin could be seen as partly defensive, in view of the past Chin support for the enemies of his clan. But there is no reason to believe that when he began his conquests he envisaged them extending as far as they eventually did. Every great empire tends to expand of its own accord, sometimes against the wishes of its rulers, as for example happened to the British in Africa in the nineteenth century. Every advance brings the conquerors into contact with new potential enemies who must be subdued to guarantee the security of the existing possessions; the perfect defensible frontier is always a little further away.

Nevertheless, there is evidence that Genghis eventually came to see his own achievements in terms of a divine plan of some sort. His comments after the capture of Bokhara, for example, have been discussed in Chapter 5. His successors certainly began to present themselves as carrying out a God-given mission to conquer the world. Matthew Paris records that, prior to Genghis' grandson Batu's invasion of Europe in 1238, he 'had sent threatening letters, with dreadful emissaries; the chief of which declared that he was the messenger of God on high, sent to subdue the nations who rebelled against him'. Perhaps the nearest thing we have to the Khan's own political manifesto in later life is a letter which he sent in 1220 to the

Chinese Taoist master Ch'ang Ch'un. His object was to persuade the sage to visit him and share the secret of immortality, and so he naturally tried to present himself in the best possible light. After stressing the austerity of his own lifestyle, in sharp contrast to the 'arrogance and luxury' encountered in China, he continued: 'I have for the common people the solicitude I would have for a little child, and the soldiers I treat as my brothers. Present at a hundred battles, I have ever ridden personally in the forefront. In the space of seven years I have accomplished a great work, and in the six directions of space all is subject to a single law.' The 'great work' was of course the empire which he had created.

This need not imply any belief in universal brotherhood. Genghis' ideas seem to have remained centred on Mongolia and its people, and although he may have occasionally tried to adopt a wider perspective, in day-to-day matters he regarded the empire as run for the benefit of the Mongols, or more specifically of his own family and their immediate entourage. Proof of this is the way in which the *Secret History* records the rewards and privileges he gave them. Whole conquered peoples were 'given' to his relatives for their support, and favoured individuals were allowed to commit up to nine crimes with impunity before they were punished. Evidently relations between the ruling class and the conquered peoples were still based on exploitation rather than the rule of law. This was probably an *ad hoc* policy intended to retain the loyalty of the people on whom the whole enterprise depended, and in this it was very successful. What struck outsiders most forcibly about the Mongols of Genghis' day was their solidarity, the united front which they presented to the rest of the world. Juvaini relates a famous story of how Genghis illustrated this point to his sons by asking them to break first one arrow shaft, then a progressively larger bunch until there were fourteen, which even strong athletes could not break. 'So it is,' he said, 'with my sons also. So long as they tread the path of regard for one another they shall be secure . . .' (This story also appears in the *Secret History*, but there it is told of the semi-legendary matriarch Alan Qo'a and her five sons. Evidently it was a popular motif in Mongol culture.) In later years this solidarity was to be severely tested, but so strong was the idea that according to Juvaini, when a falconer searching for a lost bird stumbled on a plot by fellow Mongols against Genghis' grandson Mongke Khan (reigned 1251–9), his report was at first disbelieved: 'they were quite unable to believe that such a state of affairs existed and they made him repeat himself over and over again'.

Nevertheless, opinion has long been divided on whether Genghis was a genuine empire-builder, or merely a robber baron on a vast scale. It has been argued that although he came to rule over large agricultural societies, he never understood how they functioned, but regarded them simply as sources of plunder for his armies. It is hard to maintain such a negative view, however, in the light of the innovations which he copied from these societies. Perhaps the most important of these was writing, previously unknown among the Mongols, for which Genghis introduced a script based on that of the Uighurs. It has also been argued, for example by Ratchnevsky, that Genghis introduced a formal code of laws for his empire, known as the 'Great Yasa'. However, Morgan has shown that the evidence for this is very sparse. Rashid ud-Din preserves what were thought to be fragments of this code, but they probably represent an incomplete collection of individual decrees, recorded originally by Juvaini, covering a wide variety of subjects. Based on the account in the *Secret History*, Morgan argues that Genghis appointed Shigi-qutuqu to some sort of supreme judicial position, but that rather than formalising a set of regulations he was simply to keep a record of his decisions to form the basis of a sort of case law. This was nevertheless a far-sighted policy which implies that Genghis envisaged a long-lasting state organisation based on the keeping of written records – hardly the preoccupation of a typical bandit.

In many respects, admittedly, the administration of the Mongol empire did remain rudimentary. Where possible local chiefs or governors were employed to carry out the routine running of the conquered territories according to existing local custom, though in China Khitans, Uighurs, and even Europeans like Marco Polo, seem to have been preferred to native Chinese. Morgan considers that the

Mongol taxation system was never standardised, but consisted mostly of *ad hoc* levies. As Juvaini complains, Mongol rulers were sometimes induced to farm out the collection of taxes to unscrupulous agents who resorted to violent methods of extortion. One of the dues which we know were levied systematically was the obligation to support and maintain the khan's messengers. A formal postal service, the 'Yam', was introduced during the reign of Ogodei, with permanent way stations at intervals along the main routes where the riders could obtain food and fresh mounts. The *Secret History* reveals that this was necessary because messengers had previously been abusing their position, commandeering horses and goods in excess of their needs, and placing an unbearable burden on the inhabitants of the districts through which they regularly passed. From this we can deduce that Genghis probably issued commissions to individual officers who were entrusted with messages, leaving them to make their own arrangements for their journeys. In a life of almost ceaseless campaigning, he probably never had the time to devote to regularising this and other aspects of his rule. But even here, the regime which he established can be seen to be taking steps to ensure the continued prosperity of the territories under its control. One aspect in which the Mongol regime was unusual among its contemporaries – and very progressive to modern eyes – was its attitude to religion. The Mongols believed in a single supreme being, Tengri, though they also worshipped the sun, and regarded mountains, streams and other natural features as sacred. Their taboos included polluting running water by washing in it, and eating animals which had been struck by lightning. On the whole, however, they were tolerant of other religions, and willing to accept aspects of them which they found worthwhile. When they established their rule over non-Mongol peoples, this toleration could become a source of strength. We have seen in Chapter 5, for example, how Jebei's declaration of religious freedom won over the Muslims of Qara-Khitai. William of Rubruck describes a debate which he attended at the court of the Great Khan Mongke in 1254, in which Nestorian and Catholic Christians, Muslims, Buddhists, Taoists and Shamanists all put forward their religious views: this was probably the only place in the world at that time, and for centuries afterwards, where such a gathering could have been held.

Genghis' Successors

Forty years after Genghis' death his united world empire had been replaced by four main successor states, all ruled by his descendants – the Yuan regime of Kubilai Khan in China; the Ilkhans in Persia; the Golden Horde on the western steppes; and the Chagatai Khanate based on the old Mongolian heartland. It is tempting to see this fragmentation as proof that Genghis' 'great work' had ultimately failed, but this may be an oversimplification. A recurring theme in the higher level political and military organisation of the Mongolian tribes seems to have been the concept of a central authority situated in the centre of four subordinate entities, sometimes referred to as the 'khan and four beys system'. In accordance with this tradition Genghis had divided his empire before his death into four 'ulus' or provinces, each of which was allocated to one of his sons. Similarly, in his early career, he was seen as being served and protected by the men whom the *Secret History* calls his 'four war-horses' – Bo'orchu, Mukhali, Boroqul and Chila'un-ba'atur – and his 'four hounds', Jelme, Jebe, Subotei and Qubilai. This system may have had its ultimate origins in the Chinese idea of the four directions, but in fact it was widespread throughout medieval Central Asia, where it is attested for the Turks, Koreans, Tibetans and Khitans among others. In view of the other evidence for Khitan influence on Mongol institutions, they may have been the inspiration for its adoption in Genghis' empire. From this point of view, the division of the empire into the four successor khanates can be regarded as a natural progression, which Genghis may have foreseen. The fact that at the end of the thirteenth century every one of these states was still ruled by members of his family might well have seemed to him the most important indicator of his success.

The details of how this situation had come about were, of course, less tidy than any political theory. Under the new 'Great Khan' Ogodei the empire continued to expand after Genghis' death, with the final defeat of the Chin in China and the reoccupation of the

Black Sea steppes. By this time it constituted the largest expanse of territory ever controlled by a single monarch. At a 'quriltai' in 1235 the khan and his generals planned the simultaneous invasions of Korea and Poland, something which even Stalin never attempted. Ogodei died in 1241, a setback which may have saved central Europe from becoming another outpost of the empire, and was followed after a period of uncertainty by his son Guyuk (1246–8), and then by Mongke (1251–9), a son of Ogodei's younger brother Tolui. By this time tensions within the royal family were becoming evident, and Tolui's clan secured the succession only by means of a bloody purge of their opponents. After 1259 Mongke's brother Kubilai was nominated as Great Khan as well as head of the 'ulus' of China, but he never succeeded in enforcing his authority over the other provinces. These became in effect independent and often mutually hostile kingdoms.

The Mongols who remained in Mongolia and the adjacent regions, including those of the Chagatai Horde (the descendant of the 'ulus' of Genghis' second son), increasingly saw themselves as the guardians of traditional nomad ways. Under men like Arik Boke and Khaidu, Kubilai's main rivals for the title of Great Khan, they spent much of their time fighting their fellow Mongols – though the Chagatais continued to campaign as far afield as the Delhi Sultanate for the rest of the century. Sultan Ghiyas ud-Din Balban of Delhi (1266–87) was successful in fighting off a series of incursions by the Chagatais, and became the principal focus of resistance to the Mongols in the east. He was proud of the fact that he had fifteen former sovereigns from all over Asia at his court, all of them refugees from the Mongols. The Chagatai Horde inflicted a shock defeat on the Delhi army as late as the Battle of Kili in 1299, but soon afterwards it lost its main power-base in the former Khwarizmian territories and gradually declined into obscurity.

In 1256 Mongke sent his brother Hulegu to complete the conquest of Persia and the Middle East, which had been left in an anarchic state following the original invasion a generation earlier. Hulegu destroyed the castles of the Assassins in Persia, captured Baghdad and Damascus, and established a permanent base on the grasslands of Azerbaijan, where Jebei and Subotei had rested their horses thirty-five years before. His attacks on the Muslims made him a natural ally of the Crusaders as well as the Georgians and Armenians (though he was actually a Buddhist), and he was preparing to march on Jerusalem and Cairo when news of the death of Mongke forced him to abandon the campaign. His troops settled in Iraq and Persia and established the Ilkhanid state, which fought several wars against the Mamluks of Egypt in the second half of the thirteenth century. The Mamluks were a dynasty of slave soldiers, originally imported by their Ayyubid predecessors, who had overthrown their masters in 1250. Ironically, many of them had been surplus Kipchaq prisoners of war, sold to the Ayyubids by the Mongols. The Mamluk victories at Ain Jalut in 1260, Abulustayn in 1277 and Hims in 1281 are often seen as the first real checks to the Mongols' long career of conquest, which prevented the Mongols penetrating further than the borders of Syria. The Ilkhanids converted to Islam during the reign of Hulegu's great-grandson Ghazan around 1295. The Mongol ruling class was gradually absorbed by its Persian and Turkish subjects, and Genghis' direct line came to an end with Khan Abu Sa'id in 1335.

The western steppe had originally formed the 'ulus' of Genghis' eldest son Jochi, who had died before his father and been succeeded by his son Batu. Batu extended his territory further west into eastern Europe during the campaign of 1237 to 1241. At the time his 'ulus' was referred to as the Kipchak Khanate, which reflects the fact that most of its troops were Kipchaks recruited during Batu's career of conquest, but it later became better known as the Golden Horde, after Batu's spectacular golden tent. Under his successors, the Horde kept Russia in subjection and occasionally raided further west, but most of its energies were taken up by its wars with the Ilkhans. Despite its sometimes uninspiring military record, the Golden Horde outlasted all the other Mongol successor states, surviving on the Ukrainian steppes until the sixteenth century.

When Mongke died in 1259, his brother Kubilai broke with tradition by having himself proclaimed Great Khan, not by a 'quriltai' in Mongolia, but by his own army, which he had commanded in China since 1251. In 1261 he defeated a rival claimant, Arik Boke of the Chagatai Horde, but seven years later another revolt by Arik Boke's successor Kaidu cut China off from the western 'ulus'. Kubilai was now in practice the ruler only of the Chinese portion of the Mongol empire, a fact which he acknowledged in 1271 when he proclaimed himself the founder of a new Chinese dynasty, the Yuan. This regime survived Kubilai's death in 1294 and endured until 1368, when a Chinese rebel named Chu Yuan-chang ejected the Mongols and established the native Ming dynasty. The rulers of Mongolia remained a threat to China until the Manchus finally subjugated them in the eighteenth century, but Toghon Temur, who died in 1370, was the last khan of the royal house of Genghis to rule in his homeland. After that, outside the Central Asian steppes at least, the Mongols were little more than a memory – and usually a bad one. The Yuan and Ilkhanid regimes were never very efficiently run and left behind them a legacy of economic decline, while the Russians who had once been subject to the Golden Horde remembered it mainly for oppression and extortion. But for a period of a century and a half, the Mongol conquerors and their successors had brought together regions of the Eurasian continent that had never previously had any knowledge of each other, and had presided over the flowering of science and trade that ensued. Chinese inventions like gunpowder and printing percolated through to the West during the Mongol period, not perhaps as a result of deliberate Mongol policies, but as a result of the admittedly uneasy peace that they brought. As the Muslim writer Abu'l Ghazi conceded, 'Under the reign of Genghis Khan, all the country between Iran and the land of the Turks enjoyed such peace that a man might have journeyed from the land of sunrise to the land of sunset with a golden platter upon his head without suffering the least violence from anyone.'

The Death Toll

Anyone who would like to admire Genghis Khan as an empire-builder and military commander, however, is forced sooner or later to confront the issue which has defined his reputation in the west for at least the last century. Every book on the subject seems to devote a section to the atrocities which are alleged to have accompanied his conquests, and in particular to the mass slaughter of the inhabitants of captured cities in the Khwarizmian Empire. This continues to be the basis for the charge that Genghis was not an empire-builder at all, but merely a destroyer; that he and his followers were attracted by the wealth of settled societies but did not understand how they worked; and that they were motivated by a racist contempt for non-Mongols, or perhaps non-nomads, which led them to kill farmers and traders as if they were so many vermin occupying what should rightfully have been Mongol pasture lands. Part of the evidence for this charge is near-contemporary, based on the works of chroniclers like Juvaini and Juzjani, but also often cited is the contrast between the fabulous wealth of regions like Khwarizmia, northern Afghanistan and the Hsi Hsia territories in northwest China, as described by medieval observers, and the depressed condition of the same regions in more recent times. Not only did Genghis inflict unparalleled suffering on his victims, we are asked to conclude, but he actually succeeded in annihilating whole civilisations and blighting their lands for most of the next millennium.

It would be hard to argue that the Mongol conquests did not cause a great deal of collateral damage, as we would call it nowadays. It was common practice in medieval warfare to plunder captured towns, and if they had resisted calls to surrender it was considered justified to put the inhabitants to the sword. Genghis possessed the most effective armies of the period, conquered the largest area and captured the biggest cities, so inevitably he was implicated in the greatest loss of life. But it does not follow from this that he was deliberately setting out to eliminate settled civilisation. The slender evidence for such a policy is based on two events which took place in China. The *Secret History* reports that after the second conquest of Hsi Hsia in 1227 the Khan, exasperated by their treachery, ordered the entire Tangut people to be destroyed. According to Chinese sources cited by Martin, however, this order was not actually carried out. An unusual conjunction of five constellations (or planets?) appeared in the sky, and taking this as an omen Genghis reversed the policy, ordering his men to refrain from killing non-combatants in future. Probably this excuse was concocted as a way of repudiating a rash threat made in the heat of the moment without the Khan losing face. The *Secret History* tends to confirm that many of the supposed victims survived, because it describes how after Genghis' death 'many of the Tangut people [whom we have just been told were 'destroyed'] were given to Yisui-qatun'. It could even be argued that the Khan's words quoted in the *History* – 'Let us say "That was the end, they are no more"' – might refer to the loss of their political and cultural identity rather than to their physical extermination. The Chinese biography of Yeh-lu Ch'u-ts'ai also tells how the Khitan minister learned of a proposal from some Mongol officers to kill off the entire peasantry of north China so that their farmland could be used for grazing. Yeh-lu immediately went to Genghis and argued that the tax revenues from a thriving agricultural sector far outweighed the advantages of the extra pasture. His arguments won the day and the Khan ordered that the peasants should not be harmed unnecessarily, but this source is of course concerned to show its subject in the best possible light, and there is no reason to believe that the massacre was ever seriously considered as official policy.

Certainly there was great loss of life in China, but it fell far short of genocide. We have seen in Chapter 4 how, during a temporary peace with the Chin in 1214, Genghis is alleged to have killed all his prisoners at the Chu-yung Pass rather than take them back to Mongolia. But Martin, who related this story, did not believe it, and although he gives no reasons they are fairly obvious. The Mongol army at this time was increasingly reliant on Chinese auxiliaries, and even if Genghis was prepared to sabotage the peace so soon after it had been concluded, he would hardly have ordered such a waste of manpower. Juzjani says that the Khwarizmian embassy which reached Chung-tu after its capture saw the evidence of the slaughter of many thousands of the inhabitants, but his figures are obviously exaggerated, and we know from other sources, such as the account of Ch'ang Ch'un's journey to meet Genghis in 1220, that the city continued to function. In fact the *Meng-wu-erh Shih* claims that the first act of the conquerors was to take steps to feed the starving population. The biography of the Chinese general Shih T'ien-ni in the same source tells us that in 1219 its protagonist persuaded Mukhali to restrain his men from killing and plundering in order to reconcile the population to Mongol rule rather than antagonising them. In more general terms, a comparison has often been made between the census returns for China before the Mongol conquest, which list about 100 million people, and those for the 1290s, which suggest a decline to 70 million. But it is not possible from this to conclude that the invading Mongols must have killed the missing 30 million. Their administration was not as efficient or necessarily as popular as those of the Sung and Chin, and large numbers of people may have evaded the census to escape taxation, while even if the reduction is genuine it could have owed more to famine, disease and social disruption than to outright murder.

Most of the evidence for the exceptional destructiveness of Genghis' conquests comes from the Khwarizimian Empire. Here, chroniclers including Juvaini, Juzjani and Rashid ud-Din all relate essentially the same story of mass slaughter, especially in the cities of Khorasan, in the southern part of the empire. Juvaini's comment on the results is often quoted: 'even though there be generation and increase until the Resurrection the population will not attain to a tenth part of what it was before.' Unfortunately this quotation is just as often taken out of context. In fact Juvaini was emphasising the contrast between the core regions which had suffered no more than an initial conquest by the Mongols, and those further south and west in Khorasan and Iraq. At Bokhara and Samarkand, he says, there had been no general massacre, and the Mongols had appointed governors to oversee reconstruction, so that 'at the present time' (around the year 1260), they and their surrounding districts were as prosperous as they had ever been. In fact in another passage criticising the rapacity of a later governor, Juvaini describes the Mongol conquest even in parts of Khorasan as relatively compassionate: 'when a district or village surrendered the Mongols would be satisfied with only a little fodder and ten ells of linen, or at most a hundred, according to the size of the place . . . even when they took a village by force of arms they would, it is true, carry off all the cattle and clothing they could lay their hands on, but such as had been spared by the sword they did not torment with torture and mutilation.' The *Secret History* records how when Toquchar disobeyed orders not to plunder the countryside during his march across Khurasan in 1220, Genghis was so angry that he threatened to execute him. It was in the frontier regions, which had been fought over ever since and where every town had been sacked several times, and which were furthermore prone to outbreaks of fever, that the demographic disaster described above had taken place. In a later passage, Juvaini attributes much of the damage not to Mongol armies at all, but to local warlords taking advantage of the power vacuum after the flight of the Shah: 'there was no peace in that region. An emir would suddenly appear in a district and build a castle on a hilltop. That man would attack this, and this man seize and kill that.'

On the other hand even Juvaini, who on the whole is an apologist for Mongol rule, cites some apparently damning evidence of mass murder. The worst of these come from the period after the fall of Samarkand, when Genghis' armies were pushing south and west into territory where Khwarizmian forces were still in the field under the leadership of Jalal ud-Din, and hence it was more than ever necessary to remove the threat of a hostile population in their rear. The notorious massacres at Merv and Nishapur are attributable not to the Khan himself but to his younger son Tolui, who may or may not have been acting under orders. It is quite possible that in his youth and inexperience he acted with excessive severity out of fear of letting his father down by failing to suppress all resistance. But Genghis was in command in person at Tirmiz, where the people were not only slaughtered, but cut open in the hope of finding jewels which they had swallowed, and at Balkh, whose inhabitants were brought out onto the plain on the pretext of holding a census and then massacred. Juvaini explains that this was done for fear of rebellion, but as far as we know Balkh had put up little if any resistance, and in fact had provided Jebei and Subotei with supplies when they passed by in the pursuit of the Shah. Nevertheless, Genghis appears to have had some reason to distrust the inhabitants, because when he passed by again on his return from the campaign he found survivors holding out in the ruins and ordered a second massacre, this time leaving not a single wall standing. Bamiyan also suffered badly, but here there was a personal motive for the reprisals in the death of Genghis' grandson.

Occasionally amid the rhetoric we have what at first sight appears to be incontrovertible evidence for the scale of the killing. Juvaini says that after the massacre at Merv the 'sayyid' Izz ad-Din Nassaba, 'with some other persons', spent thirteen days counting the dead. 'Taking into account only those that were plain to see and leaving aside those that had been killed in holes and cavities and in the villages and deserts, they arrived at a figure of more than one million three hundred thousand.' And yet it has not escaped observant scholars that figures of this magnitude cannot be literally correct. Morgan concluded from his own visits to the sites of Herat and Balkh that the medieval walls could not physically have contained as many people as are alleged to have been killed there, even if the population was swelled by refugees from the surrounding countryside. The actual mechanics of the alleged slaughter are also difficult to comprehend. At Merv (where incidentally Juvaini accuses the local country people of joining in the massacre), each Mongol soldier is said to have killed between 300 and 400 victims. Yet they could hardly all have been bound first without arousing their suspicions, even if enough rope to tie up more than a million people had been readily available. Neither could they easily have been searched for weapons. So did none of them attempt to escape, or to overpower their assailants? Did they simply wait patiently while the throats of their relatives and neighbours were being slit? A more plausible scenario might be that the citizens of towns like Merv – numbering in the tens of thousands, if not the rumoured millions – were assembled outside the walls while their conquerors plundered their homes and searched for fugitive soldiers. Their numbers and hostile demeanour might then have caused alarm among the outnumbered Mongols, who were then ordered to ride down and disperse the crowds. The latter would have scattered in all directions and many if not most of them would have made their escape, but being on foot and poorly armed they would have suffered heavy losses to the bows, swords and lances of their enemies. The population would then have been 'destroyed' as a coherent group in the same way as the Tanguts were, leaving the countryside littered with thousands of dead bodies like the aftermath of a major battle. This would surely be enough to fuel rumours of mass extermination among those who later passed by the temporarily abandoned city. In fact we often have evidence that the cities whose populations were allegedly annihilated continued to thrive thereafter. So after recounting the slaughter at Merv, Juvaini adds that one of the citizens was appointed governor 'of those that reassembled out of nooks and crannies', and that 'many persons' survived to be killed later by Mongol patrols acting without orders in search of loot. Despite this there were still enough citizens left to attempt a rebellion in November 1221, when a rumour spread that Jalal ud-Din was approaching.

Juvaini held high office as Governor of Baghdad under Genghis' grandson Hulegu, and it is evident from his work that he was on the whole an admirer of the Mongol empire, and of its founder. To the modern mind the mass slaughters which he chronicles are very serious crimes, and it is inconceivable that he would relate them, still less exaggerate their extent, without overwhelming evidence to support the charges. But Juvaini was convinced that the Mongol invasion had been instigated by God to punish a sinful world, with Genghis as His conscious instrument. He makes this quite explicit in his account of Genghis' arrival in Bokhara, and in his report of the words with which the Khan is said to have addressed his enemies. He never used threats, we are told, but only the standard formula: 'If ye submit not, nor surrender, what know we? The Ancient God, He knoweth.' In this context it seems less unlikely that Juvani would give credence to fantastically inflated death tolls, and he might have seen no conflict between his loyalty to the Mongol regime and his reporting of them. In any case, though the total numbers of deaths reported were exceptional, the slaughter of those whom we would consider to be non-combatants was a routine part of medieval warfare, especially in the case of a town taken by assault. Martin, for example, compares the Mongol massacres with the 15,000 citizens of the Sung town of Tsao-chia Pao killed by the Chin in 1218, and the 30,000 Hindus slaughtered by the Muslim conqueror Ala ud-Din Khilji at Chitor in 1303. Many other examples could be added. Juvaini says that Shah Muhammad had once killed 10,000 of his own subjects while suppressing a rebellion at Samarkand. The conduct of European armies was scarcely more restrained. The siege of Jerusalem during the First Crusade ended in a notorious bloodbath, as did that of Limoges by the Black Prince in 1369, during the Hundred Years War. The brutality of the sack of Limoges evoked the sympathy of the contemporary chronicler Jean Froissart, who lamented that the Prince 'was so inflamed with passion and revenge that he listened to none, but all were put to the sword, wherever they could be found, even those who were not guilty; for I know not why the poor were not spared, who could not have had any part in this treason'. And yet the perpetrators of these atrocities have remained in popular estimation heroes of chivalry.

It is hard to avoid the conclusion that some commentators, at the time and more recently, have been willing to believe the worst of the Mongols simply because their appearance and lifestyle appeared alien to them. Often quoted is the description by the Persian poet Amir Khuzru of Mongol prisoners whom he saw in Delhi during the reign of the Sultan Ghiyas ud-Din Balban (1266–87): 'Their eyes were so narrow and piercing that they might have bored a hole in a brazen vessel, and their stench was more horrible than their colour . . . Their nostrils resembled rotting graves, and from them the hair descended as far as the lips . . . They devoured dogs and pigs . . . The Sultan marvelled at their beastly countenances and said that God had created them out of hell fire.' Even allowing for the fact that prisoners of war are likely to appear unkempt and their demeanour unfriendly, this can hardly be regarded as an objective description, though it has sometimes been quoted as if it was. Martin rightly calls it 'a caricature, further illustrating the fear and horror inspired by the Mongols'. It was not, however, unique. In a letter to Pope Honorius, King Georgi IV of Georgia's successor Queen Rusudan referred them as 'a savage people, hellish of aspect'. And Friar Jordan of Giano, writing in Bohemia, described the Mongols as 'inhuman and of the nature of beasts, rather to be called monsters than men, thirsting after and drinking blood, and tearing and devouring the flesh of dogs and human beings'.

It is sometimes alleged – rather hypocritically in view of the above accounts – that the Mongols had a racist contempt for all other peoples, and even when not consciously contemplating genocide had no real place for them in their world view. In reality, like all rulers until very recent times, they seem to have regarded the population of their realm as an asset to be maximised where possible. With the exception of the Tartars, the other Mongolian tribes conquered by Genghis were incorporated into his growing nation rather than slaughtered, and even in the Tartar case the women and children were spared. Even settled agricultural peoples were on the whole judged on their individual merits. One of Juvani's stories illustrates this point. He says that Ogodei, when he became Khan, sent for a famous wrestler to perform at his court. This man was a Tajik, from the former Khwarizmian Empire, and one of the ethnic group which had suffered most severely during the conquest. The Khan was impressed with his skills and rewarded him by presenting him with an attractive wife. Some time later Ogodei met this girl and asked her – with a nudge and a wink no doubt, as the sexual prowess of the Tajiks was a standing joke of the period – how she was enjoying married life. She complained that her husband was neglecting her, so Ogodei summoned him for an explanation. It turned out that the Tajiks believed that sexual activity weakened them, and that the wrestler was anxious to be on top form to fight in front of the Khan. Ogodei immediately ordered him to give up wrestling, explaining that what he really wanted was for the couple to produce children.

There has also been a rather uncritical willingness to believe that the economic decline of parts of Central Asia must have been due to the Mongol invasions. The contrast between the fertile, populous land described by early medieval writers, and the arid, poverty-stricken backwater which it had become by the beginning of the twentieth century, is certainly dramatic. But recent scholarship has shown that most of the decline can be attributed to a much later period, and in fact in some respects it is still continuing today. The

Aral Sea, for example, was once bordered by fertile agricultural land as well as supporting a thriving fishing industry, but the saline desert which now surrounds it is largely the result of massive evaporation caused by ill-conceived twentieth-century Soviet irrigation projects. The location of thirteenth-century Samarkand has long been abandoned, and the city has been rebuilt at least twice on different sites, but its decline can hardly be laid at Genghis' door, since we have Juvaini's testimony that it was thriving in the 1260s. The city again became the capital of a great empire under the Timurids in the fifteenth century, and only entered an irreversible decline after that. More plausible explanations exist than the brief Mongol destruction as an explanation for the impoverishment of this and the other cities of the Silk Road: among those that must have contributed were the gradual replacement of overland trade by sea routes after the Portuguese navigators circumnavigated Africa at the end of the fifteenth century, and later on the military conquest of Central Asia by unsympathetic regimes in Russia and China. The agricultural productivity of Persia and neighbouring Central Asia also declined, and this has often been attributed to Mongol neglect of the complex irrigation systems and the deaths of the farmers whose job it was to maintain them, but again if Genghis is to be blamed for this we must explain why in the 1260s Juvaini was still extolling the fertility of the Samarkand region – which was firmly under Mongol control – in comparison with the damage done in the frontier zones. In Hsi Hsia the cities were not rebuilt and the fertility of the irrigated farmland along the Yellow River seems never to have been fully restored, but this is a region of light and easily exhausted soils, and the viability of the settled way of life was always marginal. No doubt the initial invasions of any country led to damage to crops and farmers as well as cities, but the rapid recovery of most areas under the ensuing Mongol government suggests that they could not have been as hostile to settled life as is sometimes assumed.

Chapter 8

Genghis – The Verdict

How old Genghis was when he died is uncertain. Rashid ud-Din says that it was well known that he lived for seventy-two years, which would place his birth around 1155. However, the evidence of the *Secret History* suggests that he was born some years later, about 1162, and this is the officially accepted date in Mongolia, where for example his 840th anniversary was celebrated in 2002. Even this later date means that at least until his mid-sixties he continued to lead his armies on campaign – an unimaginably hard life, requiring him to travel immense distances on horseback, exposed to all weathers. Even if he no longer fought in person, he remained addicted to the energetic and dangerous sport of hunting. The sage Ch'ang Ch'un had tried unsuccessfully to persuade him to give it up, explaining that although he could not confer immortality, he did know some ways in which he could improve the Khan's life expectancy. Another vice which Ch'ang Ch'un warned against was excessive sexual activity, but Genghis had ignored this advice as well; Juvaini records that in the 1260s he already had more than 20,000 living descendants. The Khan's health and vigour, until his last illness, were clearly exceptional. Juzjani, who must have known people who had seen him during the war in Khwarizmia, when he was in his mid-fifties, describes the Khan in fairly conventional terms as tall, vigorous, of strong constitution, his hair not yet grey. Only his eyes were remarkable; they reminded observers of a cat.

The portrait of Genghis which we see in the *Secret History*, however, is not one of a hero in the traditional mould, whose reputation depended on his personal feats of arms in the style of an

Alexander the Great or a Richard the Lionheart. In fact some passages in it – like the abduction of Borte, discussed in Chapter 2 – seem to cast doubt on his courage. On other occasions also he took refuge in the forests while his companions were left to hold off a pursuing enemy. According to the *Secret History*'s account of the Khan's showdown with the shaman Teb Tengri, when the latter's six brothers entered his tent Genghis was 'afraid of being hemmed in' and left the tent to join his guards, who gathered round to protect him. But in all these cases he was temporarily outnumbered, and had good reason to fear an attempt on his life. To retreat from danger in these circumstances could be seen as pragmatic rather than cowardly. Another interpretation of his actions is that he genuinely believed in his divine mission to unite his people, and so considered the preservation of his own life as of paramount importance. When the cause required that he expose himself to danger, for example in decisive battles, he did so without apparent hesitation, as the horse he had killed under him at Koyiten in 1201 and the serious wound he suffered soon afterwards, bear witness. The *Secret History*'s account of his mission to recover the eight stolen horses also shows him acting decisively in an emergency, without undue regard for his own safety. According to Rashid ud-Din, in later life Genghis used to recount other stories of his adventurous youth, in one of which he was once ambushed by six assailants. He charged them with his sword while they shot arrows at him, cut them all down, and rode on unscathed. On his return journey he found their horses still wandering loose and rounded them all up. Whether a story like this can be taken at face value is questionable, but it does suggest that the Khan was aware of the need to play the hero at times if he was to retain the respect of his warlike followers.

Genghis' personal ability as a military commander has been much discussed, but the consensus has always been that he rates among the greatest in history. The extent of his conquests and the number of his victories alone would guarantee that accolade. It seems unlikely that he introduced any major tactical innovations; his armies continued to fight in a similar style to that which we see in use among both friends and enemies in the early campaigns in Mongolia – a style which may have been inherited from their Khitan predecessors. But the almost unbroken success of the Mongol armies against a wide variety of opponents shows how little need there was for innovation. He already possessed the best cavalry in the world, and he was no doubt wise not to try to change it. He may have regularised and improved their organisation and discipline, but it is less the administrative details of his achievement that impresses than the scope of his vision. He led his armies on operations of unprecedented scale, co-ordinating their movements across vast distances with a sureness which reminds us of the young Napoleon. He had an extraordinary grasp of the importance of intelligence and reconnaissance, and of the strategic relationship between widely-separated regions – what we would now call geopolitics. For example, he was able to plan a rendezvous between his son Jochi and the western expedition of Jebei and Subotei north of the Caspian Sea – a region thousands of miles from Mongolia, where no Mongol soldier had yet set foot. Juvaini says that on his expedition into India he considered returning home by way of Hsi Hsia, more than 2,000 miles to the northeast. He abandoned the plan when local informants assured him that there was no road – he was presumably unaware of the existence of the Himalayas between him and his goal – but the fact that he could contemplate such a march across completely unknown terrain, and knew the precise direction it should take, is a tribute to his strategic awareness.

An equally important quality was his ability to select men of talent, and to employ them in areas to which their particular skills were best suited. Genghis did not, however, suffer from the delusion common among autocrats that willpower alone could overcome all obstacles. One of the sayings which has survived among his 'biligs' or 'maxims', quoted by Martin, concerned an officer named Yisun Beg. Genghis admitted that he was talented and brave, and capable of enduring great hardships, but considered him unfit to command an army because he did not appreciate that other men could not do what he did. 'Only a man who feels hunger and thirst, and by this estimates the feelings of others, is fit to be a commander, as he will see that his warriors do not suffer from hunger and thirst and that the four-footed beasts do not starve. The meaning of this is that the campaign and its hardships must be in proportion to the strength of its weakest warriors.'

There have been suggestions that he was sometimes unduly suspicious, and gave credence to rumours that his most eminent followers were plotting against him. According to the *Secret History* he accepted Teb Tengri's malicious claim that a prophecy had foretold that Qasar would replace him, and even had his brother arrested. Qasar was released only after their mother Ho'elun had intervened, and even then was not restored to his former rank. It is noteworthy that Teb Tengri's next attempt to spread dissension, by subverting the followers of Genghis' younger brother Temuge, was also forestalled by one of the women of the Khan's household – in this case his wife Borte. It has been argued that the way in which the *Secret History* depicts Genghis as influenced by women was part of a subtle campaign to discredit him. On the other hand, to a modern observer it could be seen as evidence of his open-mindedness. When Qulan Qatun of the Merkits was being brought by her father to present her to the khan, they were briefly detained by an officer named Naya'a-noyan, who insisted on escorting them. Genghis accused Naya'a of having held the girl for his own nefarious purposes, but when Qulan Qatun spoke up in his defence he accepted her arguments and rewarded the man. He could also be swayed by the counsel of his officers, as when he rescinded his order to execute his uncle Da'aritai, who had fought against him in the Kerait war, when Bo'orchu, Mukhali and Shigi-qutuqu interceded on his behalf. Compared to many other medieval monarchs – and indeed to his own successors – Genghis seems to have been relatively immune to the sort of insecurity that led them to remove or even murder their relatives and most able servants. In fact his willingness to listen to reasoned criticism and moderate his sometimes hasty anger is to a modern observer one of his most attractive characteristics. The picture in the *Secret History*, of the ruthless conqueror humbly submitting to a telling-off from his mother and confessing 'I was afraid . . . I was ashamed', goes some way towards explaining why, among his own people at least, he was as much loved as feared.

Another example of the Khan's open-mindedness was his treatment of his former opponent Jebei. In 1218, according to Juvaini, Jebei fell under suspicion after his successful pursuit of Kuchluq and conquest of Qara-Khitai. Genghis seems to have thought – or listened to those who wanted him to think – that his general might set himself up as an independent ruler in the newly-conquered territory, and so he sent a message warning him not to be too ambitious. In fact the accusation was quite incredible. Apart from the fact that Jebei had never shown any sign of disloyalty, Qara-Khitai was strategically indefensible, sandwiched as it was between the Mongol and Khwarizmian Empires, and with borders open to the steppe on three sides. And of all people Jebei, who had just conquered it, would have known this. Nevertheless, he resorted to a dramatic gesture to allay his master's suspicion. Many years before, at the Battle of Koyiten, he had killed Genghis' favourite horse, which the *Secret History* describes as yellow with a white muzzle. Now, from the teeming herds of Qara-Khitai, he rounded up a thousand horses of similar colouring and sent them as a present to the Khan. This, says Juvaini, fully restored Genghis' trust in him. Why it would necessarily do so, though, is not entirely clear. A genuinely paranoid monarch must have appreciated that such an extravagant 'gift' would enhance Jebei's reputation more than that of the recipient, especially as Genghis was always insistent that the booty from war belonged to him until he had distributed it, so that technically the horses had never been Jebei's to give. We should perhaps see Genghis' reaction as that of an old comrade, genuinely moved by the reminder of shared hardships, rather than of a tyrant mollified by the offer of a few horses. The successes of other subordinates, perhaps better placed to cause trouble than Jebei had been, seem to have attracted nothing but praise. The biography of Subotei in the Yuan Official History quotes the Khan's verdict on the Uriangqat general: 'Subotei has slept on his shield, he has prevailed in bloody battles and has exposed himself for our house, and we are deeply gratified.' Mukhali, who of all Genghis' commanders would have had the best opportunity to become independent at the head of the army in China, retained his trust until the end of his life.

It could be argued that from the beginning Genghis was as lucky in his opponents as he was in his supporters. Of his early rivals in Mongolia, Jamuqa lacked diplomatic skills and failed to inspire loyalty; Toghril was indecisive and his son Senggum too hasty; while Tayang Khan of the Naimans was easily demoralised. Tayang's son Kuchluq so alienated his own power-base in Qara-Khitai that he was overcome without a fight. Rashid ud-Din quotes the observations of a chief named Sorkat of the Baya'ut clan on the various contenders for power in eastern Mongolia in the 1190s. Jamuqa, he said, was an intriguer who set people against each other instead of inspiring them to work towards a common goal. Alak-udu of the Merkits had dignity and authority, but did not have Temujin's ability to govern. The latter's brother Qasar was admired for his strength and his prowess as an archer, but lacked leadership skills. Only the future Genghis Khan, Sorkat concluded, had the combination of qualities needed to unite the Mongol nation. Among his opponents in China, the Tanguts of Hsi Hsia seem to have lacked any tactical sophistication and the headlong charges of their cavalry were easily defeated, while their royal masters vacillated constantly between appeasing the Mongols and fighting them. The Chin were weakened by infighting, and some of their best troops, the Khitans, preferred the Mongols to their Jurchen masters. Genghis' one enemy of real stature was Jalal ud-Din, but by the time he took command of the Khwarizmian army the empire had been fatally weakened by his father's failures. However, just as he made his own luck in the matter of choosing his generals, Genghis should also be given credit for seizing the opportunities provided by his opponents.

The picture which emerges from our admittedly patchy and biased sources is of a man of enormous vision and ability, able to inspire both loyalty and fear, often ruthless and vengeful, but not gratuitously sadistic, and lacking the paranoia to which lesser men in positions of authority are prone. He may not have been the demi-god portrayed by some of his modern admirers, but neither was he the monster of the traditional western view. He left behind not just ruined cities and piles of skulls, but the nearest thing to political stability that the war-torn regions of Central Asia had ever seen.

Perhaps it is Juvaini's final verdict on Genghis which best sums up the complexity of his character, as well as the ambivalence with which people have always regarded it. The chronicler pays tribute to his 'great energy, discernment, genius and understanding', but in his view Genghis was nevertheless ultimately a warrior: 'an overthrower of enemies, intrepid, sanguinary, cruel. A just, resolute butcher.' It is not a judgement of which the Khan himself is likely to have entirely disapproved.

Source Notes

Introduction
The editions I have used for the main sources listed here are:

Onon, U. (ed. and trans.), *The Secret History of the Mongols,* New York, 2001.
Rashid ud-Din, *The Successors of Genghis Khan*, trans. Boyle, J., New York and London, 1971.
Ata Malik Juvaini, *The History of the World Conqueror*, trans. Boyle, J., Manchester, 1958.
Waley, A., *Travels of an Alchemist*, London, 1931.
De Rachewiltz, I., *Papal Envoys to the Great Khans*, London, 1971.
Marco Polo, *The Travels*, trans. Latham, R. E. Harmondsworth, Middlesex, 1958.

For Juzjani and Nasawi I have had to rely on extracts in other works, principally Barthold, W., *Turkestan Down to the Mongol Invasion*, London, 1977. The numerous untranslated Chinese records are discussed in Martin, H. D., *The Rise of Chingis Khan and his Conquest of North China*, Baltimore, 1950. A valuable general overview of the contemporary sources appears in Morgan, D., *The Mongols*, Oxford, 1986. Man, J., *Genghis Khan, Life, Death and Resurrection*, London, 2011, discusses the present day 'cult' of Genghis Khan in Mongolia and China.

Chapter 1: Genghis' World
The ethnography of pre-Genghis Mongolia is discussed in Ratchnevsky, P., *Genghis Khan: His Life and Legacy*, Oxford, 1991, and De Hartog, L., *Genghis Khan, Conqueror of the World*, London, 1989. The latter is also the main source for geography and climatic

conditions. For new research on rainfall variations see *Scientific American*, 12 March 2014 (www.scientificamerican.com-History of Science-Climatewire).

The beginnings of steppe warfare are discussed in Anthony, D., *The Horse, The Wheel and Language*, Princeton, 2007. Both Anthony and Di Cosmo, N., *Ancient China and its Enemies: The Rise of Nomadic Power in East Asian History*, Cambridge, 2002, also present evidence for the self-sufficiency of steppe economies. For the Silk Road see Franck, I., and Brownstone, D., *The Silk Road, a History*, New York, 1986. The argument for the nomads as victims appears in Beckwith, C., *Empires of the Silk Road*, Princeton, 2009. For events in China see *The Cambridge History of China, Vol. 6: Alien Regimes and Border States, 907–1368*, Cambridge, 1994.

Chapter 2: War on the Steppes

This account is based principally on the *Secret History*. Juvaini and the Chinese sources in Martin (1950) discuss the Baljuna Covenant; Martin is also the main source for the Kirghiz campaign. For the role of the Muslim merchants see Ratchnevsky.

Chapter 3: The Khan's Armies

The *Secret History* is the main source for the organisation of Genghis' armies. See also Rashid ud-Din, Marco Polo, and Atwood, C. P., *Encyclopedia of Mongolia and the Mongol Empire*, New York, 2004. On the question of numbers, see Barthold, De Hartog, and Morgan (1986). Morgan also discusses the development of the 'tamma' armies. For the Yuan dynasty the principal source is Hsiao, C. C., *The Military Establishment of the Yuan Dynasty*, Cambridge, Massachusetts, 1978. Carpini is quoted in De Rachewiltz. For Haithon see Bretschneider, E. (trans.), 'The Journey of Haithon, King of Little Armenia, to Mongolia and Back', *Medieval Researches* Vol. 1, London, 1888.

Anthony, and Karasulas, A., *Mounted Archers of the Steppe, 600 BC–AD 1300*, Osprey Elite Series 120, Oxford, 2004, discuss the origins of the composite bow. Modern research into the properties of the Mongol bow is to be found in Karasulas, and McEwen, E.,

Miller, R. and Bergman, C., 'Early Bow Design and Construction', *Scientific American*, June 1991. Also useful, though devoted mainly to European archery, are Hardy, R., *Longbow*, Sparkford, Somerset, 1992, and Roth, E., *With a Bended Bow – Archery in Medieval and Renaissance Europe*, Stroud, Gloucestershire, 2012. The classification of methods of arrow release, widely quoted in modern books but seldom acknowledged, is due to Morse, E., 'Ancient and Modern Methods of Arrow-Release', *Proceedings of the Essex Institute*, 1885. For Henry VIII's longbows see Strickland, M., and Hardy, R., *The Great Warbow*, Stroud, Gloucestershire, 2005. The limit of 85lbs for a typical archer, and the penetration tests against mail, are from Roth. T'ang dynasty archery is discussed in Ranitzsch, K. H., *The Army of Tang China*, Stockport, 1995, and that of the Manchus in Von Essen, M. F., *Eight Banners and Green Flag: The Army of the Manchu Empire and Qing China, 1600–1850*, The Pike and Shot Society, Farnham, Surrey, 2009. The effectiveness of relatively light bows is discussed, though in an earlier historical context, by Godehardt et al, 'The Reconstruction of Scythian Bows', in Molloy, B. (ed.), *The Cutting Edge: Studies in Ancient and Medieval Combat*, Stroud, 2007. The authors also make the point that cumulative damage to armour and shields by repeated hits may be as significant as a single powerful penetrating strike. For the archaeology of Mongol arrows and other weapons, and poisoned arrows, see Nicolle, D., and Shpakovsky, V., *Kalka River 1223*, Osprey Campaign Series 98, Oxford, 2001. The quotes from Fakhr-i Mudabbir are taken from Digby, S., *War-Horse and Elephant in the Delhi Sultanate*, Oxford, 1971.

Archery tactics are discussed in Turnbull, S., *Mongol Warrior*, Osprey Warrior Series 84, Oxford, 2003. The fourteenth-century Mamluk manual is quoted in Amitai-Preiss, R., *Mongols and Mamluks – The Mamluk-Ilkhanid War, 1260–1281*, Cambridge, 1995. The views of Professor J. M. Smith have been put forward in several publications dealing with the Mongol-Mamluk wars: Smith, J. M., Jr., 'Ain Jalut: Mamluk Success or Mongol Failure?', *Harvard Journal of Asiatic Studies* No. 44, 1984. Smith, J. M., Jr., 'Mongol Armies and Indian Campaigns', *Harvard Journal of Asiatic Studies*

44:2, 1984. Smith, J. M., Jr., 'Mongol Society and Military in the Middle East', in Lev, Y. (ed.), *War and Society in the Eastern Mediterranean*, Leiden, 1997. Smith, J. M., Jr., 'Nomads on Ponies versus Slaves on Horses', *Journal of the American Oriental Society*, 1998.

The Khitan military system is discussed in Wittfogel, K. A. and Feng, C., *History of Chinese Society: Liao*, Philadelphia, 1949. For the wider influence of the Khitans see Morgan (1986). The source for earlier Manchurian innovations is Dien, A., 'The Stirrup and its Effect on Chinese Military History', *Ars Orientalis* XVI, University of Michigan, 1986. The *Political and Military Institutes of Tamerlane* are quoted in Zaman, M. K., *Mughal Artillery*, Delhi, 1983. Amitai-Preiss cites the Egyptian account of the Battle of Hims. Witsen is quoted in Karasulas, and Marbot in Haythornthwaite, P., *Napoleonic Light Cavalry Tactics*, Osprey Elite Series 196, Oxford, 2013. For other Napoleonic parallels, see Nosworthy, B., *Battle Tactics of Napoleon and his Enemies*, London, 1995.

For Anna Comnena see Sewter, E. (trans.), *The Alexiad of Anna Comnena*, London, 1969. Other accounts of Turkish tactics appear in Smail, R., *Crusading Warfare, 1097 to 1193*, Cambridge, 1995, and Strickland and Hardy. Taybugha is quoted in Latham, J., and Patterson, W., *Saracen Archery*, London, 1970. For Turkish and Mamluk archery, see also Nicolle, D., *Saladin and the Saracens*, Osprey Men-at-Arms Series 171, London, 1986, and for Mamluk military exercises Smith, G. R., *Medieval Muslim Horsemanship: A Fourteenth-Century Arabic Cavalry Manual*, London, 1979.

For Yuan dynasty armour see Anon, *Ancient Chinese Armour*, Shanghai Classics Publishing House, 1996 (Chinese text). Nicolle and Shpakovsky discuss excavated swords and armour. The carrying capacity of Mongol horses is discussed in Smith (1998). Meng Hung's account of Mongol shields is quoted in Martin. For Persian shields see Heath, I., *Armies of the Middle Ages*, Vol. 2, Worthing, Sussex, 1984. Ibn Battuta is quoted in Digby. Smith (1998) discusses seated archers. Siege weapons are covered in Turnbull, S., *Siege Weapons of the Far East 1*, Osprey New Vanguard Series 43, Oxford, 2001. For trebuchets see Hansen, P. V., *Experimental Reconstruction of a Medieval Trebuchet*, Copenhagen, 1992, and for gunpowder weapons Needham, J., *Science and Civilisation in China Vol. 5, Part 7: The Gunpowder Epic*, Cambridge, 1989.

The debate about the influence of pasture on the extent of the Mongol conquests is discussed in Morgan, D., 'The Mongols in Syria, 1260–1300', in Edbury, P. W., *Crusade and Settlement*, Cardiff, 1985. See also Smith, J. M., Jr., 'Ain Jalut: Mamluk Success or Mongol Failure?', *Harvard Journal of Asiatic Studies* No. 44, 1984; Smith, J. M., Jr., 'Mongol Armies and Indian Campaigns', *Harvard Journal of Asiatic Studies* 44:2, 1984; and Sinor, D., 'The Mongols in the West', *Journal of Asian History* Vol. 33, No. 1, 1999. A contrary argument is put forward by Amitai-Preiss.

Chapter 4: The First Campaigns in the East
The narrative of the campaigns is based mainly on Martin. For the Tangut army and its wars with the Sung see Kycanov, E. I., 'Les Guerres Entre les Sung du Nord et le Hsi-Hsia', in *Études Song* Series 1 Vol. 2, Evreux, 1971. Gunpowder weapons are discussed in Needham. For the Jurchen army and the defences of the Chin empire see: Tao, J., *The Jurchen in Twelfth-Century China: A Study of Sinicization*, Washington, 1976; Lovell, J., *The Great Wall*, London, 2006; and Turnbull, S., *Chinese Walled Cities, 221 BC to AD 1644*, Osprey Fortress Series 84, Oxford, 2012.

Chapter 5: War in the West
Juvaini is the main source for the events in this chapter, supplemented by Rashid ud-Din and Juzjani. Also valuable is *The Cambridge History of Iran, Vol. 5: The Saljuq and Mongol Periods*, Cambridge, 1968. Martin deals with the conquest of Qara-Khitai and the strategic situation on the eve of the Khwarizmian war. For the Khwarizmian army see Nicolle (1986).

The Black Sea campaign is neglected by Juvaini but has been well covered by several modern writers. See De Hartog, Sinor, Saunders, J., *The History of the Mongol Conquests*, London, 1971, and especially Nicolle, D., and Shpakovsky, V., *Kalka River 1223*, Osprey Campaign Series 98, Oxford, 2001.

Chapter 6: The Fall of North China
The main source here is Martin. The *Secret History* also relates the main events of the final campaign in Hsi Hsia. See Man for a discussion of the death and burial of Genghis.

Chapter 7: A Mongol Empire?
Morgan (1986) and Ratchnevsky discuss the administration of the empire and the careers of Genghis' successors. The theory of Genghis' grand strategic plan is in Lattimore, O., 'The Geography of Chingis Khan', *Geographical Journal* 129/1, 1963. See also Schamiloglu, U., 'The Qaraci Beys of the Later Golden Horde: Notes on the Organisation of the Mongol World Empire', *Archivum Eurasiae Medii Aevi* 4, 1984.

The main sources for the massacres are Juvaini and Juzjani. Morgan, Man and (for China) Martin all attempt to put the allegations into context, but the main counter-argument is provided by Juvaini himself, in passages often ignored by sensationalist writers. Beckwith argues that the decline in the economy of Central Asia postdates the Mongol era.

Chapter 8: Genghis – the Verdict.
Liddell Hart, B. H., *Great Captains Unveiled*, London, 1927, has been very influential in presenting Genghis as a military genius. Ratchnevsky argues for the view of the *Secret History* as unsympathetic to Genghis.

Sources and Recommended Reading

Primary Sources in Translation

Ata Malik Juvaini, *The History of the World Conqueror*, trans. Boyle, J., Manchester, 1958.

Bretschneider, E. (trans.), 'The Journey of Haithon, King of Little Armenia, to Mongolia and Back', *Medieval Researches* Vol. 1, London, 1888.

Marco Polo, *The Travels*, trans. Latham, R. E., Harmondsworth, Middlesex, 1958.

Onon, U. (ed. and trans.), *The Secret History of the Mongols*, New York, 2001.

Rashid ud-Din, *The Successors of Genghis Khan*, trans. Boyle, J., New York and London, 1971.

Waley, A., *Travels of an Alchemist*, London, 1931.

Secondary Sources

Anon, *Ancient Chinese Armour*, Shanghai Classics Publishing House, 1996 (Chinese text).

Amitai-Preiss, R., *Mongols and Mamluks – The Mamluk-Ilkhanid War, 1260–1281*, Cambridge, 1995.

Anthony, D., *The Horse, The Wheel and Language*, Princeton, 2007.

Atwood, C. P., *Encyclopedia of Mongolia and the Mongol Empire*, New York, 2004.

Beckwith, C., *Empires of the Silk Road*, Princeton, 2009.

The Cambridge History of China, Vol. 6: Alien Regimes and Border States, 907–1368, Cambridge, 1994.

The Cambridge History of Iran, Vol. 5: The Saljuq and Mongol Periods, Cambridge, 1968.

De Hartog, L., *Genghis Khan, Conqueror of the World*, London, 1989.

Di Cosmo, N., *Ancient China and its Enemies: The Rise of Nomadic Power in East Asian History*, Cambridge, 2002.

Dien, A., 'The Stirrup and its Effect on Chinese Military History', *Ars Orientalis* XVI, University of Michigan, 1986.

Digby, S., *War-Horse and Elephant in the Delhi Sultanate*, Oxford, 1971.

Franck, I., and Brownstone, D., *The Silk Road, a History*, New York, 1986.

Hansen, P. V., *Experimental Reconstruction of a Medieval Trebuchet*, Copenhagen, 1992.

Hardy, R., *Longbow*, Sparkford, Somerset, 1992.

Haythornthwaite, P., *Napoleonic Light Cavalry Tactics*, Osprey Elite Series 196, Oxford, 2013.

Heath, I., *Armies of the Middle Ages*, Vol. 2, Worthing, Sussex, 1984.

Hsiao, C. C., *The Military Establishment of the Yuan Dynasty*, Cambridge, Massachusetts, 1978.

Karasulas, A., *Mounted Archers of the Steppe, 600 BC – AD 1300*, Osprey Elite Series 120, Oxford, 2004.

Kycanov, E. I., 'Les Guerres Entre les Sung du Nord et le Hsi-Hsia', in *Études Song* Series 1 Vol. 2, Evreux, 1971.

Latham, J., and Patterson, W., *Saracen Archery*, London, 1970.

Lattimore, O., 'The Geography of Chingis Khan', *Geographical Journal* 129/1, 1963.

Legg, S., *The Heartland*, London, 1970.

Liddell Hart, B. H., *Great Captains Unveiled*, London, 1927.

Lovell, J., *The Great Wall*, London, 2006.

Man. J., *Genghis Khan, Life, Death and Resurrection*, London, 2011.

Marshall, R., *Storm from the East – from Genghis Khan to Kubilai Khan*, London, 1993.

Martin, H. D., 'The Mongol Army', *Journal of the Royal Asiatic Society* 1943/1 – 2.

———, *The Rise of Chingis Khan and his Conquest of North China*, Baltimore, 1950.

McEwen, E., Miller, R., and Bergman, C., 'Early Bow Design and Construction', *Scientific American*, June 1991.

Molloy, B. (ed.), *The Cutting Edge: Studies in Ancient and Medieval Combat*, Stroud, 2007.

Morgan, D., 'The Mongols in Syria, 1260–1300', in Edbury, P. W., *Crusade and Settlement*, Cardiff, 1985.

———, *The Mongols*, Oxford, 1986.

Morse, E., 'Ancient and Modern Methods of Arrow-Release', *Proceedings of the Essex Institute*, 1885.

Needham, J., *Science and Civilisation in China Vol. 5, Part 7: The Gunpowder Epic*, Cambridge, 1989.

Nicolle, D., *Saladin and the Saracens*, Osprey Men-at-Arms Series 171, London, 1986.

———, *The Mongol Warlords*, Poole, Dorset, 1990.

———, *Attila and the Nomad Hordes*, Osprey Elite Series 30, London, 1990.

———, and Shpakovsky, V., *Kalka River 1223*, Osprey Campaign Series 98, Oxford, 2001.

Nosworthy, B., *Battle Tactics of Napoleon and his Enemies*, London, 1995.

Ranitzsch, K. H., *The Army of Tang China*, Stockport, 1995.

Ratchnevsky, P., *Genghis Khan: His Life and Legacy*, Oxford, 1991.

Roth, E., *With a Bended Bow – Archery in Medieval and Renaissance Europe*, Stroud, Gloucestershire, 2012.

Saunders, J., *The History of the Mongol Conquests*, London, 1971.

Schamiloglu, U., 'The Qaraci Beys of the Later Golden Horde: Notes on the Organisation of the Mongol World Empire', *Archivum Eurasiae Medii Aevi* 4, 1984.

Sewter, E. (trans.), *The Alexiad of Anna Comnena*, London, 1969.

Sinor, D., 'The Mongols in the West', *Journal of Asian History* Vol. 33, No. 1, 1999.

Skoljar, S. A., 'L'Artillerie de Jet à l'Époque Sung', in *Études Song* Series 1 Vol. 2, Evreux, 1971.

Smail, R., *Crusading Warfare, 1097 to 1193*, Cambridge, 1995.

Smith, G. R., *Medieval Muslim Horsemanship: A Fourteenth-Century Arabic Cavalry Manual*, London, 1979.

Smith, J. M., Jr., 'Ain Jalut: Mamluk Success or Mongol Failure?', *Harvard Journal of Asiatic Studies* No. 44, 1984.

——, 'Mongol Armies and Indian Campaigns', *Harvard Journal of Asiatic Studies* 44:2, 1984.

——, 'Mongol Society and Military in the Middle East', in Lev, Y. (ed.), *War and Society in the Eastern Mediterranean*, Leiden, 1997.

——, 'Nomads on Ponies versus Slaves on Horses', *Journal of the American Oriental Society*, 1998.

Strickland, M., and Hardy, R., *The Great Warbow*, Stroud, Gloucestershire, 2005.

Tao, J., *The Jurchen in Twelfth-Century China: A Study of Sinicization*, Washington, 1976.

Turnbull, S., *Siege Weapons of the Far East 1*, Osprey New Vanguard Series 43, Oxford, 2001.

——, *Siege Weapons of the Far East 2*, Osprey New Vanguard Series 44, Oxford, 2002.

——, *Mongol Warrior*, Osprey Warrior Series 84, Oxford, 2003.

——, *Chinese Walled Cities, 221 BC to AD 1644*, Osprey Fortress Series 84, Oxford, 2012.

Von Essen, M. F., *Eight Banners and Green Flag: The Army of the Manchu Empire and Qing China, 1600–1850*, The Pike and Shot Society, Farnham, Surrey, 2009.

Wittfogel, K. A., and Feng, C., *History of Chinese Society: Liao*, Philadelphia, 1949.

Zaman, M. K., *Mughal Artillery*, Delhi, 1983.

Index